Westerns

Postwestern Horizons

GENERAL EDITOR

William R. Handley
University of Southern California

SERIES EDITORS

José Aranda
Rice University

Melody Graulich
Utah State University

Thomas King
University of Guelph

Rachel Lee
University of California, Los Angeles

Nathaniel Lewis
Saint Michael's College

Stephen Tatum
University of Utah

WESTERNS

A Women's History

VICTORIA LAMONT

University of Nebraska Press
LINCOLN

© 2016 by the Board of Regents of the University of Nebraska

All rights reserved

The University of Nebraska Press is part of a land-grant institution with campuses and programs on the past, present, and future homelands of the Pawnee, Ponca, Otoe-Missouria, Omaha, Dakota, Lakota, Kaw, Cheyenne, and Arapaho Peoples, as well as those of the relocated Ho-Chunk, Sac and Fox, and Iowa Peoples.

Parts of this book are based on previously published material. Chapter 2 and parts of the conclusion are drawn from "The Bovine Object of Ideology: History, Gender and the Origins of the 'Classic' Western," in *Western American Literature* 35.4 (2001 Winter): 373–401. Chapter 4 is a revised version of "Native American Oral Practice and the Popular Novel; or, Why Mourning Dove Wrote a Western," in *Western American Literature* 39.4 (2005 Winter): 368–93. An earlier version of chapter 5 appeared as "Cattle Branding and the Traffic in Women in Early Twentieth-Century Westerns by Women," *Legacy* 22.1 (2005): 30–46.

All images are from *Romantic Range*, which is © and ™ Condé Nast. Used with permission.

First Nebraska paperback printing: 2024
Library of Congress Control Number: 2016937696

Set in ITC New Baskerville by Rachel Gould.

"Lamont's discoveries can be quite startling. . . . [Her] project tackles many contemporary academic issues, from gender fluidity and sexual violence to colonialist iterations of Native narrative to class-based social justice. None of these topics is imposed upon the texts: they emerge organically from Lamont's close reading of context and narrative. . . . [An] important contribution to the literary history of the West."
—Jennifer L. Jenkins, *Journal of Arizona History*

"Lamont has done some wonderful research recovering the complex an important role that women writers played in the beginning of the western."
—Maria O'Connell, *Montana: The Magazine of Western History*

"[Lamont] resurrects the work of well-known western women authors during an era when their stories of strong female characters in the frontier West enjoyed popular readership."
—Renee M. Laegreid, *Western Historical Quarterly*

"Compelling. . . . A valuable read for all those interested in the intersections of gender and culture in early twentieth-century America."
—*Michigan Historical Review*

"A readable excursion into female authors, their experiences, and their perspectives, within an important genre. In unmasking and then undoing female erasure from the beginnings of the American Western novel, Lamont makes important points and deftly defends them. Her book is enjoyable and significant."
—Thomas E. Simmons, *Journal of American Culture*

"*Westerns: A Women's History* introduces a whole new set of woman authors and texts to be included in the study and teaching of Western American literature as well as a new and compelling origin narrative of the Western literary genre."
—Randi Tanglen, *English: Journal of the English Association*

"For more than a century, the mythic western cowboy has been consistently hypermasculine. Victoria Lamont's *Westerns: A Women's History* prods the boundaries of this image while debunking the myth that literary westerns were consistently written by men."
—Cynthia Culver Prescott, *South Dakota History*

"Lamont's work rests upon an impressive amount of archival work in little-known ephemera. . . . [*Westerns*] introduces a new group of works that may be taught on courses focused on the West or inserted into other contexts and critical discussions, causing us to reorganize, question, and revise our existing frameworks."
—Nicole Tonkovich, *Legacy*

"*Westerns* is recommended reading not only for fans of classic Westerns and of feminist literary recovery, but indeed for all readers interested in the history of the American West and the origins of contemporary feminisms."
—Emma Morgan-Thorp, *Canadian Literature*

"Lamont's authoritatively written, engrossing book has much to reveal about the wider history of American feminist discourse in general, bound up in the western genre."
—Gerri Kimber, *Times Literary Supplement*

"Lamont has made the subject of the western important all over again. . . . As a piece of feminist recovery work, Lamont has reordered the scholarly record about a canonical national tradition. By definition this is a major work."
—Krista Comer, author of *Surfer Girls in the New World Order*

"This book promises nothing less than to 'tell an alternative origin story of the popular western,' and it succeeds in spades. Through a series of brilliant readings, canny archival research, sheer wit, and even laugh-out-loud moments, Lamont decisively changes the face of women's westerns. In the process she makes her reader rethink not just the genealogy of popular westerns, but the gender, class, and race dynamics of the literary marketplace, early feminisms, and scholarly blind spots. . . . This book leads the way in that rethinking, with wit, flair, and deep persuasiveness."
—Christine Bold, author of *The Frontier Club: Popular Westerns and Cultural Power, 1880–1924*

For Christine

Contents

List of Illustrations . . ix
Acknowledgments . . xi

Introduction . . 1
1. Western Violence and the Limits of Sentimental Power . . 11
2. Domestic Politics and Cattle Rustling . . 31
3. Women's Westerns and the Myth of the Pseudonym . . 53
4. Why Mourning Dove Wrote a Western . . 75
5. Cattle Branding and the Traffic in Women . . 101
6. The Masculinization of the Western . . 125
Conclusion . . 155

Notes . . 161
Bibliography . . 171
Index . . 183

Illustrations

1. Cover image from *Romantic Range*, June 1937 . . 141
2. Cover image from *Romantic Range*, September 1937 . . 142
3. Illustration from *Romantic Range*, December 1935 . . 143
4. Illustration from *Romantic Range*, December 1935 . . 144
5. Illustration from *Romantic Range*, June 1941 . . 148

Acknowledgments

In 1991, as a new MA student at the University of Guelph, I signed up for a graduate seminar on "Women and the West" with Christine Bold. I owe my subsequent career to that seminar. It was Christine who introduced me to the study of popular culture and to some of the women writers, including B. M. Bower and Frances McElrath, who figure prominently in this book. Christine also provided invaluable feedback on early drafts of this book. I am also indebted to the mentorship of Mary Chapman, who supervised my dissertation; Melody Graulich, who edited my early publications and went out of her way to welcome me into the scholarly community at the Western Literature Association, and Dianne Newell, who has been a generous mentor, collaborator, and friend. Virginia Shay, Sarah York, Natalie Blagden, Stephanie Jorgensen, and Ashna Zaidi provided first-rate research assistance to this project. I also thank Kristin Elias Rowley and the staff at the University of Nebraska Press, who have been nothing but patient and helpful throughout the process of preparing this book. I have also been fortunate to have been a part of the thriving scholarly communities at the Western Literature Association, where many of the ideas in this book were first tested, and at the University of Waterloo English Department, where I am continually inspired and energized by our dedicated staff, students, and faculty. I thank my partner, John Straube, for his patience and understanding and for looking after the dogs.

This book involved archival research at the Houghton Library, Harvard; the Library of Congress; and the Syracuse University Library.

I am thankful to the staff at all of these libraries for their assistance. The interlibrary loan department at the University of Waterloo has been tremendously helpful in tracking down many obscure documents needed for my research. This project would also not be possible without digital archives, including the Colorado Historic Newspaper Collection, the Pulp Magazines Project, and Galactic Central. I thank the many individuals who contribute to the time-consuming process of cultural preservation by digitizing and organizing important ephemeral documents. Reed Doke and Bill Bower, grandsons of B. M. Bower, contributed invaluably to this project by sharing their memories and family stories with me. I am especially grateful to Reed for allowing me to park in his sunroom for days on end while I poured over his grandmother's extensive archives and for making excellent turkey sandwiches.

Research for this book was generously funded by the Social Sciences and Humanities Research Council of Canada, with additional support provided through the Bob Harding and Lois Claxton Humanities and Social Sciences Endowment Fund at the University of Waterloo.

Westerns

Introduction

This book argues that the popular western, widely considered a male-authored tradition, was founded as much by women writers as by men and played a significant role in American women's literary history at the turn of the twentieth century. The popular western acquired the substance of its current shape in the form of "quality" novels that, during the late nineteenth and early twentieth centuries, reclaimed the popular West from the dime novels and other cheap publications in which stories of the West and the frontier had flourished. These new "quality" westerns were within the purview of both male and female authors. Indeed, the first known cowboy novel outside of the dime novel tradition was written by a woman, the Colorado suffragist Emma Ghent Curtis, and published in 1889, thirteen years before the popular western was supposed to have been reinvented by Owen Wister, who published his novel *The Virginian* in 1902. *The Virginian* was itself based on the Johnson County Rustler Wars of 1892, as was a competing novelization of those events written by a woman, Frances McElrath's *The Rustler,* also published in 1902. One of the most prolific authors of serial westerns to profit from "imitating" *The Virginian*, B. M. Bower, was also a woman. Indeed, women were active at every turn during the period, between roughly 1880 and 1940, when the American frontier myth, after years of ghettoization in the dime novel, was supposedly "reborn" as a dominant myth of American identity. This book is a revisionist account of the origins of the popular western that takes into account the many women who helped constitute the genre.

Despite decades of feminist literary recovery in English literary studies, the recovery of popular western women writers engages problems identical to those faced by feminist scholars of the 1970s, 1980s, and 1990s as they recovered many women writers who are now commonly taught in literature classrooms. "How can feminism speak of the relentless silencing of women," writes Mary Eagleton, "while at the same time maintaining that there is a formidable tradition to uncover?" (2). Yet this book makes just such a claim. I address this problem partly by tracing precisely the material relations that have sidelined most women writers of popular westerns while privileging the voices of male authors such as Owen Wister, Zane Grey, Louis L'Amour, and others and partly by tracing common patterns of representation that run through diverse women's texts despite the fact that they wrote from within male-dominated cultural networks. Women authors of popular westerns remain virtually invisible largely because they specialized in what came to be known as a denigrated, popular form and because gendered categories of popular fiction invented by marketers in the 1920s became so deeply entrenched that the "women's western" eventually became a contradiction in terms. When feminist literary scholars began their recovery of a "women's West" in the 1970s, the popular western had been naturalized as a masculine genre, popular fiction was widely regarded as unworthy of serious study in any case, and most western writing by women was out of print. The first books about women writers of the American West, appearing in the early 1980s, reflect these conditions through their focus on domestic writing, memoir, and other "private" genres or on the few women—like the Pulitzer Prize–winning Willa Cather—with established literary reputations upon which scholars could build a woman-centered canon.[1] What began as a systemic omission eventually morphed into explicit denial of the possibility that women *could* write westerns in the popular tradition: In her widely cited book *West of Everything* (1992), Jane Tompkins conceived the popular western as a male-authored backlash against the woman-authored sentimental novel and asserted that, "when women wrote about the West, the stories they told did not look anything like what we know as the western" (41–42). The first monograph to take popular westerns by women seriously, Norris Yates's *Gender and Genre* (1995), also marks them off from the "western" proper by categorizing them as "domestic westerns" (4), which is equally misleading insofar as women's westerns do not concern themselves wholly with domestic themes, nor is the domestic ignored in male-authored texts.[2] When we cordon off women writers in a feminized subcategory, we tacitly endorse their continued exclusion from discussions of the genre when we should be rethinking our understanding of the genre in order to account for them.

This book recovers selected women writers active during the emergence of what we now call the "popular western," loosely dated from 1890—the year the federal census pronounced the frontier "closed"—to the outbreak of World War II. By "popular western" I mean fiction set on the post–Civil War cattle frontier, written for a popular but "respectable" audience of adult readers. In this respect my study does not include dime novels and related cheap fiction, such as Street & Smith's Buffalo Bill and similar series (although it does address novels that respond to them). These publications targeted primarily juvenile readers and featured stories built around series characters. The paradigm for the twentieth-century popular western, however, was established in two new and related venues: western novels published by "quality" publishers who distinguished their literary goals from the commercial interests of the "cheap" press (Radway, *Feeling* 141–42), and a new category of pulp fiction magazines that, following in the footsteps of Frank Munsey's *Argosy* (established 1882), offered pulp fiction to "respectable" adult readers. Women readers constituted a significant, if not dominant, proportion of the "respectable" readership for "quality" books and pulp fiction (Bold, *Frontier Club* 108–9), and women authors considered this a cultural terrain well within their purview. The women I focus on in this book all published novels with "quality" publishers such as Little, Brown, as well as periodical fiction in the new, adult-oriented, and "respectable" pulp fiction magazines.

While a short-lived chapter in the history of the American West, open-range cattle ranching supplied the raw ingredients for the western as we now know it: the unfenced, wide open landscape, the lonely homestead, the rough frontier town, the outlaw, the schoolmarm, and, of course, the cowboy. While in reality cowboys were a racially and ethnically mixed group that included large numbers of Mexicans and African Americans, popular westerns depicted the cowboy hero as an Anglo Saxon whose rough exterior concealed an innate nobility that is now widely identified with classic American values of masculinity and meritocracy. His fate looms large in the novels I discuss, is intimately tied to broader social commentary, and is inextricably bound up in the story of a woman. Rather than melt into the cowboy's arms, however, most of the fictional women I discuss play an active and independent role in the narrative, avenging the cowboy's murder (Curtis, *The Administratrix*), showing him the error of his ways when he turns outlaw (McElrath, *The Rustler*), or simply choosing not to accept his offer of rescue (Bower, *Lonesome Land*).

This is not a comprehensive survey of women writers of popular westerns, nor does it claim to offer a master narrative of the woman's popular western. It does, however, respond to Janet Dean's call for a revisionist method that recovers *both* marginal writers and texts *and* the relations that canonize some texts while excluding others: "It is not enough to dig up texts long buried, catalogue them, and set them in a museum display for us to admire; we also must find new ways of understanding both the texts and the mechanisms that have excluded them from view" ("Searching" 950). In particular, I challenge both Tompkins's account of the popular western as masculine backlash against a female-dominated sentimental culture, and Yates's characterization of women's westerns as domestic texts. Instead of reifying the centrality of the male-authored tradition, I offer an account of the western as a complex cultural field in which both men and women participated, although not always on equal footing. The fact that these women did not always reach vast readerships (although they often did) should not exclude them from discussion of the genre: To do so would be to reconstitute the power relations that marginalized them in the first place. In this regard I am particularly indebted to the methods of Pierre Bourdieu, which take marginal texts seriously for what they tell us about both the structure of a field as a whole and the perspectives that have been sidelined by more powerful cultural agents (42).

This book has implications for the broader study of American women writers because it recovers their contributions to American frontier mythology during a crucial period in its history. At the turn of the twentieth century, ideas about the American frontier shifted profoundly in response to so-called frontier closure, leading to an explosion of public interest in fiction, photography, and art about the "disappearing" West. The popular western as we now know it emerged during this period of frontier anxiety, and many of its familiar conventions and tropes are responses to the loss of a so-called safety valve of "free" land. While this era of frontier anxiety has been well documented by David Wrobel, the significant contributions of women writers to this body of writing have yet to be examined.

I begin my study in chapter 1 by examining the earliest-known "quality" cowboy novel, written in part to correct misrepresentations of the cowboy that were appearing in national and local newspapers, dime novels, and tobacco cards. In the late nineteenth century, westerners were aware, as they are now, of the penchant for the eastern media to produce distorted images of their region and its people. Colorado educator, reformer, and woman suffragist Emma Ghent Curtis attempted to set the record straight in her 1889 novel *The Administratrix*, published more than a dozen years before Owen Wister's *The Virginian*, yet featuring characters and motifs now familiar in classic westerns, including a chivalric cowboy, a tenderfoot schoolmarm, outlaws, vigilantism, and gun violence.

Although widely mythologized, open-range cattle ranching proved to be an unsustainable practice that eventually led to conflicts among large and small ranchers, homesteaders, and so-called rustlers. In April 1892 in Johnson County, Wyoming, these tensions erupted in vigilante violence and the subsequent arrest of dozens of stockmen and their hired mercenaries. *The Virginian* was not the only novel inspired by these events, which were widely reported in national newspapers. The Montana author Francis McElrath also wrote a novel, titled *The Rustler*, based on the Johnson County War, which was published virtually simultaneously with *The Virginian*, in April 1902. In chapter 2 I argue that these two novels represent positions in the larger cultural conversation that constituted the popular western: In contrast to Wister's more familiar justification of the vigilante violence enacted by his cowboy hero, McElrath resolves the conflict between cattlemen and rustlers through female-authored reform.

Although situated well outside of what Christine Bold has called "the frontier club"—the elite circle of men including Owen Wister who exerted powerful influence over the idea of the West at the turn of the twentieth century—most women writers of popular westerns were complicit with frontier club colonialism. Curtis, McElrath, and Bower accepted the displacement of Indigenous peoples as an inevitability and were less concerned with racial conflicts between Indigenous people and white settlers than they were with class tensions within settler communities. In her western *Cogewea*, Mourning Dove (Okanagan), member of the Confederated Tribes of the Colville Reservation, challenges this erasure. In chapter 4, I map out the discursive and material relations within which Mourning Dove was able to reinscribe an Indigenous presence in the space of the popular western. I also position the popular western in relation to other colonial discourses in an attempt to understand why Mourning Dove preferred the western, a genre so closely identified with violent conquest, over the ethnographic narrative that she would eventually also write. I argue that ethnographic and popular western narratives were intimately linked despite their different conventions and fields of practice and that the popular western was the more subversive choice for Mourning Dove because it enabled her to translate Indigenous culture into print as a living, rather than a "dying," culture and to address white readers from the position of storyteller rather than Native informant.

Cogewea was published as a novel "by Mourning Dove" but "given through Sho-Pow-Tan," one of the Indian names that her editor, Lucullus McWhorter, had adopted. This complex signature reflects the thorny editorial relationship between the Indigenous woman author and her white male editor (Bernardin, "Mixed Messages" 494). Nonetheless, the collaborators insisted upon the authenticity of the text; indeed, its value depended upon readers' acceptance of it as authentically "native." This is a particularly complex example of the authenticity issues that dogged popular westerns in general during this period. As representations of the West proliferated, publishers and authors were under increasing pressure to differentiate authentic western images by "real" westerners from inferior copies by imposters. Although authentic "westernness" was identified with masculinity, women writers were not necessarily excluded from this category. I am often asked whether the women in this study used male pseudonyms to be taken seriously as western authors. It is an attractive idea: a subversive community of women infiltrating an exclusive men's club, hitherto unknown to literary history. The reality, I reveal in chapter 3, is less romantic, more complex, but equally interesting. Through a comparative case study of two authors of similar class and regional backgrounds, B. M. Bower and Caroline Lockhart, I demonstrate that western authority was structured within complex relations of class, gender, and region that resulted in very different choices for each author. Whereas Bower was persuaded by her editor at *Popular* magazine to avoid publicity and effectively conceal her gender, Lockhart, who began her career as the popular journalist Suzette, switched to westerns in order to publish "serious" fiction in her own name. In this chapter I analyze these choices in the context of the early twentieth-century popular fiction marketplace, arguing that claims to western authenticity played an important role in constituting women's authority as writers of the popular West. By "western authenticity" I mean a form of cultural capital deployed by authors who lived or traveled extensively in the West and therefore claimed the ability to depict it truthfully. Like Handley and Lewis ("Introduction" 5), I do not judge the authenticity of western texts; rather, I analyze the ways in which this concept was defined and deployed by authors, publishers, and other cultural agents. My analysis of women's literary authority is also informed by depictions of gender and authenticity in their fiction. That both Bower and Lockhart depict women as imposters in the West is not a coincidence. In Bower's *Chip, of the Flying U* (1906), a genteel eastern woman poses as the artist behind the rugged western landscapes painted by her cowboy lover, while Lockhart's *The Lady Doc* (1912) depicts an unscrupulous woman doctor who misleads and exploits the naïve townspeople under her thrall. In different ways, both texts reveal "westernness" to be a complex and contradictory construct rather than a simple matter of bearing witness to a "real" West.

Although I argue that women writers of popular westerns have been sidelined by male voices, I nonetheless also claim that something like a women's popular western tradition exists. "Tradition," however, is too strong a word, for it implies the existence of woman-centered cultural networks capable of its transmission. The women in this study wrote in relative isolation both from each other and from the male-centered frontier club that dominated western cultural production at the turn of the twentieth century. Nevertheless, their westerns are linked by certain themes, tropes, and motifs, suggesting that women writers put the western to different uses than did their male counterparts. In chapter 5 I explore a pattern in women's westerns that I argue is particularly significant: Whereas cattle herds are a familiar backdrop in popular westerns, women's westerns foreground the particular identities of cattle as female bodies that both signify and reproduce patriarchal power. I trace this pattern through novels by Frances McElrath, B. M. Bower, and Katharine Newlin Burt; through early twentieth-century feminist writing by Charlotte Perkins Gilman and Emma Goldman; and into contemporary feminist theory, arguing that women's popular westerns have much to tell us about the broader history of American feminist discourse.

Until 1915, popular westerns by women circulated primarily in "quality" novels and in general pulp fiction magazines, where they appeared alongside detective fiction, love stories, stories of urban life, adventure stories set in foreign lands, nautical fiction, college stories, sports stories, and other topics publishers believed would help them attract the broadest possible readership. Not until 1915 did popular fiction magazines begin to splinter into the genres we know today, in particular the detective story, the love story, and the western. In chapter 6, I demonstrate that the western love story magazine emerged in tandem with the male-oriented action western as publishers developed specialized titles and catered increasingly to gendered or otherwise specialized readerships rather than families. Although men's and women's western titles were developed simultaneously, the masculine version became known as the "original" version of the genre while the western love story magazine—which incidentally outlasted all other pulp magazines—was deemed an inferior imitation in early scholarly books about the pulp western. Although western love story magazines featured a relatively narrow set of plots and characters and naturalized patriarchal and heteronormative ideals, they also contested these ideals through content such as Muriel Newhall's series character Sheriff Minnie, a cross-dressing forty-something law woman who was a staple of the publisher Street & Smith's Romantic Range series in the 1930s and 1940s.

Collectively, these linked case studies tell an alternative origin story of the popular western. Women writers have been active at virtually every stage in the history of this iconic genre, from its nascent period in the late nineteenth century, when cowboys and cattle wars became subjects of national fascination, to its proliferation in cheap genre magazines between the wars. This book is an attempt both to recover some of the many women's texts that have helped shaped the western and to help expose and dismantle the processes and structures that have hitherto excluded them from view.

1
Western Violence and the Limits of Sentimental Power

The late nineteenth-century cattle boom of the far West set the stage for a new frontier hero—the cowboy. Although widely regarded as a descendent of James Fenimore Cooper's Leatherstocking, the colonial frontier scout who guided "civilization" into the wilderness, the cowboy differed from the scout figure as a wage-earning laborer rather than a semiautonomous scout contracted by colonizers to guide their incursions into the wilderness. Cowboy westerns thereby brought postindustrial class tensions into the frame of the frontier encounter between "savagery" and "civilization." Considered the founding modern western, Owen Wister's *The Virginian* (1902) deployed the cowboy hero to advance the interests, not of the laboring class from which he originates, but of the men constituting what Christine Bold calls "the frontier club": a cadre of elite men from some of America's wealthiest families (*Frontier Club* xvii). By working his way up from cowboy to ranch manager to cattleman in his own right, Wister's cowboy figure bridged two classes who, in reality, were sharply divided in the West: The ranch owners, known as "cattlemen," owned the cattle and were mainly businessmen from the eastern United States and Europe. The term "cowboy" marked the socially inferior status of the cowboys, young working-class men who managed the herds but did not own them or have much of a prospect of transcending the ranks of labor (Moore 34). In cowboy fiction, the western cattle range became a mythic space in which ideological struggle between labor and capital played out, its outcome carrying the weight of natural law. While *The Virginian* has been canonized as the foundational text of the cowboy-western tradition, it was preceded by more than ten years by *The Administratrix*, a novel about cowboys written by Colorado populist and suffragist Emma Ghent Curtis, published in 1889. Although remarkably different in political vision from *The Virginian*, *The Administratrix* is generically very similar: Its narrative of the cattle frontier is structured around a romance between a well-bred eastern schoolteacher and a humbly born but innately noble cowboy; it envisions the struggle between legitimate and illegitimate pursuit of wealth and power in terms of a narrative vocabulary that has become familiar in western films and novels: cowboys, schoolmarms, outlaws, large powerful cattle outfits, entrepreneurial cowboys, lynchings, and violent confrontation. Indeed, *The Administratrix* looks very much like the form that we know as the western. This novel raises key questions, then, about the emergent period of the western and its relation to women as readers and writers.

Emma Ghent Curtis was a prominent populist and woman suffrage activist in Colorado during the 1880s and 1890s. She was born in 1862 in Jackson County, Indiana, to parents Ira Ghent and Mary Palmer Ghent. Her father's occupation was listed in the 1860 Census as farmer. By 1885, according to the Colorado state census of that year, Emma had married James Curtis, a farmer who had immigrated from England and was living in close quarters in Fremont County, Colorado, where she, James, and their three-year-old son shared a home, apparently with James's brother and sister-in-law, their child, and two other adults, one male and one female. The 1900 Federal Census reveals that, in 1886, Emma's daughter Mary was born. Although a farmer's wife with two small children, Emma managed to publish her first novel, *The Fate of a Fool*, in 1888 and her second, *The Administratrix*, in 1889. At some point before or in the early years of her marriage, she was also the editor of the Canon City newspaper the *Royal Gorge Review*. Perhaps her female housemates and she shared childcare, enabling Emma to become active politically and as a writer. Her earnings from her writing were likely welcome contributions to the family income.[1]

Curtis was a central figure in the 1892 campaign for woman suffrage in Colorado. Writing in 1910, Alice Hubbard remembered Curtis' appearance at the convention of the newly formed Colorado People's Party:

> In that meeting appeared a little woman named Emma Ghent Curtis, from Canon City, who buttonholed the delegates in favor of putting a plank in the platform for woman suffrage. Our convention was the first of all the parties. I was not favorable to it at the first, not because I was opposed to it, but because I felt it was not expedient just at that time—I had not progressed far enough to demand right because it was right, and as my influence was really a dominant one in the meeting she had to have me. I could not reason her out of it, and finally agreed to let the plank go in. The Democratic Convention met, then she went to get it in that, and then she got it into the Republican platform—so that all the platforms had the demand for woman suffrage. . . . And it was made into law because that little lone woman left her home and her babies and battled for it alone. (Hubbard 127)

Although remembered as a lone heroine for the cause, Curtis was probably one of a community of political women in Colorado. A dozen women attended the Denver convention of the Colorado People's Party as elected delegates; however, an article in the *Woman's Journal* credited Curtis's influence with their election. Clearly she was a political force in the Colorado suffrage campaign (Washburn 276). Curtis remained politically active throughout the 1890s: In 1894 she ran for the Colorado State senate, and in 1898 she was nominated to the Populist ticket for the state election. She was also a commissioner of the Colorado Industrial School for Boys. Curtis continued to write and publish, mostly poetry, until her death. Her poems appeared in various national and regional magazines and newspapers. One of her short stories was featured in a special issue of *Century* featuring western authors, in which her name appeared alongside the likes of Mary Austin. She died in Canon City in 1918, at the age of fifty-eight, and her funeral received a prominent headline in the local paper, suggesting her significant stature in her community.[2]

The Administratrix was published in 1889, four years before woman suffrage was passed in Colorado. It is impossible to know how much Curtis's novel influenced Colorado voters, who had defeated the first suffrage referendum in 1877, but the novel has much to tell us about the emergence of the cowboy as a rhetorical figure who could be deployed in the interest of woman suffrage advocacy. Contrary to later theories of the western as a genre constituted in opposition to women's culture and authority (Tompkins, *West* 41–42), the first known cowboy hero represented outside of the dime novel tradition was a vocal woman suffrage advocate. How is it that Curtis recognized in this figure the potential for legitimizing a political movement that was still widely regarded as radical, if not an aberration of nature? To answer this question, we need to explore the political and cultural context in which *The Administratrix* was written.

Historians have attributed the successful passage of woman suffrage in Colorado in 1893 to the formation of an alliance between woman suffragists and Colorado populists, culminating in the formation of the Colorado People's Party in 1891, of which Emma Ghent Curtis was an active member. Curtis had been a member of the Farmers' Alliance (Diggs), which, along with the Woman's Christian Temperance Union, women's clubs, and voluntary associations, provided a new institutional home for the woman suffrage movement after the defeat of the first suffrage referendum in 1877 (Mead 59). When the Farmers' Alliance joined forces with various labor and reform organizations to form the Colorado People's Party (Mead 61), woman suffrage played a prominent role in debates about the new party's platform. While Colorado populists were generally more supportive of women's political engagement than other major parties (Edwards 102), many populists believed that open support of woman suffrage could harm the party's chances in the short term and advocated shelving it for a later day (Mead 62). Emma Ghent Curtis, who was the Colorado delegate to the national Populist conventions of 1891 and 1892, wrote and published *The Administratrix* in 1889, two years before the formation of the Colorado People's Party. At that time, she was probably already involved with the Farmers' Alliance, one of the key groups that contributed to the formation of the Colorado People's Party and a key locus for woman suffrage activism in Colorado.

Curtis was well aware that the success of woman suffrage in Colorado depended on the support of men, particularly working-class, Hispanic, black, and immigrant men, who were largely blamed for the defeat of woman suffrage in 1877 (Mead 58). Indeed, veterans of that first campaign may well have warned Curtis about the hostile reception that greeted national woman suffrage organizers, who had come to Colorado to assist the 1877 campaign. They were maligned in the local press as "men in petticoats and women in pantaloons" who had come from afar to mettle in Colorado's business (quoted in Mead 59). Curtis found in the figure of the cowboy a vehicle for woman suffrage rhetoric with which the working-class men whose support she courted could identify, whose proven masculinity answered suspicions that woman suffrage would emasculate men, and whose identity was strongly associated with Colorado, rather than with eastern elites.

The "administratrix" referred to in the title is the novel's heroine, Mary, who, like Curtis herself, moves from Indiana to Colorado. She secures a post teaching school and soon falls in love with and marries a local cowboy named Jim. A successful rancher in his own right, Jim is also a vocal critic of the plight of women and advocate for women's rights who frequently lectures Mary about the need for women to assert their rights more forcefully and resist their passive role. Jim also embodies populist politics as an "ordinary" citizen beset by greedy, wealthy, and powerful elites. A cowboy who gradually acquires his own herd, Jim is soon regarded as a threat to established cattlemen. Jim finds himself the subject of malicious and false rumors that he is a cattle thief and is murdered by vigilantes while in the sheriff's custody, leaving his widow, Mary, the titular administratrix of his estate. To find Jim's murderers and avenge his death, Mary cross-dresses as a cowboy and secures a job at the ranch operated by Jim's killers and eventually confronts and kills them in a violent shootout. This remarkable novel is the most significant known work of fiction written by a nineteenth-century westerner to deal specifically with woman suffrage in the West. In the remainder of this chapter, I argue that the *Administratrix* registers and attempts to resolve the multiple tensions that framed Curtis's position as a westerner, a woman suffrage advocate, and a populist.

The familiar story of the cowboy's reputation before Buffalo Bill and, later, Owen Wister redeemed him is that he was regarded as a dangerous criminal, but this generalization obscures the complexity in early depictions of the cowboy that would have influenced Emma

Ghent Curtis's novel. If we presume that she penned her novel in the mid- to late 1880s, Curtis would have been familiar with representations of cowboys circulating in the Colorado press as well as in national American popular forms such as dime novels, tobacco cards, wild west shows, and tournaments (now known as rodeos), which were varied and contradictory. Warren French's 1951 study concluded that the earliest dime novel cowboy, dating to the mid-1880s, "was not the same person we expect to find in contemporary romances" (221). These early cowboys were idiosyncratic, reflecting the points of view of their creators in the absence of a predominant set of conventions. Some were heroes, some were criminals, some were flawed, some were idealized (French 221–32). Christine Bold sees populist class affiliations in early dime novel cowboys, as well as depictions of violence that are more ironic and self-reflexive than the frontier club westerns that would eventually dominate the popular western market (*Frontier Club* 90–94).

Colorado newspapers of the 1880s were equally varied in their depictions of cowboys. Generally they took a more paternalistic tone toward the cowboy than did the dime novel, suggesting their affiliation with the dominant members of Colorado society. They certainly highlighted the criminality of the cowboy, but they regarded him as much with class-based derision as they did with fear. In her study of Texas cowboys, Jacqueline Moore demonstrates the class lines that were drawn between socially inferior, infantilized cowboys and the cattlemen who ran the cattle industry and commanded respect as community and industry leaders (49). The *Alamosa Journal* echoed this ideology, describing the cowman as "a proprietor, a steady, sagacious, and useful citizen" and the cowboy as "a rough hireling, taking pride only in his pistol, his lariat, and his ability to drink without limit and fight without cause."[3] The *Castle Rock Journal* derisively satirized the close relationship between the cowboy and his pony: "[They] have developed into an inferior kind of Centaur.... Some scientists, however, dispute this, as several specimens of cowboys have been from time to time discovered, who . . . detach themselves from their mustangs and disappear into certain business houses, where their wants are attended to by a man wearing a diamond breastpin and white apron." Hinting scornfully at the Hispanic men who made up a significant segment of the cowboy population in Colorado (Moore 40), this same article noted that the cowboy uses profanity "equally well either in Mexican or United States language."[4] In the hierarchy of one small town in Colorado, according to the *Aspen Times*, cowboys rated lower than the local saloon owner, who was lauded for his ability to keep the peace with the cowboys who were his main clientele.[5] When, in 1882, two cowboys terrorized the village at Fort Garland before opening fire on the fort itself, the *Aspen Times* described them with more contempt than fear: The ringleader was "a blow-hard. . . . He aspired to be a desperado, and was a success in so far that he became notorious; but no great crime of any consequence has ever been fastened upon him: He hadn't grit enough, nor was he sharp enough to plan a stage robbery, drive off a herd of cattle, or rob a national bank. He made his name by bull-dozing over the weak, getting drunk and running small border towns."[6] Colorado papers exaggerated the criminal activity of cowboys by reporting on cowboy violence in other states and territories. An article entitled "Cow Boy's Fun" in the *Aspen Weekly Times* reported a shooting between rival cowboy gangs in "Whichitaw," Kansas, that left one dead and two wounded.[7] Similar articles reported on cowboys shooting each other in a drunken dispute in Albuquerque, New Mexico,[8] and cowboys in Wyoming who terrorized stagecoach passengers by pretending to fire at them.[9]

Cowboys were depicted as harmless buffoons in an *Alamosa Journal* story describing a gang that stole agate stones from a dealer on a train, not knowing that they had little real value except to naïve tourists, and a cowboy-miner who slid down a snowy slope in a copper mining pan was derided for not realizing that snow friction heats copper seven times faster than fire: "There was weeping and wailing and gnashing of teeth," the paper mocked.[10] A cowboy arrived in Virginia City

> on the hurricane deck of a sad-eyed mule and was amusing a crowd on C street by causing the animal to perform numerous tricks. Chief of Police Henderson appeared on the scene and ordered [the cowboy] to move on with his mule and be p.d.q. about it too, or he would arrest both him and the animal. Smith expressed a doubt of the chief's ability to take the mule into custody. The officer approached the mild-eyed mule and reached for the bridle rein. Its owner quietly remarked, 'Butt him over, Ned." The

next instant the chief lay on the broad of his back in the middle of the street from a pile-driver butt from the mule's head.[11]

Not all representations of cowboys in the Colorado press were disparaging or condescending. Acts of violence carried out by cowboys against the Ute Tribe were considered a normal part of a cowboy's duty in confrontations with cattlemen over rangeland and were reported without commentary in an article that described one such skirmish, emphasizing the bravery of an officer but barely mentioning the cowboys: "The engagement between the cowboys and Indians, which took place more than two weeks ago, near the mouth of the San Juan river in Utah was fraught with interesting incidents, showing the demoniacal savagery of the Indians in the battle and the bravery of an army officer."[12] A similar article commended as "righteous" the murder of several Ute by cowboys.[13] An early example of romanticized images of cowboys, an article titled "Life in a Cow Camp," emphasized the cowboy's work ethic and ability to withstand privation: The cowboy "springs from his bed as if he had been wide awake, pulls on his boots and coat, buckles on his spurs, takes his bridle out of his bed—for a cowboy's bed is his harness room and portmanteau—catches up his hat, flips his tarpaulin back over his bed, and stumbles off over the rough prairie to where his night horse is staked. Three movements of his hands and the horse is bridled and free from the rope." Meanwhile, his counterpart, relieved from night duty, "gives a sigh of relief as he wets his throat, dry with dust of two hours on the trampled bed grounds, shivers as the cold water reaches his stomach, turns to warm himself at the fire, then decides that he is too sleepy, and rolls himself in his heavy blankets."[14]

Buffalo Bill's Wild West Show, which was first held in Omaha, Nebraska, in 1883 and included cowboys in its repertoire, played a significant role in redeeming the cowboy's reputation in Colorado (Reddin 59, 68–69). Perhaps influenced by Buffalo Bill, a "cowboy tournament" was held in Denver in the fall of 1887. The *Aspen Weekly Times* reported that it was the first event of its kind in Denver and had attracted 12,000 spectators.[15] A particular turning point in the reputation of the cowboy in Colorado was Buffalo Bill's European tour in 1889, after which newspaper accounts of cowboys are much less ambivalent and more laudatory than previously. That year, the *Aspen Morning Chronicle* reported that a "cowboy inauguration excursion train" set out for Washington to represent Colorado in the inauguration of Benjamin Harrison as president.[16] The movements of Buffalo Bill's cowboys were closely followed: Newspapers described the spectacle of buffalo and horses loading onto a steamship destined for Paris[17] and lauded the exploits of cowboys in Europe: "Cowboys in Paris" ran one headline.[18] The *Aspen Daily Chronicle* reported that Buffalo Bill's cowboys were able to subdue horses previously thought untrainable.[19] With the rise of celebrity cowboys, Colorado newspapers started to object more vocally to their undeserved reputation: The *Carbonate Chronicle* blamed the cowboy's bad reputation on Texas cowboys, claiming that Colorado cowboys were different: They were hard workers who minded their own business, got drunk only occasionally, and used their guns only in extreme situations. "This may not be the cowboy the eastern mind pictures him, but it is the cowboy—at least the western Colorado cowboy—of today."[20] Newspapers reported less on cowboys' criminal activities and spent more time explaining the "real" cowboy to their readers. The *Aspen Daily Chronicle* explained in detail how a lasso was made.[21] The same paper corrected misrepresentations of cowboys on tobacco cards and in wild west shows: "Outside of Wild West shows there is scarcely any of this headlong throwing of heavy cattle which has common illustration in cigarette pictures." Cowboys wore high heels, the newspaper reported, not out of fashion, but so they could dig into the ground when roping cattle with one foot.[22]

The Administratrix was published in 1889, on the cusp of this emergence of the cowboy hero in Colorado print culture as well as in the midst of the second major campaign for woman suffrage in Colorado. Curtis saw in this emerging hero a vehicle for popularizing woman suffrage in a state that had resoundingly defeated it in 1877. On the one hand, the cowboy had paid his dues as a denigrated member of the working class. Labor and populist groups in Colorado, whose members included workers and farmers of various ethnicities, could identify with the cowboy as one of their own—an exploited worker and victim of the prejudice of eastern Anglo-American elites. On the other hand, the cowboy had amassed enough cultural capital to make him a viable spokesperson in favor of woman suffrage. Whereas the 1877 campaign suffered from the identification of suffrage with eastern elites, Curtis's cowboy-suffragist took advantage of the cowboy's emergence in Colorado print culture as a marker of authentic Colorado identity.

Curtis included a short preface to her novel that signals her entry into debate about the "real" cowboy: "I have attempted to depict the cowboy as he is" (*The Administratrix* 5). Despite the celebrity that cowboys were beginning to enjoy when Curtis published her novel, she still represents them as objects of the prejudice that cowboys are racially mixed and dangerous. Her cowboy hero, Jim, is introduced as a potentially dangerous figure in the eyes of the novel's heroine, a schoolteacher newly arrived from the East, who is at first put off by his appearance. "I don't believe he'd look so bad if he were dressed like a white man. And so that is a cowboy—a real, genuine cowboy. And yet he didn't eat me" (13). That Jim is not dressed like a "white man" invokes the racism that inflected negative images of the cowboy discussed above. Although the narrator reassures readers that Jim is white, he can easily be mistaken for Hispanic or Native American because of his tanned skin and Native dress: "His face would have been fair but for exposure to the scorching Colorado sun; the eyes were blue, intense and searching" (10). We are subsequently told that Jim comes from New York State, not Texas, differentiating his Anglo-Saxon ancestry from the Hispanic ancestry of many Southwestern cowboys. As the plot develops, Jim vies for Mary's affection with another cowboy, Stan, who makes a better first impression on Mary with his finer dress and manners. Readers learn to decipher conflicted ideas about cowboys in the broader culture as Mary attends a roundup, learns to drink water from a hat brim, acquires a taste for baked beans, and, most important, chooses a husband. At first, Mary is duped by appearances, taking an instant dislike to Jim, preferring the attentions of Stan. The kind elderly couple that Mary boards with insists that Jim is hardworking and honest, while others, like the well-to-do Chellis family that befriends Mary, are suspicious of Jim because of his mysterious origins. From Mary's negotiations of these competing versions of the cowboy emerges Curtis's cowboy hero.

The danger that Mary will marry the wrong man, also the theme of Curtis's first novel, *The Fate of a Fool*, was a particularly resonant theme for Colorado suffragists. As historians of western women such as Glenda Riley have demonstrated, women in the nineteenth-century West depended on a good marriage for their economic future, given their very limited economic opportunities, which consisted primarily of service, sex work, or, for women with some education or capital, teaching and certain small businesses. Of primary concern to them was whether or not a prospective husband would be a stable provider and a fair head of household. It was not uncommon for women to negotiate terms with prospective husbands "regarding such habits as smoking, drinking, and gambling. . . . They also converted men to active Christianity and defined their own decision-making powers in future relationships" (Riley, *Building and Breaking* 23). To misread a prospective husband's character was a mistake with potentially dire consequences, from the scandal of divorce to having to care for children without a reliable male provider. Mary comes close to such a mistake when she spurns Jim in favor of the attentions of Stan, but she is saved at the last minute from a bad marriage when she overhears Stan brag to Jim that she is his for the taking: "These girls all come out here to marry," he says, "Most anybody can get 'em" (115). Learning that Stan is only interested in her as a servant to look after him and his aging mother, Mary rejects him and realizes that she has feelings for Jim, which she has been repressing because of her prejudices against his inferior dress, manners, and "dark" features. The subsequent marriage between Mary and Jim resolves the novel's opening conflict over the nature and character of the cowboy.

Curtis deploys the hero she has constructed as the main mouthpiece of her woman suffrage message in the novel. Significantly, her heroine, Mary, is not vocal politically. Despite similarities to Curtis herself—both have moved to Colorado from Indiana, work as teachers, have written for newspapers, and marry ranchers—Mary is not modeled entirely on Curtis, who, as we have seen, was highly politicized. Jim, rather than Mary, is the vehicle Curtis uses to articulate arguments in favor of woman suffrage and other reforms that will improve the condition of women. The novel is particularly concerned with prostitution, which was a pressing issue for Colorado reformers. Prostitution flourished in Colorado in the 1880s and 1890s, fueled by the large population of young, single men working in the territory's booming mining industry (MacKell 71). Despite ordinances against it, prostitution was tolerated by authorities because of the large amounts of money it contributed to city coffers in the form of fines and because powerful mining companies resisted antiprostitution ordinances. Not until the early 1900s did efforts begin in earnest to stop the blatant practice of prostitution in Colorado's dance halls, saloons, gambling dens, and brothels (MacKell 198–99). Prostitution was also a touchstone issue for the national Populists, who condemned the established political parties for creating the poverty and joblessness that forced women into prostitution (Edwards 95). In *The Administratrix*, prostitution is the key symptom of women's unjust state as a disenfranchised class. Dependent on men, women too easily succumb to men's sexual advances in hopes of a good marriage, only to be abandoned, often with children to care for. For such women, prostitution is the only means of survival left. To drive home this point, Curtis devotes a chapter of her novel to a cowboy's deathbed confession of such abandonment: Influenced by fellow members of his "gang," Hen Hall had seduced a young girl, then abandoned her when she told him she was pregnant and asked him to save her from disgrace. She was forced to work in a dance hall to support herself and her child. Such institutions, where women were paid to dance with male patrons, were widely regarded as one step away from prostitution (MacKell 13). Mother and child eventually died from exposure after both were thrown out of a dance hall during a blizzard.

While the novel's heroine voices no opinions about prostitution, the cowboy hero Jim claims, in his many speeches on the subject, that prostitution would end if men were forced to marry the women they seduced, who would then have legal recourse for support. Women, Jim further pontificates, must exercise their influence over men in order to improve their condition:

> I don't justify-men's faults—I think them contemptible—but if women would stand up for their own rights, and have nothing to do with men who mistreat their sex, or who drink and carouse around, there's be an improvement in things. Women could lead men anywhere if they'd just set about it. Instead of that, they hand over the reins to the man, and consent to *be* led. . . . I know the women are not used right. . . . It's a shame,

and I'd like to see things righted; but the women ought to show more spirit. They keep too still under their ill-treatment; they don't say a word about wrongs that men would raise the devil about. Women don't know their power. . . . If the women would keep ding-dingin' at [the men] all the time, they'd wake up and do something. (*The Administratrix* 83–85)

Jim invokes an ideology of women's power that was pervasive for most of the nineteenth century in debates about woman suffrage and women's political role. It is well established in scholarship on American woman suffrage that its rhetoric combined arguments based on natural rights with arguments based on expediency. While rights-based arguments emphasized women's equality with men as persons in their own right, arguments based on expediency suggested that enfranchised women would improve American political life because of their superior moral nature (Chapman and Mills, "Introduction" 2). Suffrage would enable women to exercise in American political life the same moral influence that enabled them to create in the home a haven from the competitive and amoral public sphere. Women's organizations such as the Woman's Christian Temperance Union argued that "women's vote . . . would express her higher, selfless nature" (Baker 95). Frederick Douglass similarly argued for woman suffrage on the grounds that women were natural pacifists who would bring peace to an America riven by Civil War (Chapman and Mills, "Introduction to Part 1" 15).

In the remainder of this chapter I show that, in *The Administratrix*, this moral form of female political power proves illusory, but let me first set up my reading by appealing to a classic example of women's moral power, which Jane Tompkins has called "sentimental power" (*Sensational Designs* 122–46): *Uncle Tom's Cabin* dramatizes women's political engagement through the figure of Mrs. Bird. She persuades her husband to shelter the fugitive slave Eliza despite the fact that he voted for the Fugitive Slave Act. Mrs. Bird's inherent Christian morality moves her to interfere in the political affairs of her husband when she learns he has voted for the act that would criminalize citizens in free states who harbored escaped slaves: "Her husband and children were her entire world, and in these she ruled more by entreaty and persuasion than by command or argument. There was only one thing that was capable of arousing her, and that provocation came in on the side of her unusually gentle and sympathetic nature;—anything in the shape of cruelty would throw her into a passion, which was the more alarming and inexplicable in proportion to the general softness of her nature" (Stowe 68). Mrs. Bird's inherent moral superiority goes hand in hand with a feminine mode of power, exercised not through mannish assertiveness, but through the natural, womanly influence she exercises as a wife and a mother. She intervenes politically only when Christian sympathy arouses her passions sufficiently to engage in the political world. This impassioned political engagement is rendered all the more powerful in comparison to Mrs. Bird's normally passive state. Her rare interventions in political matters leave Senator Bird virtually powerless to resist.

The concept of women's moral superiority to men was a facet of Barbara Welter's well-known theory of the "cult of true womanhood," an ideology of womanhood composed of the values of piety, purity, domesticity, and submissiveness (21). This discourse of womanly authority has been identified with a particular class of women: white, middle-class, and eastern (Hewitt 2). Subsequent scholarship in American women's history has demonstrated that it falls far short of describing the multiple experiences of American women in the nineteenth century (Hewitt 11). While it was a powerful rhetorical means of combating the position that woman suffrage was an aberration of women's nature, the discourse of women's moral influence was incompatible with the material conditions of frontier living, even for women such as Curtis, whose writing suggests that she identified with middle-class values of womanhood. As Glenda Riley has shown, conditions on the "female frontier" were at odds with many of the values attached to middle-class womanhood: Owing to the structure of frontier economies and the relative shortage of women, marriage was more obviously "a matter of economic necessity" on the western frontier than it was in the East, compelling many couples to set aside sentimental ideals in their choice of a mate (Riley, *Female Frontier* 18). Life was hard for both rural and urban women. The former were expected to perform both their domestic duties and fill in for the men when required, and many worked outside the home to provide needed income for the family. Women in cities waded through muddy streets, lived among (or worked in) saloons, dance halls, and brothels, and were not considered safe at night without a male escort (Riley, *Female Frontier* 76–101, 121–47). Riley concludes that, despite these obstacles, women on the "female frontier" were, at the end of the day, expected to fulfill their domestic roles: "Rather than changing women's established routines and concerns, [the frontier] simply made women's pursuits and lives more difficult" (*Female Frontier* 101). Under these conditions it would be difficult for Colorado women to experience their gender as a source of power and authority. This gap between the material realities faced by Colorado women and the discourses that attributed to them an innate, womanly ability to influence others to a higher morality manifests itself in the violent ending to *The Administratrix*.

The Administratrix superficially subscribes to ideals of women's "natural" moral influence, but the novel does not model this influence in any of its female characters. Such an ideology underlines Mary's roles both as a schoolteacher and harbinger of civilization in the West and, once she marries Jim, as female head of a ranching household. In an article for the Kansas woman suffrage and populist newspaper *Farmer's Wife*, Curtis wrote that it was the ranch "queen's" responsibility to combat the influence of saloons over the cowboys by providing wholesome entertainment for them at the ranch. "If the home is made the pleasantest place in the world then the showy, lively, inviting saloons will have less success in enticing young men to their downfall and death" ("Woman on the Ranch" 1). Accordingly, her novel's heroine organizes regular entertainments at the ranch, where neighbors and cowboys gather to tell stories, recite poetry, and sing songs. Nevertheless, she has precious little influence over the bawdy cowboys that work and board there. One of the workers, Lat, an unrepentant womanizer, declares that "they's nothing in this world that's so plentiful and so easy got as women. They're so d—d servile that they'll take any kind of kick, and are always standin' ready to marry anybody they can get. They're easier to get than Texas cows. You've got to have twenty-five dollars to get a Texas cow, but a man, no matter what he's done, can get a woman with a little soft talk" (*The Administratrix* 245). Lat makes sexual advances toward Mary, further challenging her stature as the female head and moral center of the home. When Mary complains to Jim about Lat's unwanted attention, Jim conveniently forgets his advice to Mary that women should stand up for themselves and admonishes her to put up with him because Jim can't afford to lose him. While Mary's cultural evenings service the text's secondary aim of showcasing the cowboy's civilized graces, they have little influence on the cowboys most in need of moral uplift.

The didactic message of this pro–woman's rights text, then, is not borne out by its representation of women's influence inside or outside of marriage. Single women are prey, and in their search for a provider they are too often misled by displays of wealth. Although Jim frequently lectures on the power of women to influence men, there is no character in the novel that models this ideology. Rather, Curtis's female characters are subject to the kinds of limitations on their authority that most Colorado women were likely to experience. They are vulnerable to sexual exploitation and reliant on marriage for their economic survival. Various subplots relate the plight of particularly vulnerable women: For example, during one of the storytelling sessions, we hear the story of the poverty-stricken Louise Hay, whose father plans to marry her off to the wealthy but coarse Bug Johnson. The hero of the story "rescues" Louise by marrying her himself. Another subplot of the novel relays the story of dance-hall girl Eulalia, another victim of the womanizer Lat. We learn that she was lured away from her home in French Canada by promises of wealth and was then virtually enslaved, traded from one dance hall to the next: "Just as the world was one great cotton-field to the slave who was dragged from post to pillar for the money he could earn for idle hands, so to her the world was one great dance-house" (*The Administratrix* 269–70). The novel's main female characters are more privileged but are far from moral exemplars: The well-to-do Amy Chellis finds practicing piano too much work and enjoys toying with the affections of cowboys. Mary's sister, Iola, dresses extravagantly and cannot focus enough to read a novel through to the end. Mary is deemed "a missionary among the wild men" when she first marries Jim and sets out to "civilize" him (129), but, as we have seen, her influence over the "wild men" is limited.

In order to reconcile this tension between the rhetoric of female moral influence and the realities of women's authority in the West, Curtis transforms her heroine into a man with a gun. At the turning point in the novel, Mary's woman suffragist cowboy husband is wrongly accused of cattle rustling by a rival cattle outfit and lynched. The widowed Mary is named the administratrix of his estate and inherits both his ranch and his role as the text's central authority figure and voice of women's rights rhetoric. Seeking to bring her husband's killers to justice, Mary disguises herself as a young cowboy named Mose and infiltrates the ranch where the men she suspects of killing her husband work. Whereas she had no power over the womanizing Stan when she was dressed as a woman, the cowboy Mose soon has the cowboys completely in his thrall. He delivers lengthy lectures on the evils of saloons and prostitution to which the cowboys listen with rapt attention:

> He explained to the men how they were laying up want, disease and vagrancy for their old age; how they were throwing away in the purchase of these curses the money that might found for themselves comfortable homes. His remarks, merciless and caustic in the highest degree, spared no one; he commended all honest pastime, but scourged without moderation all injurious folly. (321)

In the guise of a cowboy, Mary is transformed into a model example of the sentimental heroine. This newfound authority as Mose is represented as an authentically feminized essence that penetrates her masculine attire: "Now the depressed, handsome, childlike, frank and honest appearing Mose was making a strong impression on the hearts of these rough men. Sex may be hidden, but its effect remains" (319). Ironically, it is only when Mary's sex *is* hidden that it has any real effect on the men around her. This irony undermines the discourse of feminine sentimental power, revealing this power as having its origins in the trappings of patriarchy. When alive, for example, Jim admonished Mary to exert herself, but his refusal to fire Lat for harassing her exposes him as the ultimate arbiter of the limits of her authority. Similarly, Mary can only infiltrate and influence the cowboy community by masquerading as a man.

Whereas sentimental power conventionally operates by converting its subject to a superior moral position, Mary's goal is not conversion but revenge. Using her feminine power to win the trust and admiration of Jim's killers, Mary as Mose bides her time until conditions are ripe for exacting revenge. During a roundup, she waits until she is alone with each of her intended victims and kills them in a violent and rhetorically charged confrontation in which she reveals her true identity and delivers a scathing indictment of their crime before dispatching them with her gun: "Know that I am Mary Madnau. . . . In less than half an hour you will be giving an account of your crimes before the bar of God. . . . Now stand still while I pass sentence on you, and do not disturb me. Your father was the head of the ring that made me a widow . . . and for it, *you shall die* (356). Mary's victim then "fell rather than knelt upon the ground, covering his face with his hands. Mary sat upon her horse . . . the revolver in [her hand]. . . . Her face was like marble, and tears were coursing down her cheeks. . . . The shot rang out clear and sharp. Harry Talbert sank to the ground. Blood spurted from a huge hole in his breast. His unclosed eyes took on the death stare" (357). Claiming the sentimental heroine's power as God's intercessor, and crying the sentimental heroine's tears, Mary nonetheless uses a gun to drive her message home.

The text's most intractable exploiters of women are purged in this final scene of bloody violence, including Stan, Mary's would-be seducer. Mary's act of revenge is also an act of sacrifice, for she is subsequently shot to death by her victim's defenders. Also meeting his end is Lat, the womanizing ranch hand. Although not part of the murder plot, Lat is so overcome by Mary's act of revenge and subsequent death that he rides during a storm into the wilderness and certain death, but not before delivering the last word on women's rights in the text: "It's the result of our nature to love women, and it's the result of our trainin' and theirs, for us to pursue 'em forever and never be satisfied. O, sometimes I think, if I could, I'd destroy 'em all. . . . O how I hate the system that trained this fever in me!" (369) The most intractable womanizer in the text is converted, not through exposure to the influence of a good woman, but through a bloody scene of purging violence.

The ideal subject of mainstream American woman suffrage discourse was the middle-class white woman—among the least vulnerable classes of women in American society. They were educated and often encouraged to exert their independence through professional and volunteer work, and they had access to far more economic and political capital than working-class women. In Colorado and other western states, however, women who identified as middle class faced material obstacles to exercising their presumed superior moral authority. The resulting tension is embedded in *The Administratrix*: While the novel admonishes Colorado women to exert their "natural" power over men in order to achieve their full rights as citizens, it takes men's clothes and a gun to convert Colorado to the cause of woman suffrage.

2

Domestic Politics and Cattle Rustling

Through the 1890s the cowboy transitioned from a regional curiosity to a familiar figure in American popular culture. A number of factors contributed to this process: The pronouncement of frontier closure in the 1890 U.S. Census triggered the memorialization of a way of life that many assumed would shortly disappear. Cowboys figured prominently in Buffalo Bill's Wild West Show and the dime novels of Prentiss Ingram (French 229–31). The cowboy had also begun to appear more frequently in "quality" fiction by Stephen Crane, Florence Finch Kelly, Frances McElrath, Owen Wister, and others. Kelly, McElrath, and Wister all drew particular inspiration from the so-called range wars, or conflicts over the unfenced western ranges, which were widely reported in national newspapers.[1] These conflicts between wealthy cattle ranches and smaller ranchers and settlers resonated nationally given the rise of corporate monopolies and labor unrest in America more generally (Slotkin, *Gunfighter* 171–74). The most well known of the range wars, the 1892 Johnson County War in Powder River, Wyoming, was the backdrop for the two novels I consider in this chapter: Frances McElrath's *The Rustler* and Owen Wister's *The Virginian*, both published in April 1902. Much attention has been paid to Wister's representation of the conflict in the archetypal terms of good (ranchers) versus evil (rustlers); indeed, Wister's version has been credited with making the cowboy an exemplar of American ideals such as self-determination, a strong work ethic, and an innate sense of moral virtue. However, Wister's was one voice, albeit a powerful one, in a broader debate about the origins of the range wars and their national significance. In this chapter I demonstrate that this debate engaged women as writers and readers by calling attention to social divisions that, many women reformers argued, resulted from women's exclusion from full participation in American political life.

The Virginian references the Johnson County War during a pivotal event in the text: the lynching of Steve, best friend to the novel's eponymous hero, after Steve becomes a cattle rustler. Although haunted by his part in the murder, The Virginian justifies his role in the lynching by referencing the Johnson County War: "You leave other folks' cattle alone, or you take the consequences, and it was all known to Steve from the start. . . . He knew well enough the only thing that would have let him off would have been a regular jury. For the thieves have got hold of the juries in Johnson County" (Wister 266). The Johnson County War pitted large corporate-style cattle companies against small, independent cattle owners, homesteaders, and cowboys in a struggle over control of the cattle trade. The Virginian adopts the large cattle owners' version of events by branding their competitors as thieves who must be eradicated. This character is Wister's answer to historical cowboys such as Jack Flagg and Nate Champion, who fought against the monopoly of Big Cattle by participating in labor strikes and daring to start their own herds in defiance of policies designed to keep cowboys in positions of servitude.

McElrath also took as her subject the Johnson County War, using it as the backdrop for a romance between a cowboy and a socially superior eastern woman and as the inspiration behind many of her key characters and events. McElrath's cowboy hero starts his own ROB brand in competition with large ranch owners. McElrath's fictional gentleman cattle rancher Horace Carew leads a vigilante attack on the cattle rustlers that culminates when the vigilantes set fire to a rustler's hideout and then shoot him as he flees, events that mirror almost exactly the vigilante murders of Nate Champion and Nick Ray.

The similarities between the two novels certainly invite speculation about possible contact between the two authors; however, I am equally interested in two intriguing and related differences. First, the two novels take quite different positions on the maverick question, a debate over how to distribute unbranded cattle that proved pivotal in sparking violent confrontation between cowboys and large ranchers. Calves of unknown origin posed a unique problem for the cattle trade throughout the period of about 1870 until the close of the nineteenth century. During the great roundups, when ranchers banded together to sort, count, and brand their herds, orphaned calves became objects of explosive tension because of the way in which they disrupted the discourses of class and property on the free range: Cowboys hired to manage the roundups were usually ordered to turn mavericks over to their employers, but some considered these animals part of the public domain and established their own small herds by branding mavericks as their own. Although maverick cattle constituted a relatively small proportion of industry profit, the ideological stakes were high enough to start the "war" in Johnson County, Wyoming. Beginning in the spring of 1892, when two accused cattle rustlers, Nate Champion and Nick Ray, were murdered by a group of fifty vigilante stockmen, this war played out anxieties over class and property ownership in a particularly unstable and difficult- to-control social space. Whereas *The Rustler* foregrounds the maverick debate in its fictional account of the conflict, *The Virginian* is strangely silent on the matter of mavericks. This distinction, I argue more fully below, is a fundamental one. Given that Wister had lived for a time in Johnson County and was likely familiar with the nuances of the maverick debate, his evasion of the maverick question in his fictionalized version of the rustler wars suggests that this debate was somehow incompatible with his own desire to read the conflict as a straightforward contest between the thieving rustlers and honest, hardworking ranchers. *The Rustler*, in contrast, spells out the maverick debate in considerable detail, a move that I argue interprets the Johnson County War as a class conflict rather than a moral one and clears a space for female domestic authority on the frontier.

A second crucial difference between the two novels has to do with their depictions of the cowboy hero. By successfully winning battles on moral, sexual, and economic fronts, The Virginian shows America how to sustain its frontier values post–frontier closure; Wister's hero, known only as The Virginian, is the foreman of a large Wyoming ranch who must break with his cowboy brethren in order to fulfill his duties to his employer. Hanging rustlers—including his best friend Steve—is among The Virginian's more unsavory duties. Such is his loyalty to his employer, however, that The Virginian steadily climbs the ladder of ranch society. Meanwhile, his romance with the refined easterner Molly Stark Wood supplements his increasing salary with the cultural capital necessary to make him a true gentleman. At the novel's climax, The Virginian jeopardizes his social achievements by accepting an invitation from the rustler Trampas to settle their differences in a gunfight, knowing full well that Molly despises violence. But when her fiancé returns victorious, it is Molly who renounces her sentimental principles in thankful surrender to The Virginian's embrace. Marriage to Molly and a partnership in his employer's cattle business are the rewards for our hero's steadfast loyalty and unyielding principles.

The Rustler introduces a cowboy hero named Jim who is very similar to The Virginian: a trustworthy worker of exemplary skill who falls in love with Hazel, an eastern woman above his station. Whereas The Virginian wins Molly's hand in marriage and legitimate entry to the class she represents, Jim learns that Hazel has been leading him on. Disillusioned, he turns cattle rustler and kidnapper, vowing to obtain by criminal means the status he cannot come by honestly. Hazel is also transformed: She realizes her culpability in Jim's criminal turn and transforms from coquette to reformer, eschewing marriage to any man in order to devote her life to reforming the children of cattle rustlers.

The different ways in which these plots unfold envision different root causes of violent struggle in the West and posit equally different remedies: Whereas Wister represents frontier conflict in moral terms, as a struggle between good, hardworking cowboys and evil rustlers, McElrath denaturalizes this narrative by highlighting the role of social inequality in engendering violence. To heal such divisions, McElrath makes a case, not for the gunfighter who will violently eradicate criminals, but for the woman reformer who will peacefully eradicate social injustice. That these two novels answer to each other so closely suggests that whether or not Wister had ever read McElrath's work, or vice versa, these novels occupied opposing positions in a broader cultural debate that included both men's and women's voices. Perhaps the genre that we now recognize as the western became insistently masculine precisely because it had once been well within the purview of women's culture and authority. In order to map out the terrain of this debate, it is necessary first to return to the historical materials used by Wister and McElrath to ground their novels.

Class, Property, and the Rustler Wars

In 1884 the Wyoming government attempted to put an end to ongoing disputes involving maverick cattle by passing the controversial Maverick Law, giving control of calves of unknown origin to the Wyoming Stock Growers Association (WSGA), an elite society of stock owners, many of whom were investors from the eastern states and from overseas. Under this legislation, mavericks were to be turned over to the WSGA, who would be responsible for distributing them at regular auctions.[2] Opponents of the WSGA—including cattle-owning cowboys and homesteaders—bitterly resented the legislation as yet another step in the monopolization of the Wyoming cattle industry by the "cattle lords," an elite inner circle of wealthy cattle owners.

The Maverick Law was supposed to put to rest a problem that had existed for as long as the industry itself but that had become particularly pressing as the cattle industry in Wyoming became more fiercely competitive. Although the practice of grazing cattle on the open range was appealing to the entrepreneurial fantasy of limitless economic expansion, it made the task of determining property ownership problematic. Inevitably, a few animals would escape branding at the yearly roundup, and once they were separated from their mothers, their origin became impossible to determine. This unmarked property was not so much a material as a discursive problem: The orderly distribution of maverick calves required an ideological framework for determining who could legitimately own them. To many cowboys, the maverick calf was a just reward for their skill and resourcefulness. A. S. Mercer, an early historian of the conflict sympathetic to the so-called rustlers, claimed that there was a long tradition of rustling mavericks on the Great Plains: "It was quite common for herd owners to pay the boys from $2.50 to $5 per head for all the 'mavericks' they could put the company's brand on, and 'rustling for mavericks' in the spring was in order all over the range country. . . . This practice taught the cowboy to look upon the unbranded, motherless calf as common, or public property, to be gathered in by the lucky finder" (Mercer 14). Cowboys' claims to the animals, however, were regularly challenged by the owners of large cattle companies, known locally as "lords" or "barons," who claimed title to mavericks found on their property or roped by one of their employees. It was common practice for larger operations to offer salary bonuses to cowboys who turned mavericks over to their bosses and to prosecute cowboys who "mavericked" for themselves. The issue, however, had as much to do with what was implied ideologically by the availability of such animals in the public domain as it did with their formal economic value. The cattleman Granville Stuart averred, "It was only a step from 'mavericking' to branding any calf without a brand, and from that to changing brands" (quoted in H. H. Smith 57). To define mavericks as part of the public domain and concede to their more or less arbitrary distribution had implications for the stability of the institution of property itself.

Contrary to popular fantasies of the West as a timeless refuge from the afflictions of modernity, then, the consolidation of huge economic power blocs and the emergence of a highly vulnerable wage-earning class implicated the cattle industry in debates that were violently engaged in urban settings. Indeed, there are significant correspondences between labor disturbances in Johnson County and those in Chicago, such as the Haymarket massacre of 1886 and the Pullman strike of 1894.[3] The Wyoming cattle trade was not immune to the pattern of boom-and-bust economics, labor unrest, and violent class antagonism that underlined these crises. The boom began in the late 1870s, when the industry began to attract major investors—hailing from such far-flung locations as New York, Philadelphia, Boston, England, and Scotland—who saw in open-range cattle ranching the seemingly ideal realization of laissez-faire corporate capitalism. These investors purchased huge herds, left them to graze on the open range, and reaped the profits in the spring. Boosters such General James S. Brisbin, author of *The Beef Bonanza; or, How to Get Rich on the Plains* (1881), contributed to the popular belief that raising cattle on the open range amounted to a license to print money for those with enough capital to make the initial investment. Such material attracted investors with claims that open-range cattle ranching delivered high dividends with little expense aside from the initial capital investment and that the only skills required were those that came naturally to the well-rounded businessman who enjoyed vigorous outdoor life—"merely a form of outdoor sport that paid dividends" (H. H. Smith 11). The imaginary dimension of the industry infected even its accounting procedures: Entire herds were bought and sold on the basis of the "book count," determined through crude (and wishful) calculations meant to save the expense of actually rounding up and counting the herd. More often than not, the numbers on the books were not borne out when the herds were finally tallied before going to market. Many stockowners went bankrupt this way.

Poor management and harsh weather took their toll, profits dwindled, and in many cases labor was asked to absorb the losses. In 1886, the year of the Haymarket massacre, Wyoming stockmen attempted to implement a significant wage cut, which was successfully resisted through a cowboy strike. Relations between cowboys and their employers deteriorated rapidly in the ensuing years, as did the stability of the industry itself. The crushing blow was delivered when the disastrous winter of 1887 decimated herds and bankrupted ranchers, reducing community morale to an all-time low.

Class struggle in Johnson County was both articulated and enacted through the discourse and practice of cattle rustling. "Men ordinarily honest," writes the Johnson County historian J. Elmer Brock, "stole cattle from the big outfits and did not consider it dishonest but an act justifiable in a war of classes" (quoted in H. H. Smith 115). The WSGA drew up blacklists of cowboys barred from employment, using the term "rustler" in its pejorative sense to label strikers and thieves as well as cowboys who ran their own small herds. Jack Flagg, among the most notorious cowboy activists of the time, had been blacklisted by the WSGA for his part in the 1886 strike. In 1888, he and a group of other blacklisted cowboys formed the HAT brand, sealing their reputations as cattle thieves through this challenge to the WSGA monopoly. With its local newspaper advertisements appearing in brazen proximity to those of established outfits, the prosperous HAT brand signified to many that the rustlers had indeed gotten hold of Johnson County.

Wyoming courtrooms were bogged down with rustling cases in the late 1880s, including various charges against the HAT partners, but popular opinion weighed so heavily against larger cattle companies that most juries refused to convict rustlers, no matter how convincing the evidence. When legal channels failed, some stockmen apparently resorted to vigilante justice. In 1889, the suspected rustlers Ella Watson and James Averell were murdered. Eyewitnesses named a well-known cattle lord as the leader of the lynching. In October 1891, Nate Champion, another well-known cowboy activist and reputed rustler, was attacked in his bed by four men, one of whom Champion identified as a detective working for the WSGA. On separate occasions, in December of that same year, two men with connections to the HAT brand were murdered, both under similar circumstances. Hindsight has prompted historians of Johnson County to look on these events as precursors to the "war" that broke out in April 1892, when a group of vigilante stockmen invaded Johnson County in order to exterminate every suspected rustler in the county, apparently with the blessing of the Wyoming governor Amos Barber.[4] Lurking in the immediate vicinity of this violent confrontation was the figure of the maverick calf. The proceeds from mavericking figured insignificantly in the income of the large cattle companies and can hardly account for the energy spent to prevent cowboys from accessing them. Given the way in which the branded bodies of cattle functioned as representations of property, however, a reading of their structural place in the discourse of free-range capitalism is more likely to account for the way in which the maverick calf was almost always implicated in the property disputes between cowboys and cattle companies.

Within the discourse of property on the open range, the cow's branded body occupied the structural place of what the Lacanian theorist Slavoj Žižek calls the "sublime object" of ideology. The sublime object is an ordinary, everyday object that finds itself occupying the place of the impossible/real object of desire. Such objects appear to transcend the insurmountable gap between signifier and signified—the gap on which the symbolic order is constituted—but in fact they only mask the absence of the impossible/real object within the symbolic. Žižek explains this principle using money as an example: "In the social *effectivity* of the market we . . . *treat* coins as if they consist 'of an immutable substance, a substance over which time has no power, and which stands in antithetic contrast to any matter found in nature'"

(18). Žižek's emphasis here is on the behavioral rather than the intellectual dimension of the illusion: "What [individuals] 'do not know,' what they misrecognize, is the fact that in their social reality itself, in their social activity—in the act of commodity exchange—they are guided by [a] fetishistic illusion" (31). Ideology is, therefore, manifest in social behavior: The social effect of capitalism is such that subjects behave as though money were a sublime object.

The orderly flow of capital within the free-range cattle industry depended on all participants behaving as though cattle were born branded with the transcendental mark of their owner. As Blake Allmendinger has shown in his study of cowboy culture, the brand filled the place of absent owner—or, rather, marked the owner's absence:

> Before fencing transformed the public space of the open range into a series of privately controlled segments of land, cattlemen let their livestock graze with other ranchers' wandering herds; hence animals could easily mix and become confused with one another in promiscuous groups that roamed the unfenced frontier. Ranchers used brands to distinguish their stock from that of the other cattlemen and to protect their possessions from outlaws who could rustle and sell unbranded mavericks. Ranchers invented hieroglyphic economic inscriptions, or forms of language, to inform readers that no one could take ranchers' cattle or mistake their bulls, heifers, calves, and castrated steers for other men's real estate. (4)

The discourse of private property on the free range required its subjects to treat the brand as though it embodied the transcendent, sublime presence of the owner watching over his or her property. Maverick cattle disrupted this illusion by exposing the absence masked by the brand, requiring the industry to confront regularly the arbitrary naming that underpinned the institution of private property.

The fact that rustling convictions were rare was read by cattle companies and their supporters as evidence of a legal-judicial system controlled by rustlers, but most property disputes were grounded in the difficulty of distinguishing between theft and purchase on the open range. Individuals accused of altering or removing existing brands or of driving calves away from their mothers could always legitimate their claim by insisting that the animal in question was found a maverick. The fundamental illegibility of the brand made it possible for competing fantasies of ownership to vie for legitimacy. The social effect was not, however, a general breakdown in the institution of private property; rather, the struggle was articulated as an antagonism between two distinct classes: the wealthy cattle companies, which controlled the range and most of its resources, and an alliance of cowboys, homesteaders, and small-business owners. As Helena Huntington Smith observes, the conflict focused on the figure of the maverick: "To the big stockman the maverick is a symbol of property and the property is mine, not thine. To the little stockmen who came along later, the maverick is a symbol of his own rights on the public domain. The maverick is a source of hatred and strife. The maverick is a boil on the neck of body politic. The maverick is a motherless calf" (86).

In keeping with the class-based underpinnings of the dispute, mavericking was considered a problem only when it disrupted the subordinate status of certain groups, especially cowboys, whose expertise in managing cattle already threatened the dominance of their tenderfoot employers. Attempts to regulate the distribution of maverick cattle throughout the 1880s affected particularly the access of cowboys to mavericks. The 1884 Maverick Law required all mavericks to be turned over to the WSGA for auction but deliberately made no provision for how the auctions were to be carried out, enabling the WSGA to exclude cowboys by demanding expensive bonds and by auctioning the animals in large lots that no cowboy could afford.

Rustling became a crisis in Wyoming in the years following this particular piece of legislation: Cowboys refused to turn mavericks over for auction and were branded rustlers; others deliberately altered the brands of cattle from large stock companies in retaliation against their monopoly. Juries increasingly preferred the claims of the little stockmen to those of the cattle barons. Histories of the Johnson County War tend to dwell on the difficulty of distinguishing the real rustlers from the honest cowboys and attempt to settle the vexed question of which side of the dispute stood on the moral high ground. Such questions are unanswerable because the conflict was, in fact, engendered by a structural fracture in the discourse of property itself. Maverick legislation served only to call attention to the arbitrary naming that underpinned the institution of property, infecting virtually every property dispute with the maverick's scandalous ambiguity.

The crisis exploded in violence when, after months of planning and preparation, a number of wealthy ranchers, frustrated by the difficulty of securing rustling convictions, decided to take the law into their own hands. On April 6, 1892, at 4:00 AM, a party of fifty-two men, including hired mercenaries, eastern tenderfoots who had come to help defend their western interests (and no doubt to indulge their heroic fantasies), local cattlemen, and two journalists arrived via train in Casper, Wyoming. On Saturday, April 9, the "invaders" surrounded the ranch house where Nate Champion and Nick Ray were staying. Both men were well-known members of the "rustlers" side, but Champion was a particularly desirable target. A blacklisted cowboy who ran his own herd of allegedly rustled cattle, Champion had become a local celebrity because of his open defiance of Johnson County's most powerful cattlemen. At dawn, an unsuspecting Ray emerged from the ranch house and was shot and mortally wounded. Champion managed to drag him back to safety, and the two remained under siege for several hours, with Champion firing at every opportunity, until the impatient invaders finally forced him out by setting fire to the ranch house: "In his sock feet he burst out on a dead run. There are all kinds of reports about how many bullet holes were in his body" (Gage 58). The invasion went no further, thanks to the timely arrival of Jack Flagg, who stumbled on the scene en route to, of all places, a Democratic state convention in Douglas, Wyoming. Flagg had no difficulty mobilizing more than enough armed men to stop the invaders, who were eventually forced to retreat to a ranch house just outside the town of Buffalo, remaining under siege for several days while a huge and menacing crowd gathered around their precarious refuge. Friends of the invaders, meanwhile, were for a time unable to telegraph for help because the invaders themselves had cut the telegraph lines.

Although reluctant to deliver his allies into the hands of the authorities, Governor Barber had no choice but to telegraph President Benjamin Harrison for military assistance, which he was finally able to do on Tuesday, April 12, 1892.[5] Federal troops arrived the following day and took custody of the invaders, who were subsequently held in various facilities until, in August 1892, they were released on bail. When, after numerous delays, the invaders were finally brought to trial in

January 1893, every single case was dismissed because of legal technicalities—an outcome facilitated, no doubt, by the invaders' many influential supporters.

The Woman Reformer as Frontier Heroine in McElrath's *The Rustler*

Owen Wister's interest in the Johnson County War is no surprise given his immediate involvement with many of its key players, places, and events. His first western journey took him to Wyoming in 1885, one year after the Maverick Law was passed. His host in Wyoming was Major Frank Wolcott, the manager of the VR ranch and a key participant in the invasion (Bold, *Frontier Club* 8). And of course, Wister was a member of the frontier club, to borrow once more Bold's useful term describing the inner circle of men who powerfully influenced frontier discourse at the turn of the twentieth century. Clearly, the Johnson County War was also of interest to Wister because industrial expansion and class conflict in the West spoke to his interest in articulating the national importance of western American culture and history.

But Wister was not alone in recognizing the implications of the Johnson County War with respect to the national cultural imaginary. In the spring of 1902, Frances McElrath's *The Rustler* was published—a "coincidence" made all the more intriguing because of the implied relation between the two novels: So closely do they resemble each other, some critics have commented, that "the two authors of the two books, could have been accused of collaboration" (Frantz and Choate 160–61). *The Rustler* raises questions about the relation between gender and genre with respect to the emergence of the "classic" western. Representing rustling as a form of class antagonism constituted by the indeterminate status of the maverick calf, McElrath makes explicit the authorizing function of the maverick's (absent) mother.

Because this novel is not well known, some detailed plot description is useful here. In the opening chapter of *The Rustler*, the heroine, Hazel, refuses an offer of marriage from the English ranch owner Horace Carew. "You do wrong in thinking that in settling down you would be giving up your entire freedom," he tells her in the novel's opening line. While Horace is absorbed in his proposal, Hazel "[chances] to look over the edge of the cut-bank along which her horse was slowly walking and she [sees] Jim [the foreman of the ranch belonging to Hazel's cousin].... Their eyes met, and that was the beginning of all things" (9–10). Although Hazel is a regular guest at the great houses of Newport, the recent death of her father, whose affairs are in some disarray, has forced her to economize by staying at the Wyoming ranch until it can be discovered whether she has been left "an heiress or a pauper" (51). As in *The Virginian*, a love relationship evolves between the silent, virile cowboy (a self-proclaimed woman hater) and the well-bred lady tenderfoot, but with highly suggestive differences in outcome.

Jim is at first indifferent to Hazel, who considers him beneath her but nevertheless expects him to admire her refined looks and manners. When he does not, Hazel hatches a plan "to make Jim know that I've been on the ranch before I leave it" (49). To this end, "Hazel stoops to conquer" (57), ridding herself of her expensive dress and demeanor and seducing Jim through various performances that make her appear humble and vulnerable. Her strategy works too well. For Jim, "Miss Clifford rich and cared for would have been somebody altogether outside the pale of possibility. But the simple young woman earning a scanty subsistence by teaching—poor, proud, and alone—was someone whom he dared offer his protecting arm to support" (113). Yet Hazel takes no pleasure in her triumph. Sensing the shift in Jim's feelings for her, Hazel is overcome with panic: "The strong spirit of the man looked out at her for once and she quailed before it.... In her sudden revulsion of feeling she hated the vulgar and trivial impulse that had prompted her all winter. She was sanely herself again" (106–8).

Unfortunately, Hazel's awakening comes too late for Jim, who, devastated and disillusioned by her rejection, becomes the most notorious rustler in the county. Over a period of time, he becomes the leader of a highly organized gang of rustlers whose ROB brand flaunts both their crimes and their imperviousness to the law. A vigilante army, led by Hazel's spurned suitor, Horace Carew, is organized to stop Jim's gang. The two plots converge when Jim abducts Hazel and takes her to his rustlers' hideout in an attempt to force her to acknowledge his wealth and power.

While Hazel is in captivity, the rustler war breaks out in a way that closely follows the historical record of Johnson County. McElrath's romantic plot is intertwined with these events. A secondary romance also develops when Horace Carew conducts a covert investigation of local rustler activity. Suspecting the involvement of a man named Nathan Grimes, Horace cultivates a relationship with Grimes's adopted daughter, suggestively named Mavvy (short for Maverick), in order to learn details about the rustlers. Mavvy, who falls in love with Horace, learns of a plot by the rustlers to kill him and risks her life to prevent the murder: She first warns Horace of the danger and then, by disguising herself as Horace, takes a bullet meant for him. Mavvy narrowly survives; meanwhile, Horace and his "gentlemen army" kill Nathan Grimes and Nick Lowry, clearly modeled after Nate Champion and Nick Ray, after a prolonged siege at their cabin. Jim stumbles on the spectacle, escapes under gunfire, and rides through the county warning its inhabitants of the invasion—a deed carried out in Johnson County by Jack Flagg. McElrath closes the rustler war in a way that is similarly consistent with the historical record: The vigilantes are arrested by the local law enforcement with the assistance of enraged citizens, who did not know "that practically the stockmen's interests were their own" (248). Later, "through the exertion of considerable money and outside influence, the stockmen were let out of jail on heavy bail with the understanding that the case would never be brought to trial, and the forty gentlemen, with the charge of murder still against them, were set at liberty" (258).

Jim comes through the crisis, his rustling operation for the most part unscathed, and focuses his attention on flaunting his power and wealth before Hazel's captive gaze. Unimpressed by Jim, Hazel is deeply moved by the hard life of the rustlers, especially their children, who are uneducated, in poor health, and in need of moral guidance. Among these children is Jim's adopted son, Tips, left an orphan by the American war against the western tribes. When Tips dies of a fever epidemic that has swept the rustler colony, Hazel blames herself for exposing him to the unhealthy environment of the rustlers' hideaway (since she blames herself for Jim's turn to rustling). She does her penance by taking responsibility for the welfare of the rustler families, teaching the children to read and offering their mothers advice on parenting and other domestic matters. Jim is also stirred by the death of Tips, but his repentance comes too late; while he is busy returning stolen cattle to their appropriate ranges, he is shot and fatally wounded by an unseen assailant. He manages to make his way back to the rustlers' hideout, where he spends his last days under Hazel's care. Jim's death marks the end of the reign of the rustlers and helps determine Hazel's decision to continue her work with the former rustlers' families rather than marry Horace. That role is reserved for Mavvy, who finally manages to win Horace over with her self-sacrificing devotion.

Like *The Virginian*, *The Rustler* constructs the East-West split through its composition of gender relations and marriage. It negotiates a very different resolution, however, on behalf of its heroine, who manages successfully to evade the marriage that looms over her in the novel's opening paragraph. This evasion, moreover, is the novel's central project and is explicitly tied to McElrath's domestic-feminist reading of the rustler war. Whereas *The Virginian* articulates the clear distinction between good and evil (and erases the class content) in the rustler wars by evading the maverick issue, McElrath explains the nuances of the debate in the chapter following Jim's turn to rustling. She represents the rustler wars as a phase of class antagonism marking the transition from "baronial conditions" to a more "commercial condition. . . . The cowpuncher was beginning to feel dissatisfied with the mere romance of his occupation, and was whispering to himself that the profits on the range were rather more one-sided than need be" (164). The maverick, according to McElrath, was pivotal in this "evolution of the *rancher*" (165). In considerable detail, McElrath explains that "maverick-branding became a recognized feature of the cattle industry," eventually encouraging the cowboy to compete with this employer: "If his employer could make thirty of forty dollars out of the maverick which *he* found and branded, the cowpuncher argued, why should not he himself have that large profit instead of the paltry sum paid him?" (165, 167). This in turn leads to "quasi-honest" branding practices: "Then the cowpuncher who had used to go out and 'rustle' mavericks for his employer became on his own account a 'rustler'" (167).

McElrath's account of mavericking makes clear how the uncertain status of mavericks destabilizes the power relations of class and property ownership. This is precisely what *The Virginian*'s moralized version of class struggle, founded on the transcendental signification of private property, disallows. The latter text recuperates the ideological fantasy of Wister's "natural aristocracy"—which rationalizes his "democratic" class system—through its depiction of The Virginian's social mobility, founded on his "naturally" conceived aristocratic status. The transcendental signification of property supplies the linchpin of this narrative: The most significant difference in the text is that between The Virginian, who earns his property, and his former friend, the rustler Steve. This construction rewrites the economic struggle between cowboys and their employers as a moral distinction between "natural" aristocrats and criminals. As both a cowboy and an aristocrat, The Virginian embodies the fantasy of unequal equality.

The marriage narrative is crucial to the signification of property and class in both novels. The historian Nancy F. Cott supplies a model for reading these marriage plots: "The differentiation of public from private [in the late nineteenth century] was incomprehensible without marriage, which created couples who made homes and families that amassed and transmitted property. Because marriage bears a formative relation to both private property and domestic intimacy, it not only inhabits but undergirds the domain of privacy" (110). As Cott argues, the cultural work of marriage in constructing the public-private distinction meant that it was read as a matter of both public and private interest. Because the intelligibility of the boundary was maintained through the denial of citizenship to women and their containment within the private sphere, the signification of private property and the social status of women were inextricably linked. Women political activists, therefore, enjoyed more cultural legitimacy when advocating on behalf of the moral and economic stability of the family; they figured prominently, for example, in efforts to ban the sale of alcohol because of its effect on the family, particularly the women and children who were victimized by alcohol-related violence and unemployment. Women's political activism met with far more resistance when it advocated empowering women as an end in itself rather than as an extension of women's domestic duty.[6] In both *The Virginian* and *The Rustler*, the marriageability of male heroes denotes their social status, which in turn formulates a particular epistemology of social organization: Molly Wood signifies the power and status to which The Virginian is "naturally" entitled because of his inherent physical and moral virtues. To subordinate herself to him, as she finally does on the eve of their marriage, is to signify The Virginian's natural entitlement to the status that she represents. In contrast, Hazel's rejection of Jim marks his "awakening" from this ideological fantasy: He, too, possesses all the right virtues and is seduced by Hazel into believing that he can therefore aspire to a higher status; however, the novel stops short of representing a social reality in which this dream can be realized. Jim is thus stunned by "the absurdity of his thinking for a moment that a refined lady would love him—and marry him—and that he should have children of his own and a home, and live a respected man in some good community" (137).

These two novels, then, are in agreement with respect to the national orientation of their western narratives and to their engagement with an entire apparatus of assumptions about class, gender, and social organization. The crucial difference between them has to do with their arrangement of the gender hierarchy and its link to a way of processing certain contradictions inherent in American democratic ideology. In *The Virginian*, Wister argues that democracy is a social reality despite the stratification of American society because the latter is the effect of a natural hierarchy formed through a social-Darwinian process of struggle. *The Rustler* exposes this view as an ideological fantasy, arguing that class stratification and antagonism are socially constituted processes that undermine the achievement of real democracy. The distinction between the social reality of class and the ideological fantasy of "unequal equality" is articulated through the Jim-Hazel courtship: Hazel's pretense of making herself available to Jim is the dream, while her return to her former self marks Jim's awakening. The novel endorses Jim's aspirations. They are a sign that by cultivating the capacity to recognize Hazel's attractions he has "simply come to his own, to his better self" (111). The problem is that he does not yet inhabit a social reality in which these dreams can be realized. Hence Hazel ends her performance upon recognizing that she is not prepared to become, in her own social reality, the poor proud governess with whom Jim had fallen in love: "The play was at an end. The sudden revelation of the soul of the man had been too much for Hazel. It had stirred her into a deeper comprehension of him and of what she had been doing, and she had dropped the rôle she had assumed. . . . She was sanely herself again" (108).

The narrative does not simply return to the status quo (a Hazel-Horace marriage), however, because it is the marriage myth that is itself at stake: As the crucial naturalized social relation—differentiating classes on the basis of female desire—the marriage myth must be deconstructed in order to make democracy a social reality for men and women alike. This procedure is entwined with the novel's feminist project. The maverick dispute—specifically the way in which the ambiguous status of the maverick calf disrupts the articulation of private property—supplies the basis for raising Hazel's consciousness once the limitations of her earlier performance are exposed. A clear homology is drawn, first of all, between the status of women in classic patriarchy and the status of calves as property. Most explicitly, the link is embodied by the character of Mavvy, whose symbolic name invokes a reading of gender and property as mutually implicating discourses. Mavvy is introduced in a chapter that follows directly Hazel's successful evasion of advances from both Jim and Horace. Seeking distraction from Hazel's rebuffs, the dejected Horace attends a nearby ball, where, during an illustrative square dance, the (male) dancers are instructed to "lock horns with your own heifers, and rassle 'em to their places" and to "corral the fillies, rope your own, and back to your claim with her!" (144). Whereas Hazel has just escaped the marriage "roundup," the less fortunate orphan Mavvy is brought to the dance, apparently to be prostituted by her adoptive father, who forces her to accept the crude advances of another rustler. She is rescued by Horace, who is glad for the opportunity to restore his recently bruised masculinity.

Just as the ambiguous status of the maverick upsets the symbolic economy through which private property is articulated, so it also raises questions about the status of women, who are treated within the marriage market just like cattle. To recognize the status of women as property as the effect of a symbolic economy is one step toward upsetting the apparatus of social relations through which this status is determined. Hence McElrath explores the enabling potential of the women/cattle analogy as well as its more disturbing implications. On the one hand, for example, Hazel's situation is as precariously contingent as that of the calf whose brand can easily be altered or plagiarized: If her social identity is constituted through symbolic processes, then what is there to distinguish her from the destitute Mavvy, especially given Hazel's eroding income? The possibility of marriage to Jim is, thus, "an impending avalanche" (108) threatening to subsume Hazel's identity. On the other hand, when Hazel becomes aware of her place in the marriage market, she is able to behave in a way that effects substantive changes to her social situation. By refusing marriage, she disrupts the gender economy that commodifies women in order to constitute the fundamental privilege of citizenship—the right to own property—as masculine.

Hazel awakens to the social reality of the marriage economy after her seduction generates an unanticipated outcome. Her initial plan is simply to make herself desirable in an economy in which her highly refined manners, dress, and accomplishments are not valuable. Jim, the only remotely eligible bachelor in the novel, is initially "as insensible to her charms as a post" (45). Hazel decides that, because Jim is "too independent to allow himself to be taken up by people socially" (64), it is up to her to go, like Mohammed, to the mountain. Her plan, however, is based on a fundamental misrecognition of her status within the marriage market. Her adaptability, we are told, is "true to [Hazel's American] breeding and nationality," which gives her the "capacity of 'fitting in' in any environment" (60). Accordingly, she adapts to the local marriage economy, inspiring Jim to dream of what a life with her could mean: "I might get to be a partner some day," he muses. "With Hazel beside him he could strive for any glory" (114). However noble these aspirations may be, they are fundamentally antidemocratic because they merely replace one form of inequality (based on class) with another (based on gender). Hazel is repulsed by Jim precisely because his awakened desire exposes her transformation as nothing more than crude adaptation to an economy in which her fundamental status as marital property remains unchanged.

On the basis of this rupture between two ideological fantasies—both of which are at some level consistent with democratic ideology but neither of which constitutes democracy as a social reality—*The Rustler* formulates a domestic-feminist position, advanced as a step toward realizing democracy as social practice. McElrath argues that the subordination of the subject to the arbitrary forces of the market economy is effected specifically by the mother's negated authority, for the brand both marks the subject as property and subordinates the authority of the mother to that of the market. The authority of the mother, then, is the necessary alternative to the symbolic violence of the branding iron. Jim's turn to rustling is the symptom of social trauma originating specifically in the objectification of women and the consequential neutralization of their moral authority as mothers. Immersed entirely in the world of work, Jim and his adopted son, Tips, inhabit a motherless, misogynist landscape: "*Women*," observed Tips, "may be all very well in their place, but their place ain't on the range nor anywhere near it!" (21). The role of Tips's mother in this landscape has fallen to Jim: "Can't see what a feller'd want of a mother when he'd got Jim" (27), Tips belligerently informs Hazel. Jim is himself the product of a motherless, dysfunctional, and impoverished home: His father was an outlaw, and his mother "was always too hard-worked" (75) to have time for him.

Having inscribed Jim's fall in terms of a seduction plot that explodes both the myth of the classless society and the commodification of women within marriage, McElrath undoes the negation underlining these fantasies in order to repair the social damage that they cause. Hazel's maternal consciousness is awakened by the death of Tips, which Hazel blames on her own "vulgar" behavior. Accepting the blame for this and virtually every other crisis in the novel, Hazel recognizes her own power to effect change in the social world and atones for past wrongs through acts of social mothering: "She had set one discordant note jarring through the world; now she wanted to atone by bringing others into harmony" (325). She opens a school for the rustler children, tends to the sick, and advises the rustlers' wives on domestic matters. Jim's ROB brand eventually dominates the local cattle industry, but his power has no effect on Hazel, nor can he compete with her growing popularity in the rustler community: "Her gentle measures were designed to frustrate the very work he was carrying on. He had brought her to camp to witness with her own eyes his supremacy, and instead of bowing before it like the rest, she had quietly gone to work to undermine his power" (340–41). In her new role as a prototypical social worker, Hazel repairs the trauma that

Jim had experienced when his earlier fantasies had been shattered. At first seduced by Hazel and the democratic fantasy that she performs in order to mislead him, Jim is ultimately redeemed by the example of her newly realized maternal authority: "Witness the little weeping child beneath the mesquite bush vowing to bear an honest name. Witness his years of faithful labor as foreman of the K cattle company and the first worthiness of his love for Hazel. It had sent him widely astray, that love, but it had come from an intrinsically true source and it had finally brought him back to the right" (353).

Hazel's domestic feminism places *The Rustler* in the tradition of both domestic-feminist discourse and broad cultural anxiety about frontier closure. Domestic-feminist reformers argued that, with respect to issues such as poverty, disease, unemployment, crime, and exploitation, "cleaning up" the Republic was the task for which women were best qualified because their moral authority supplied an antidote to the corruptive impulses of unbridled individualism, associated with male domination in business and politics. Domestic-feminist rhetoric unsettled the very basis for a gendered distinction between public and private space in American society at the turn of the century. By arguing that the public sphere was, in practice, an extension of the domicile, they simultaneously reinvented the domicile as a public space, fundamentally enmeshed in the political and economic worlds rather than eternally isolated from them. Predicated as it was on conventional, middle-class representations of gender, domestic feminism nevertheless expanded political and professional opportunities for women. Hence the progression in Hazel's range of choices in *The Rustler*. At the beginning of the novel, Hazel's choices are circumscribed by the seeming inevitability that she will marry—the only question is, Will she marry Horace? In the end, however, the successful suitor proves to be her profession, for Hazel chooses to remain unmarried so she can continue to oversee the reformation of the rustlers' children. Like The Virginian, Hazel embodies frontier values in a postfrontier context, but through her democratizing social work rather than by economic competition.

Complementary, rather than antithetical, to its feminist concerns, prevalent ideas about the frontier support McElrath's feminist project: With the "disappearance" of the "free land" widely believed to underwrite equality of opportunity in America,[7] American democracy must be reinvented in a way that addresses the now undeniable reality of increasing competition for ever-scarcer recourses. In *The Virginian*, Owen Wister blames the resulting social unrest on criminals and posits a frontier hero capable of keeping them at bay. McElrath, in contrast, focuses on the social conditions—including poverty, disease, poor education, and resource scarcity—that produce criminality and posits a domestic-feminist reformer as heroic antidote to frontier closure. Far from occupying separate, gendered cultural spheres, both frontier heroes emerged from a complex matrix of debates, discourses, and motifs from which emerged the "western" as we know it.

3
Women's Westerns and the Myth of the Pseudonym

The success of *The Virginian* stimulated a market for "quality" western novels and magazine fiction in the early twentieth century. Owen Wister's book topped bestseller lists, a new phenomenon at the time, and was reprinted multiple times. Western stories were sought after by editors of "quality" mass-market magazines such as *Argosy* and *Popular*—magazines that promised the "best" fiction at a cheap price. While *The Virginian*'s popular success has helped underwrite the novel's canonical status as the foundational western, recent scholarship demonstrates the considerable resources contributing to Wister's success, including his social ties with powerful publishers (Bold, *Frontier Club* xix–xx, 53–54). Few women writers enjoyed comparable power, yet they were quick to respond to the rising demand for western fiction. Surprisingly, perhaps, these women for the most part did *not* use male pseudonyms. On the contrary, only one of the authors considered in this study, B. M. Bower, wrote under a pseudonym of sorts, using a gender-neutral nom de plume that most readers assumed was masculine. Legitimate authorship of "respectable" westerns depended on more than simply the gender of the author; other factors included regional, racial, and class affiliations. Certainly, gender and class enabled the likes of Wister and Theodore Roosevelt, both born to established, eastern families, to fashion personas as red-blooded men of the West.[1] But masculinity and social power were not entirely outdone by the authenticity believed to inhere in writing by those who lived and worked in the West, including women. All of the writers in this study could make some kind of claim to authenticity as westerners because they lived, worked, or became established members of western communities. They could claim to write a West based on an authentic original, not one copied from the numerous other copied wests that proliferated in American print culture (Handley and Lewis, "Introduction" 2). In this chapter I focus on how two of these authors, B. M. (Bertha Muzzy) Bower and Caroline Lockhart, accessed authority as western writers. My objective here is to debunk the myth of the western's masculine origins and shed light on the ways in which women writers were positioned as western cultural producers. Lockhart and Bower are particularly instructive case studies in this respect because they came from very similar class and social backgrounds, yet their literary reputations followed very different trajectories: B. M. Bower's editors and publishers discouraged Bower from publicizing herself as a woman author, fearing to negatively affect the sales of one of their most profitable authors. Conversely, Caroline Lockhart, who had begun her career as journalist writing under the byline "Suzette," claimed legitimacy as an author writing in her own name through articles about her western travel experiences, through which she made the transition from journalist to serious novelist. Clearly, cultural authority over the emergent western novel was not a simple matter of being a man.

The Social Construction of Western Literary Authority

In the early twentieth century, claims to authenticity were central to establishing the legitimacy of western authors and their fiction. Of course, such claims were subsequently—and rightly—problematized. William Handley and Nathaniel Lewis observe that the scholars in their collection on the theme of western authenticity "refuse to judge a text's or author's authenticity, but rather study how the idea of authenticity is deployed" ("Introduction" 5). Claims of textual or authorial authenticity are often deeply embedded in ideologies of race, gender, and class that are exceedingly difficult to disentangle from matters of textual fidelity to reality. For example, Indigenous-authored texts were routinely authenticated by Anglo-American editors, while Indigenous authors were equally excluded from representing the Euro-American West because they were not authorized to speak for or about Anglo-

American experience. Class relations similarly structure claims to authenticity in *The Virginian*, in which the most authentic cowboy just happens to be the one most loyal to his capitalist boss. In these examples, authenticity functions as a form of cultural capital implicated in ideologies of race and class.

With the exception of Mourning Dove, the women in this study accessed authenticity through their racial, social, and regional positions as Anglo-Americans and as middle-class westerners. B. M. Bower deployed inside knowledge of cowboy culture, which she acquired mainly through her relationship with her friend, later husband, Bertrand Sinclair while he worked as a cowboy on the TL ranch in Montana. Bower claimed a position as a western author on the same terrain as Owen Wister and other male authors, whom she satirized as pretenders in some of her fiction.[2] However, my aim here is not to judge whether Bower's westerns are any more intrinsically "authentic" than Wister's, whose fiction is probably a very faithful rendering of a socially privileged, heterosexual male experience of the West. Rather, I am more interested in the way in which Bower constructs and deploys authenticity to stake her claim to the literary terrain of the western.

The demand for authenticity in western representation was tied to its status as region. As Nathaniel Lewis has demonstrated, early nineteenth-century western writers wrote largely for an eastern audience fascinated by stories of an alien landscape that most had access to only through print culture. Western authors were expected to depict the authentic western landscape, unimpeded by their subjectivity or creativity as authors. Lewis argues that later western authors labored under this precedent, in which the western landscape superseded the creativity of the author, relegating western writers to second-class status, unable to demonstrate their genius since doing so would contradict their role as *western* writers obliged to represent the region (23–25). Scholars of American regionalism have suggested that women writers had greater access to regionalism than other literary models precisely because of the subordinate role of the regional writer (Fetterley and Pryse 13). To authentically represent the region, the writer occupied the position of passive receptacle, recording what was already there rather than engaging in an act of creation. Fetterley and Pryse complicate this account, however, by deploying Frank Davey's distinction between region as a discursive by-product of the nation-state and regionalism as an inherently critical discourse that challenges the nation/region hierarchy (5). "When regionalist texts challenge . . . touristic images and allow regional persons to insert articulations of their own understanding of region, they . . . reveal regions themselves to be discursive constructions" (5–6). From this vantage point, regionalism is not so much a ghetto to which women writers have been disproportionally relegated as it is a powerful critical discourse. Emma Ghent Curtis and B. M. Bower both engaged critical regionalism in their fiction by insisting on the specificity and difference of the western states they wrote about—Colorado and Montana, respectively.

Writing of the American West differs from other regionalisms, however, because of the legacy of the West as representative of nation. By arguing in 1893 that the frontier is the crucible of American culture, Frederick Jackson Turner differentiated the West from other American regions by suggesting that America as a whole was defined through a shared frontier experience. As descendants of frontiersman, all Anglo-Americans had inherited the essence of the western character, along with the potential to write authoritatively about the West. According to what Alison Calder calls the "autochthonous theory of regional writing" (56), regional identity originates in the landscape, which shapes the subjectivity of those who live there. Regional insiders are therefore uniquely qualified to represent the region by virtue of having been "made" by it. Since the geographic location of the American frontier had shifted historically, the position of regional insider in the West could be claimed by select easterners—those whose deeds proved them worthy descendants of their frontiering ancestors. Wister and Roosevelt reinvented themselves as authentic men of the West by proving their mettle in initiation activities such a pioneering, hunting expeditions, and cattle roundups, which enabled them to access their real origin as Americans. Of course, not all Americans had equal access to this identity: Wister was aided by social connections with wealthy cattle ranchers who hosted him and by publishers who were willing to finance his western adventures, as well as by his status as a white male (Bold, *Frontier Club* 55–57). Chinese immigrants, African Americans, and Hispanics also endured the privations of western living yet were excluded from the discourse of West as proving ground. Anglo-American women writers, however, could claim this hereditary insider status: In particular, Caroline Lockhart, born in Illinois and raised in Kansas, went West to authorize her literary practice, tapping into an idea of the West as frontier, as American proving ground. In the following discussions I analyze in more detail the ways in which region, gender, race, and class enable Bower and Lockhart differently as woman writers of the popular West.

B. M. Bower and the Masculine Pseudonym

B. M. Bower is the most prolific author considered in this study and the only one to have used a nom de plume. It is certainly tempting to generalize from her example that the western as a whole was a genre barred to women writers, but in fact Bower was an anomaly. Indeed, her contemporary, Caroline Lockhart, received positive reviews for her first novel, *Me—Smith* (1911), despite the fact that its controversial protagonist remained a recalcitrant outlaw to the end. Why, then, did Bower, whose early fiction was far less controversial than Lockhart's, use a pseudonym throughout her career? Fortunately, her archives hold several clues that point to class and gender relations as key in the production of Bower's literary reputation.

Born Bertha Muzzy in 1871 in Cleveland, Minnesota, Bower moved with her family to Montana in 1889 when she was in her late teens. She attended eight years of school, standard for pioneer families of the time, and was taught music and encouraged to read widely by her father, Washington Muzzy.[3] A woman of Bower's cultural background and interests living nearer the great publishing centers of Boston or New York might well have tried her hand at writing, but Bower began teaching school, a more opportune career for a young woman with few social connections living in the remote state of Montana. When she was nineteen, she eloped with Clayton Bower. Bertha and Clayton had three children—Grace, Harry, and Roy—but the marriage was not a happy one. In her unpublished biography of Bower, Kate Baird Anderson, Bower's granddaughter, describes Clayton as violent, ill tempered, and a poor provider.[4] According to family oral history, Bertha had social and financial ambitions to which Clayton, who drifted between odd jobs as a cowboy and laborer, did not measure up. The vivacious Bertha enjoyed attending dances and making social calls, making Clayton jealous. There is strong evidence that Clayton physically abused Bertha, which may have precipitated her separation from Bower.[5] In any case, by all accounts the unhappiness of her first marriage spurred Bower to write fiction. It was work she could do at home while she cared for her children, the youngest of whom was her son Roy, who was four years old when Bower published her first story.[6] Potentially, it could also earn more money than virtually all other options available to her.

Bower began her career as a writer during a period of rapid expansion in the field of professional fiction writing, fueled by the emergence of mass-market magazines and the corresponding increase in demand for content to fill those magazines (Ohmann 23–30). This expansion created more opportunities for professional writers from the working and middle classes, who also benefited from the expansion of access to education and corresponding increase in literacy rates. Magazines such as *Authors* catered to budding writers with how-to articles on becoming a professional writer and by holding contests, the winners of which received cash prizes accompanied by publication in the magazine. *Authors* included a section of "ads interesting to Authors and Writers" that promoted typewriters, agencies, and correspondence schools.[7] One of B. M. Bower's earliest publications was in *Authors*, and she probably followed its advice for aspiring authors.

About 1900, Bower purchased a typewriter and began spending her mornings writing, a routine that she would keep up for the rest of her life. "Mornings were dedicated to writing," her daughter Dele later recalled, "no one must intrude upon [Bower's] morning regime of writing."[8] Once a story was finished, Bower would submit it for publication in one of the "quality" magazines—*McClure's* was usually her first choice, although she was never successful there. If a story was returned, she would resubmit it to a lower-tier publication, repeating the process until it found a publisher. She kept meticulous records of manuscript submissions in record books manufactured especially for the purpose, which she must have ordered by mail. She recorded her submissions, returns, publications, and income, noted whether the manuscript received a form-letter rejection or a personal note from an editor, and tracked her income. On December 15, 1900, she made her first entry for a story entitled "The Backsliding of Sister Stewart." It was rejected six times before it was finally published in *Authors Magazine*, earning Bower $12. For the next two years, she wrote about one story each month and earned from $10 to $15 per story, usually after multiple submissions. In 1904 her breakthrough came when Street & Smith paid $50–75 for short stories appearing in *Ainslee's* and $225 for her first novel, *Chip, of the Flying U*, which was the lead story for *Popular*, Street & Smith's new "quality" mass-market story magazine.[9]

Bower's early correspondence with her publishers has been lost, but it is possible to piece together the relations of cultural authority that enabled her to stake a claim as a writer of authentic western fiction from what is known about Bower's background, conditions in the literary marketplace of the period, and Bower's fiction, which often engaged explicitly with issues related to the cultural production of western fiction. In selecting *Chip, of the Flying U* to launch its new magazine venture *Popular*, Street & Smith clearly capitalized on the success of *The Virginian*. This same popularity fed a demand for authenticity in a western fiction market flooded with imitations. Here was an opportunity for Bower, as the wife of a cowboy and resident of the cattle-ranching state of Montana, to compete with the likes of Wister, who knew cowboys from his privileged vantage point as the guest of Frank Wolcott, manager of one of the wealthiest ranches in Wyoming (Bold, *Frontier Club* 74). The irony that an effete easterner like Wister would become an authoritative chronicler of the West probably motivated Bower as it did Bertrand Sinclair, a cowboy who boarded with Bertha and Clayton during the winter of 1902 and who would become Bower's second husband and fellow author of western fiction. In a 1930 letter, Sinclair recalled that *The Virginian* was among the books making the rounds of the bunkhouse when he was a young cowboy at the TL ranch, making him wonder "why no cowpuncher ever wrote about his own time and his own people" (quoted in Keller 26).

Despite the claims to authenticity that Bower could make as the wife of a cowboy living on the cattle range, as a woman she was still an outsider to the cowboy class she depicted in her fiction. Bower lived most closely with cowboys when, in the fall of 1900, Clayton began working for the TL Ranch and the couple moved with their three children into a small, three-room cabin located on one of its ranges.[10] Bower's personal albums from this period are full of photos of cowboys performing roping and riding tricks and riding in roundups (B. M. Bower Papers). However, Bower, who never appears in these photos (probably because she took them), was an onlooker, rather than participant, in cowboy life. Cowboy culture was governed by a masculine ethos demonstrated at work through skills with cattle and horses and in leisure time through hard drinking and demonstrations of sexual prowess (Moore 21). The women who cowboys interacted with most were likely to be prostitutes and the wives of the ranchers they worked for. Cowboys tended to idealize respectable women as their moral and social superiors (Moore 141–67). As a "respectable" married woman, Bower was separated from the cowboy class by vast social barriers despite the fact that she lived in their midst. This reality was not lost on Bower, who turned to Sinclair as her "native" informant. While he boarded with the Bowers, she enlisted him to critique her accounts of cowboy life and provide her with material for her stories. Bower returned the favor, typing his first story and using her submission system to help Sinclair secure his first publication.[11] Their partnership was an exchange of the different forms of cultural capital they each possessed: Bower's professional know-how, and Sinclair's insider knowledge of cowboy life.

The popular marketplace Bower entered into was not as interested in the West she knew best as a wife and mother living on the range as it was in cowboys. Not until 1912 did she publish a woman-centered novel set on the cattle frontier: In the semiautobiographical *Lonesome Land*, discussed more fully in chapter 5, Bower depicts the unhappily married Val Fleetwood, who befriends a local cowboy named Kent. Out of loneliness and to earn extra money, Val starts to write fiction, and Kent is her first reader and critic. His comments on Val's early efforts are suggestive: "He had . . . a dim impression that it was a story with people in it whom one does not try to imagine as ever being alive, and with a West which, beyond its evident scarcity of inhabitants, was not the West he knew anything about" (237). Kent seems to be suggesting that Val's picture of the West is inauthentic, but the passage can also be interpreted as a commentary on the gendering of the West— perhaps Val's West is one he knows nothing about because it depicts her gendered position as the wife of a rancher. Kent's comment points to the existence of multiple experiences of multiple wests—rather than a single, homogenous, authentic vision—some of which were in more popular demand than others. In a post-*Virginian* literary marketplace, the cowboy and the cattle frontier had become representative of the American frontier. Lacking social or regional ties to the nation's publishing centers, Bower paid close attention to the demands of the marketplace and did her best to meet them.

The conditions that led to Bower's virtual anonymity as an author were complex, more than being a simple matter of a woman writing masculine texts. Bower used the pseudonym "Bertha May Happ" for her first story, "The Strike of the Dishpan Brigade," a story of rural domestic life that was published in a Minnesota farm journal.[12] She probably had good reasons for using a pseudonym: She might not have wanted Clayton to know about her attempts at publication since her motive in doing so was to gain independence from him. In their tiny cabin, however, it would have been difficult to conceal the fact that she spent her mornings typing and her afternoons at the post office sending packages to Boston, Chicago, San Francisco, and New York. Bower subsequently published short stories as "Bertha Muzzy Bower" before changing her author name to "B. M. Bower" in the fall of 1904,[13] when her breakthrough novel was serialized in *Popular*. This was probably at the behest of *Popular* editor Charles MacLean. He not only concealed Bower's identity from his own readers at *Popular* but was adamant that her book publishers follow suit. Thus, when Little, Brown, with whom Bower signed in 1911, wrote asking for pictures and biographical information, Bower responded,

> I cannot reply as freely to the request as I should like to do, because the idea that B.M. Bower is a man has been carefully fostered ever since my Western stories began to attract attention. Mr. MacLean, of the Popular, is very much averse to having my identity revealed. If you have ever read his "Chat With You" [an editorial column in *Popular*] you will observe how deftly he avoids the personal pronoun in speaking of me. The question was raised by Dillingham's [publisher of the book version of *Chip, of the Flying U*], and Mr. MacLean urged me so strongly not to make any announcement of my sex, that I have never done so.[14]

Although MacLean's point of view was to profoundly influence Bower's career, it was not representative of the culture as a whole: Both of

Bower's book publishers—Dillingham and Little, Brown—had been prepared to publicize her until MacLean intervened, demonstrating that Bower's anonymity was not a cultural inevitability.

The plot of Bower's first novel sheds further light on gender as one facet of the complex and often contradictory relations that structured western American cultural production generally and Bower's situation specifically. It concerns a cowboy-artist whose first successful painting is sold under a pseudonym, clearly drawing inspiration from Bower's own position as a cultural producer and a brand name. The eponymous cowboy hero of the novel—named after Bower's brother Roy, nicknamed Chip—sketches in his spare time and demonstrates raw talent.[15] However, it does not occur to him that his art can be more than a pastime. His romantic interest, Della, is an eastern woman of good breeding who is well connected socially. Like many women of her class, Della has had a well-rounded education that includes some training in painting; however, she lacks Chip's natural talent. When Chip is rendered bedridden by a riding accident, he passes the time by completing a western landscape painting that Della had left unfinished. It is the first time Chip, who usually sketches in pencil, has had access to paint. In the foreground, Chip paints a scene he had witnessed of "a poor, half-starved range cow with her calf... [surrounded by] five great, gaunt wolves intent upon fresh beef for their supper" (*Chip, of the Flying U* 174). When Della sees the painting, she recognizes that Chip has created a genuine work of art, but Chip is too bashful to show it to anyone, so, with Chip's permission, Della signs it in her name and, taking advantage of her social status as a relation of the ranch owner, displays it in the ranch-house parlor. There, it can be viewed by Chip's social superiors, including the ranch owner and his well-to-do guests. One of them uses his connections to display the painting in a hotel in a nearby city, where it can be viewed by the wealthy cattlemen who constitute the local market for western art. Through Della, then, Chip accesses the prestigious medium of paint, as well as a well-heeled market for his art.

Although Della's social connections help sell the painting, Chip is the source of its authenticity as western art. Before Chip had completed the foreground of the painting, Della had planned to fill it with "Indian tepees and some squaws," a suggestion that Chip rejects because "there were no Indians in that country" (171). Whereas Della paints the West of her imagination, imitating established popular western representations, Chip paints the West of his experience. Sensing that Della, a sheltered eastern gentlewoman, could not have painted such a powerful scene of western realism, viewers of the painting doubt that it could have been painted by a woman. However, Bower complicates any easy reading of gendered authenticity by placing female experience at the center of Chip's authentic western scene. Titling his painting *The Last Stand*, the fictional Chip revises Frederic Remington's painting of the same name, a famous image of male bravado besieged by savagery, and supplants it with a scene of besieged motherhood. That fictional painting references a real painting by Bower's close friend Charles Russell, also called *The Last Stand*, a painting that privileges the mother's experience as a site of western authenticity. As I argue in chapter 5, women writers of popular westerns deployed the metaphoric language of the cattle frontier to engage feminist social critique within the field of the popular western, of which Chip's fictional *Last Stand* is another example.

Della's class and gender together compromise her ability to paint an authentic western scene, even as they enable her to access the field of cultural production on Chip's behalf. Until Della intervenes, it does not occur to Chip that he can transform his art into an income. While his habitus—a concept invented by Pierre Bourdieu to refer to a social agent's ability to effectively occupy a given social position or field—enables the cowboy to *produce* authentic cowboy art, it excludes him from the social circles and cultural institutions with the power to confer on him status as an artist. The well-connected Della clears a path for Chip to enter a cultural field dominated by both eastern cultural elites, represented by Della, and western economic elites—represented by the wealthy cattleman who eventually buys Chip's painting. Moreover, the authenticity of the painting as an original rendering of the West executed by an artist who knows it ultimately overshadows the ruse that Della uses to get people to take Chip's art seriously, for Della eventually succumbs to questions about her authorship of the painting and reveals Chip to be the real artist. With the revelation of Chip's identity, relations between institutional and aesthetic values are righted: Real westerners have access to status as western artists. Chip's situation is a variation on Bower's as an author: A nom de plume enabled her to gain access to a cultural field. In *Chip, of the Flying U*, however, Bower points to class and place, above gender, as the more salient barriers to Chip's entry into the cultural field, for in lending her name to Chip's painting, Della lends him both her social connections and access to spaces inhabited by the wealthy—her host's parlor, a hotel in the city—that prove crucial to finding a market for Chip's art. Class and place were equally important factors for the remotely located Bower, who acquiesced to Charles MacLean's wishes to hide her gender rather than risk her lucrative career as a pulp writer for *Popular*. It would have been difficult for a woman from rural Montana, with relatively little formal education and few social connections, to stand up to the publishing juggernaut of Street & Smith. Bower later regretted her early choices, writing to the literary agent Edith Burrows in 1938 that "my market absorbed everything as fast as I could turn it out, and I fear I followed the line of least resistance."[16]

Bower subsequently made two unsuccessful bids to "come out" as a woman writer. Power relations between Bower and her publishers, rather than widespread taboos against women's westerns, kept her identity hidden from most of her readers until her death in 1940. In 1912, on the heels of the success of *Lonesome Land*, her most woman-centered novel to date, Bower wrote to Little, Brown that "I have decided to come out boldly and declare myself a woman writer who has succeeded in doing a man's work as a man would do it. It's bound to come soon, in spite of me, so that it is perhaps making a virtue of necessity." She had a professional portrait taken and asked that it be included in the front material of her new novel *Good Indian*. Although Little, Brown published the photo in their book catalogue, *Good Indian* was published without the portrait and advertised in the *Bookman* as "another popular Western ranch story by the author of 'Lonesome Land.'"[17] In 1922, Bower reopened with Little, Brown the issue of publicizing her identity in an exchange of letters that demonstrates the uncertainty surrounding the question of whether publicity would help or harm Bower's sales. At that time, Hollywood celebrity culture was starting to influence profoundly modes of authorship in the transatlantic world, with the result that the celebrity of the author and the distinctiveness of his or her writing became closely linked (Hammill 17). Magazines used photographs of authors to advertise the distinctiveness of their writers, and authors began to capitalize on their fame for further opportunities in the literary marketplace and to counter the influence of more powerful cultural gatekeepers (Hammill 39). For example, when in 1919 Dorothy Parker was fired from *Vanity Fair* for upsetting theater producers with her blunt and acerbic criticism, she was able to cash in on her celebrity to find a new job as critic for *Ainslee's* (Hammill 42). Bower had recently attracted local publicity for her activities as the only woman founder and president of a mining company near Las Vegas. Nevada papers had also publicized her identity as the woman behind the author B. M. Bower, which spurred Bower to suggest to Little, Brown vice president Alfred R. McIntyre that such publicity could actually benefit her book sales: "The fact that I am a woman and the author of many Western books lends a certain glamor, it appears, to the pioneer work I have done [in mining] for the past year. That I am the only woman who is president and general manager of a mining corporation seems to have caught the attention of the general public."[18] McIntyre, however, was reluctant to tamper with the Bower name. Since Bower's books were already selling apace, he had little incentive to do anything differently. McIntyre replied to Bower that "it has been our experience that readers of Western stories are apt to be prejudiced against those which they know to be the work of a woman, and we have always been careful to say nothing at all about the sex of B.M. Bower."[19] Bower, however, had already experienced more gains than losses from the little publicity she had already received: "I have known of just one man who was unhappily affected by the disclosure. . . . [He] is the one exception. . . . Since this mine venture has brought my name before the public, I have received many letters from strangers who seem glad to know B.M. Bower is a woman."[20] This publicity was also resulting in public appearances and speaking engagements in Los Angeles and expanding opportunities in the film industry, where Bower was gaining a foothold as a scenario writer and consultant. "I have discovered an invariable increase of interest on the part of readers who learn that 'Bower' is a woman. The women are proud of the fact that another woman has succeeded in 'putting one over' on the men. While the men seem tickled to think that a woman could fool them so long. I believe the theory [that revealing her sex will hurt sales] works out—probably without exception—with a new writer. But I am now convinced that B.M. Bower, after seventeen years of continuous writing, will lose nothing by the disclosure of her sex."[21] Letters from readers in the Little, Brown archives corroborate Bower's account. Those that show awareness that she was a woman are not deterred by the fact: "Gentlemen: I have heard many discussions among people who have read B.M. Bower's books as to who the author really is; some say these books are written by a man and some have heard that B.M. Bower is a woman. . . . Could you settle this question for us . . . ? I would appreciate this very much as I have read almost every one of the books written by B.M. Bower and am very much interested in them."[22] In hindsight, the evidence is compelling that publicity might have increased, or at least not harmed, Bower's sales. However, Little, Brown had more to gain than Bower from the status quo. In McIntyre's final letter on the matter he cited the opinion of his head salesman: "I have always contended that it is a mistake to advertise the fact that B.M. Bower is a woman, and I hope you will not advertise this fact to the buying public, especially in the West. I feel positive it will have an unfavorable result. The big trade know she is writing under a nom-de-plume, but they do not advertise this fact to the public."[23]

Had Bower pushed back just a little harder, she might well have won the battle. As a leading author of westerns, she certainly had some leverage. However, she lacked the habitus for high-stakes negotiation with a powerful cultural institution like Little, Brown, which did its part to keep Bower in a subordinate position: In its negotiations with foreign publishers in June 1920, Little, Brown freely touted Bower's importance to the firm: "The Bower books are now one of our best pieces of publishing property. The sale of these Western stories in the United States is exceeded only by the Zane Grey novels."[24] However, their communications with Bower about her book sales were not so glowing. In a letter to Bower the following February, the company stated that "considering business conditions, *Cow Country* is having a fairly satisfactory sale, but we do not think it will do as well as [previous books]."[25] Had Bower known just how valuable she was to Little, Brown, she might have fought harder.

Bower's anonymity had serious consequences for her ability to withstand the 1929 economic crash and for the long-term trajectory of her reputation. The pulp fiction market, upon which Bower depended for half of her income, shrank dramatically, and Little, Brown also reduced its payments to authors. Without a reputation to capitalize on in this new climate, Bower found herself at a serious disadvantage: "The smooth paper magazines did not know me.... After the debacle in the magazine world [brought about by the 1929 crash] my market was pretty well shot." Bower blamed Little, Brown for leaving her handicapped after the pulp magazine market failed: "They have wanted the public to believe that B.M. Bower is a man, and therefore have suppressed me as much as possible. I have long called myself the number one skeleton in the Little Brown closet. My sex has been against me there."[26]

After Bower died in 1940, there was little foundation upon which to sustain her reputation, and her memory died with the last generation of her readers. By the time scholars began reclaiming the value of popular genres including the western, Bower had been relegated to status as a minor footnote in the history of the genre.

Caroline Lockhart: From Eastern Stunt Journalist to Serious Western Author

Although Caroline Lockhart was Bower's contemporary, she used very different strategies to gain access to the cultural field of the popular western. Lockhart transitioned from anonymity as the journalist "Suzette" to public stature as a woman writer precisely by claiming a western persona, which she publicized at every opportunity. Furthermore, Lockhart's first novel, *Me—Smith* (1911), was favorably reviewed despite its moral ambiguity. Reviewers were drawn to Lockhart's unredeemed outlaw protagonist and praised her depiction of a morally complicated West (Clayton 74). Her example demonstrates that women's avenues to popular western writing were diverse and not solely structured by their positions as women.

Lockhart and Bower came from similar class backgrounds: Both were daughters of Civil War veterans who migrated westward in search of social, economic, and political opportunities in the context of postwar economic setbacks.[27] As such, they were part of a distinct subset of the American middle class (Jackson 1–8) and self-identified as such, even though the pioneering experience meant that they lived in harsh conditions, without many of the conveniences enjoyed by their eastern counterparts. These middle-class pioneers valued civic engagement and volunteerism, through which they contributed to the growth and progress of their communities (Jackson 6–7). They often migrated several times when their first homesteads did not pan out or to take advantage of greater economic opportunities created by further western expansion (Riley, *Female Frontier* 29). Montana was the Bower family's second homestead; Caroline Lockhart's father made a considerable fortune from land speculation, moving his family several times around homesteads and towns in Illinois and Kansas (Clayton 9–19). Bower and Lockhart both received an upbringing that, in many respects, was conventionally middle class. Although Bower did not attend college, she received enough education to qualify her to teach school in Montana, and she was a voracious reader. Lockhart attended college in Boston, where she studied drama and elocution in hopes of pursuing a career in acting (Clayton 31–32). For both women, a middle-class upbringing equipped them with cultural capital that eventually enabled them to access careers as authors. Both Bower and Lockhart capitalized on their western locations to write for the expanding popular western market.

Despite these similarities, however, their careers followed very different trajectories that complicate any simplistic explanation of the relationship between gender and genre. Whereas Bower's publishers regarded her gender as an obstacle to legitimacy as a popular western writer, Lockhart self-consciously cultivated a western persona *in order to* claim a public identity as a woman writer. Before writing western fiction, Lockhart had been a successful stunt and investigative journalist, first in Boston and subsequently in Philadelphia, where she gained considerable popularity under the pen name "Suzette" (Clayton 34–52). Although journalism proved lucrative for Lockhart, she aspired to be taken seriously as an author of fiction. She began this transition by publishing fiction in *Lippincott's* under her own name coupled with her more familiar byline "Suzette" (Clayton 55–56), a strategy that enabled her to simultaneously capitalize on and disassociate herself from her popular byline. In August 1902, Lockhart published "A

Girl in the Rockies," a western initiation story that announced her new vocation as a western author.

"A Girl in the Rockies" capitalized on Lockhart's success as an investigative journalist. This autobiographical narrative relates Lockhart's journey through the Canadian Rockies, which she had taken the previous year precisely in order to, as John Clayton so elegantly words it, "prospect for stories" (59, 62). As a stunt and investigative journalist, Lockhart had already put herself through a wide range of precarious situations in order to write about them. On the one hand, her trip through the Rockies was yet another one of these stunts. On the other hand, her western trip was also part of the well-established tradition of the eastern tenderfoot's western initiation, tracing back to figures such as *The Last of the Mohicans's* Duncan Heyward. By proving himself able to adapt to frontier conditions, the frontier initiate figure claims his rightful inheritance as an authentic westerner. "A Girl in the Rockies" performs this function for Lockhart's authorial persona. As a woman, she can take up the feminized position of "tenderfoot" and then leverage that position through a western initiation to claim an identity as an authentic westerner.

"A Girl in the Rockies" relates Lockhart's journey on horseback through the American and Canadian Rockies. In keeping with the tradition of the tenderfoot narrative, Lockhart makes a point of describing plainly the feelings of fear and inadequacy she experiences as she embarks upon her journey, as well as the bumbling—and life-threatening—mistakes she makes upon the trail. Shortly after setting off, alone, on her journey, she meets two Indians driving a herd of horses, and her courage "ooz[es] away" as they approach. After a brief exchange in which the Indians offer guidance for the journey, she continues on her way without incident. Lockhart then gets hopelessly lost on the trail, and her fear and anxiety begin to mount. "I became so thirsty that once or twice I drank the alkali water which in a couple of coulees had seeped into the hoof-tracks of cattle. It was sickening, and made me more thirsty than before. I began to fear that something was wrong." After an opportune meeting with a local, Lockhart eventually reaches the ranch where she is to stay for the first night of her journey. This first phase of the tenderfoot narrative establishes the tenderfoot as a regional outsider, helpless and dependent on the kindness—or at least tolerance—of the locals.

At the ranch, Lockhart meets with a range of colorful western characters, who, over dinnertime banter, taunt and provoke her, further reminding her of her outsider status. Angered, she rashly makes a bet that she will be the first woman to cross the notoriously dangerous Swift Current Pass, Montana. The next day, Lockhart embarks, along with two seasoned mountain men, on the treacherous journey. Her narrative describes in detail the precariously narrow trail, the terrifying height, and the dangerous incline, which eventually forces her to dismount her horse and travel on foot, sometimes on all fours. Throughout the journey, she refuses to betray her fear to her companions, who travel ahead of her, periodically asking "How goes it?" to which Lockhart only replies "I'm coming" (13). At the narrative's climax, her footing gives way, and she finds herself sliding down the face of the mountain to what she thinks will be her death. Her fall is broken when her foot catches hold on a rock that does not give way. This time, when her companions call out "are you coming?" a desperate Lockhart replies "No, no!" Only in the face of death does Lockhart disclose her fear. Her companions quickly come to her rescue, forming a human chain in order to reach her and lift her safely onto the trail. The chastened Lockhart believes that she has failed the test and apologizes for being so much trouble to them, but her companions are struck by her courage. "There ain't no yellow streak up your back," she is told. Lockhart wins the bet and is paid her winnings—a gun and cartridges. We are told in the coda that she and her adversary become "the best of friends." A real confrontation with death, gun ownership, and the friendship of a western insider complete Lockhart's initiation into authentic westernness.

Lockhart soon made Cody, Wyoming, her permanent residence and quickly established herself as a well-known local journalist and community leader. Her first novel, *Me—Smith*, received positive reviews, favorably comparing Lockhart to Owen Wister. However, it is her second novel I want to examine here because it focuses directly on the question of gender and western authenticity, enabling further analysis of Lockhart's position as a woman western writer.

Like Bower's *Chip, of the Flying U*, Lockhart's novel *The Lady Doc* includes substantial autobiographical material: The novel's central character is, like that of *Me—Smith*, a villain: Dr. Emma Harpe. She is a transparent depiction of Dr. Francis Lane, a doctor and community leader in Cody, and at first a good friend of Lockhart. The two traveled together on horseback expeditions and appear photographed together in Lockhart's photo albums (Clayton 83). However, Lockhart and Lane fell out in highly publicized fashion when Lockhart began a scathing muckraking campaign focusing on Lane's activities in her capacity as doctor for a local mining company. In articles she wrote for various local and state newspapers, Lockhart accused Lane of incompetence and corruption. So over-the-top were some of her accusations that some newspapers refused to publish them. Lane, whose supporters rallied around her, was able to weather the negative publicity spearheaded by Lockhart, while Lockhart's own reputation suffered, compelling her to leave Cody for a time. Cody residents were somewhat mystified by Lockhart's unprovoked attacks on Lane. Not until 2007, with the publication of a new biography by John Clayton, was the mystery of the Lane-Lockhart feud solved: Lockhart's memoir, written while she was in her eighties and never published, revealed that Lane had propositioned Lockhart sexually while the two shared a Pullman car. The extremely homophobic Lockhart not only recoiled from Lane's advance, but made a calculated attempt to use her power as a journalist to ruin Lane's reputation (Clayton 82–86, 274).

The Lady Doc was part of Lockhart's character assassination of Lane. Its main character, Emma Harpe, is a doctor who moves to the far West from Nebraska to escape legal action after killing her best friend in a botched surgery. The nature of the surgery is not explained, but there are implications that it was an abortion and that she and the victim had been lovers: The surgery was forbidden by her friend's husband—who "had not liked the intimacy between [Harpe] and his wife"—and, Harpe is told by the coroner, was "in violation of all recognized methods of medical science" (18, 19). Given an ultimatum to either leave town or be reported to the authorities and sued by her dead friend's husband, Harpe moves to the fictional western town of Crowheart. There, she uses her stature as a doctor to ingratiate herself with the leading citizens of the town and quickly assumes a position of power and influence. The text is as critical of the townspeople as it is of Lane. For the most part they are midwestern-born, new arrivals to the far-western town of Crowheart. Their manners are provincial, and they are easily fooled by Harpe's professional credentials and public display of the social graces she has acquired in the East. Behind the screen of her respectable status in the town, Harpe manipulates various town affairs to her advantage, particularly the romantic life of the belle of the town. She is also an incompetent and greedy doctor. When she is not botching surgery or turning away the wounded unless they can pay up-front, she is stealing from incapacitated hospital patients. Significantly, the male frontiersman is the only one able to see through her performance. Just as this figure authenticates Lockhart in "A Girl of the Rockies," he publicly exposes Harpe as a fraud, and the novel concludes with her dramatic flight from the furious mob.

Lockhart's attack on Lane was not only a homophobic response to her sexual advance but also an attempt to shore up Lockhart's own authenticity as a western woman through an act of scapegoating the one woman in Cody with whom Lockhart had the most in common. Both Lane and Lockhart were members of an emergent class of professional women, Lane as a doctor and Lockhart as a journalist. Both remained unmarried and had ambitions as both community leaders and as professionals. While Lane was heavily involved in community building and women's organizations, Lockhart was an energetic town booster who helped found the Cody Stampede and commission the statue of Buffalo Bill Cody that still stands in the town (Clayton 82, 188–91). Both had migrated to iconic western states in order to fulfill social and economic ambitions. Although increasing numbers of women like Lane and Lockhart were gaining a foothold in the professions, they faced considerable opposition and criticism. Professional women were widely believed to be mannish and an aberration of nature. It is not surprising that Lane and Lockhart became friends, for they were women of like interests and class identity. It was precisely this likeness, however, that eventually led Lockhart to make a public scapegoat of Lane: Doing so could potentially deflect onto Lane criticism to which Lockhart was also vulnerable, namely that Lane was an aberration of nature and a fraud. Lane's attempt to seduce Lockhart triggered this act of scapegoating.

In contrast to Lockhart's self-representation in "A Girl in the Rockies," in which Lockhart stakes her own claim to authentic westernness by earning the admiration of bona fide frontiersmen, these same arbiters of western authenticity immediately recognize Harpe as a fraud and ultimately expose her as such to the broader community. Her fraudulence is codified in terms of her transgressive gender identity, which she conceals beneath a screen of appropriately womanly behavior. She performs her femininity well enough to deceive the townspeople of Cody, while in private she is depicted as greedy, coarse, and mannish. The text implies that she is sexually attracted to the town belle, even hinting at one point that she attempts to seduce her. It takes the frontiersman's heterosexual male gaze to see through this performance to the transgressions it conceals. As a professional woman herself, Lockhart was also subject to suspicions about her femininity and sexuality (Glazer and Slater 7). Indeed, that Lockhart feared being the victim of such attacks herself may explain her sudden and disproportionate public attacks on a former friend. By attacking Lane's authenticity and sexuality, Lockhart attempted to shore up her own authenticity as a western woman.

Lockhart's attempt at character assassination backfired, damaging her reputation both locally and nationally. Offended and perhaps ashamed that the majority of Cody residents were not on her side, Lockhart left the town for a time (Clayton 103). Lockhart also proved to have been overly zealous in her desire to publicly humiliate Lane, for reviewers reacted negatively to the novel's graphic depiction of a female villain. While they had praised *Me—Smith* for its realistic antihero, they found Emma Harpe "such a horrible character that you didn't want to read about her" (Clayton 90). Indeed, Lockhart had herself violated norms of female conduct by writing such transparently angry and self-serving accounts of her enemy. Lockhart had risked her own reputation to destroy Lane's, and she lost the bet.

The examples of Bower and Lockhart demonstrate that relations of gender and the popular western were far more complex than is accounted for in the few scholarly works that address the question at all. Both Bower and Lockhart negotiated gendered obstacles to western authenticity, but these obstacles were mitigated by factors of class and region. Bower was able to leverage her regional location in her negotiations with eastern publishers but became a victim of her own success when publishers became reluctant to take any risks with the lucrative Bower brand and exerted tight control over her reputation. Bower herself was probably more obedient to these publishers than she needed to be; who knows what impact she might have had on public perceptions of the popular western had she resisted her publishers and gone public? We know from Caroline Lockhart's example that a woman writer could write popular westerns in her own name—indeed, somewhat subversive ones—and achieve success. Certainly Lockhart used western authenticity as a means by which to make the transition from stunt journalist to legitimate author. By the same token, Lockhart was insecure enough in her position as an unconventional woman and author to launch a vicious attack on a former friend whose only mistake had been to misread [or read too well] her sexuality. Such accounts of women victimizing other women are rare in scholarship on women's writing, which has emphasized the role that female communities and friendships have played in fostering women's culture. The example of Lockhart and Lane demonstrates a more disturbing social dynamic that was also at play, whereby at least one woman was compelled to victimize a friend in order to valorize her own authority and legitimacy.

4
Why Mourning Dove Wrote a Western

Most women authors of westerns were Anglo-Americans who tacitly or explicitly reproduced colonial and racist ideologies in their fiction. Even as they probed and revised some of the western's central conventions and investments, they aligned themselves in certain respects with the frontier club, that network of elite white men, well connected to the leading publishers of the day, who "seized the West as a source of cultural power" (Bold, *Frontier Club* 1). Indeed, Brigitte Georgi-Findlay and Amy Kaplan have demonstrated that Anglo-American women were deeply implicated in American imperialism. For example, Emma Ghent Curtis, writing before the frontier club formula became entrenched, suppressed the cultural diversity that characterized late nineteenth-century Colorado, the setting of *The Administratrix*. Although Frances McElrath, in her fictionalized version of the Johnson County War, casts the cattle rustlers in a sympathetic light, she does not go so far as to question the legitimacy of the dominant cattle-owning class. B. M. Bower countered Owen Wister's elitist vision of the heroic cowboy with a perspective more closely aligned with cowboys as a class but participated in the racism that characterized frontier club fiction. For the most part, as Bold observes, the more distantly a writer was located from the social circles that constituted the frontier club, the less their writing followed the frontier club formula (223).

Mourning Dove (Okanagan) was situated well outside of frontier club circles. Her novel *Cogewea* was published in 1929 but written as early as 1914 and was influenced, according to Mourning Dove's autobiography, by the "yellowback novels" that she read growing up. The term "yellowback" referred to cheap novels of all kinds, including the Buffalo Bill and Young Wild West series novels, the most "lowbrow" of early twentieth-century narratives of the West, eschewed by the other authors mentioned in this study as reading primarily for juveniles and subliterates (In chapter 6 I discuss the relations among the different categories of western narrative in more detail). Another key influence upon *Cogewea*, Therese Broderick's hardcover novel *The Brand*, about a white woman who marries a mixed-blood man, was published in 1909 by the Seattle-based publisher Alice Harriman. Finally, Mourning Dove was profoundly influenced by tribal storytelling practices, which had more in common with "yellowback novels" than is conventionally assumed.

Mourning Dove's ancestry is uncertain. By her own accounts she was of mixed Okanagan and white ancestry. She spoke Salish and was a member of the Colville reservation in Washington State, formed in 1872 to confine several nomadic tribes displaced by U.S. expansion into the Pacific Northwest (Brown, "Mourning Dove" 285). In this chapter I reconstruct the cultural and material relations within which Mourning Dove wrote and published *Cogewea* in an attempt to understand why Mourning Dove chose to write a western, and I trace the ways in which Mourning Dove puts the western to use politically and creatively. I believe that we have as much to learn from thus probing the margins of a genre as we do from focusing on its "classic" or "representative" texts. Westerns on the margins often put the genre to uses for which it was not originally designed or intended, exposing more clearly the genre's blindnesses and boundaries, as well as the resourcefulness and genius of the authors who put it to subversive use. Specifically, I argue that Mourning Dove deployed the popular western as a more radical, Indigenist alternative to the dominant, ethnographic discourses available to Indigenous authors of English language texts at the turn of the last century.

Believing that their mission was to preserve Native American culture in print before it "disappeared" forever, early twentieth-century ethnographers engaged an approach James Clifford has termed "salvage ethnography" (112). It was in this context that Mourning Dove wrote *Cogewea, the Half-Blood* (1927).[1] Its editor, Lucullus McWhorter, considered *Cogewea* an important work because, as he writes in his preface to the first edition, he believed it to be the first novel written by a Native American woman (9), but he also felt that one novel was enough and discouraged Mourning Dove from writing another one. Instead, he convinced her to devote her energy to the ethnographic "fieldwork" that resulted in the 1933 collection *Coyote Stories* (Brown, "The Evolution" 162–65; Bernardin 490–91). In her original draft of the preface to *Coyote Stories*, Mourning Dove writes, "I first wrote my lines of these stories much against my will" (quoted in Brown, "The Evolution" 173). Clearly, Mourning Dove began writing with intentions that were set aside for the sake of ethnographic fieldwork. Scholars of the text have been trying to recover these intentions ever since, collectively demonstrating that *Cogewea* highlights crucial issues in Native American literary studies. Paula Gunn Allen considers it a foundational text in twentieth-century Native American literature because of its resolution, in which the main character, a mixed-blood woman, realizes that ritual tradition has relevance in her life (83–85), a theme taken up by later writers, including N. Scott Momaday (Kiowa), Leslie Silko (Laguna Pueblo), and Gerald Vizenor (Anishinaabe). In different ways, Louis Owens (Choctaw-Cherokee) and Susan Bernardin interpret *Cogewea*'s subversive appropriations of Anglo-American literary forms—the popular western, the sentimental novel—as a historically important moment in the development of a Native American literary tradition (Owens, *Mixedblood Messages* 28–34; Bernardin 495–504). The text's adaptations of Anglo-American forms draw heavily on Indigenous oral tradition, as Martha L. Viehmann, Michael Wilson, and Joanna Brooks have demonstrated. *Cogewea* has also become an important text in scholarship on alternative modernisms by Justine Dymond, Alicia Kent, and others. Debates about the authenticity of *Cogewea*, arising from extensive participation by its non-Native editor, speak to the complex and difficult questions about the politics of Native American representation.[2] As Christine Bold points out, such questions of authenticity are themselves the cost of frontier club dominance over the meaning of the West in American culture (*Frontier Club* 215).

Most of this scholarship represents the popular western as an antagonistic genre that Mourning Dove subverts, troubles, or satirizes. I would like to cast the popular western in a more enabling light by situating it in relation to both the ethnographic discourse that Mourning Dove would later practice and the indigenous oral stories and practices that informed all of her writing. The popular western appealed to Mourning Dove because it enabled an Indigenized literary practice that did not equate writing with the assimilation and disappearance of Indigenous culture.

The focus on the crucial relationship between oral and literary storytelling practice in scholarship on contemporary Native American literature overturns the assumptions of early twentieth-century Anglo-American ethnographers, who equated orality with the "primitive" and writing with a more advanced, Anglo-American "civilization," overlooking the fact that oral and written cultural forms had long coexisted in Indigenous cultures.[3] They regarded writing as both a vehicle for assimilating Native Americans into the American melting pot and a medium for preserving their supposedly dying oral traditions. Both assumptions were based on the binary construction of oral storytelling as the "primitive" opposite of written culture, to be eradicated once Native American people "progressed" toward literacy. *Cogewea* is a groundbreaking novel created as an act of resistance against precisely this binary model of the relationship between oral and literary practice. Rejecting the belief underlying ethnographic narrative that the death of Native American nations and cultures was inevitable, Mourning Dove gravitated toward the popular western as a vehicle for inscribing a *living* Indigenous culture in print. Early ethnographers did not imagine that Indigenous storytelling practice would survive, let alone become a highly valued aspect of Indigenous literary aesthetics, epitomized by Leslie Silko's classic *Storyteller* (1981), which combines poetry, prose, photography, autobiography, fiction, and traditional Pueblo narratives. In addition to challenging the primacy of writing, an oral literary aesthetic challenges the Anglo-American cultural hegemony through the various ways in which it constructs its audience, such as assuming a reader with knowledge of Native American oral history and mythology rather than taking responsibility for imparting such knowledge to a presumably non-Native reader (Owens, *Mixedblood Messages* 10). Kimberly Blaeser explains how, in Gerald Vizenor's writing, the printed word is secondary to the "real enduring" that is manifest "beyond the published versions" (29), an idea Vizenor articulates through textual devices such as minimalism, suggestion, and implication—all of which stress the contingency of the written word and invite the reader to engage with the oral world beyond the text (32). Theoretical work has also been done to provide frameworks for reading oral writing, such as Susan Berry Brill de Ramírez's theory of literary "conversivity," which she applies to the work of a diverse array of contemporary Native American authors. Such works have established the profound significance of oral practice in Native American literary studies. More recently, Christopher B. Teuton has troubled this emphasis on oral aesthetics in Native American writing by demonstrating a long history of interplay between graphic and oral communication in Native American culture (1–52).

By the late twentieth century, contrary to the predictions of early ethnographers, this oral aesthetic had become a widely recognized and prized characteristic of Native American writing. However, it circulated primarily in literary forms accessible only to a small, cultural elite. Louis Owens commented on this issue:

> What we are calling Native American literature is represented largely, if not exclusively, by the sorts of privileged texts . . . created by those migrant or diasporic Natives who live lives of relatively privileged mobility and surplus pleasure. As a group, we published Native American authors have an impressively high rate of education. . . . We may go back to our families and communities periodically or regularly . . . but we are inescapably both institutionally privileged by access to Anglo-American education and distinctly migrant in the sense that we possess mobility denied to our less privileged relations. (Owens, "As If" 22)

Whereas the late twentieth-century oral aesthetic circulated in the literary field, Mourning Dove—writing at a time when Native American access to the production of print culture was more narrowly restricted—adapted the conventions of popular pulps she had read as a child. Her experimentation with the interplay between oral and written language goes beyond the novel's mimetic representation of oral practice (embodied especially in the figure of the storyteller-grandmother). Mourning Dove also experimented with the formal conventions associated with both oral storytelling and mass-produced popular fiction to challenge the binary and hierarchical relationship between oral and written storytelling, a goal similar to that of later practitioners of Native American oral writing. *Cogewea* would eventually be identified with the subliterary formula western (which, as I discuss in chapter 6, was not yet consolidated when Mourning Dove began writing *Cogewea*). Consequently, it would be regarded as protoliterature by some late twentieth-century scholars engaged in the formation of a Native American literary canon, a text representative of a period before the emergence of "mature" Native American literary tradition.[4] While Lucullus McWhorter's position as editor certainly played a role in compromising the status of *Cogewea* as a Native American text, I believe another important factor contributing to the contested status of *Cogewea* as a Native American text was the literary hegemony that has underwritten the value of much Native American oral writing. Whereas late twentieth-century oral writing derived its legitimacy from its authors' demonstrated proficiency with literary language, *Cogewea*'s place in the emerging Native American literary canon was less certain because of its indebtedness to popular narrative. By drawing attention to this literary hegemony, I do not mean to devalue or lessen the achievements of any Native American literary author; rather, my goal is to highlight and valorize Mourning Dove's innovations with form, plot, narrative structure, and generic convention. As Laura Godfrey has deftly argued, there is much to lose if readers, guided by hegemonic norms of literary language, dismiss this important novel because of its "jarring, fractious" narrative language (70).

It is clear from the extensive correspondence between Mourning Dove and Lucullus McWhorter that ethnography was not Mourning Dove's first choice of genre. McWhorter was an Anglo-American advocate for Native American rights in the Pacific Northwest, as well as a historian and ethnographer working at a time when ethnographic practice was dominated by the method of Franz Boas.[5] Mourning Dove and McWhorter met in 1914 at a fair in Walla Walla, Washington. When McWhorter heard that Mourning Dove was working on a novel, he offered to help her edit the manuscript and secure a publisher, an offer that Mourning Dove, with few contacts in the literary world, appears to have readily accepted. McWhorter soon engaged Mourning Dove's help with his ethnographic project, hiring her to collect and transcribe Okanogan narratives. In this way, Mourning Dove joined the ranks of many so-called Native informants, the use of which was advocated by the Boasian method as a desirable way to gain insider knowledge of an alien culture (H. Carr 198). These "informants" were recruited by Anglo-American ethnographers to collect and record Native American oral stories and folklore, a project predicated upon the assumption that Native American and other minority oral cultures would soon "disappear" through the mechanism of assimilation and must therefore be preserved in print. Despite his track record as a strong advocate of Indigenous rights, McWhorter shared in this assumption: "I see many on this trail," he wrote to Mourning Dove in 1915, "'They are bearing bundles which glow and shine like the gold that is washed from the river beds. These bundles are the traditions and history of the tribes.' But they 'pass with their bundles of light—the history of their people—into the cloud and are seen no more'" (quoted in Brown, "The Evolution" 163). By her own account, Mourning Dove answered McWhorter's call quite reluctantly. Left to her own devices, she preferred popular narrative over ethnography, quite possibly because the former supplied a more powerful vehicle for furthering Mourning Dove's goals as an activist storyteller.

The assumed death of Native American culture was implicit both in the methods of salvage ethnography and in its narrative conventions. Ethnographers preferred material deemed to have prepreservation origins, regarding Native Americans living on reservations as products of a culture contaminated by white contact (Womack 57; H. Carr 155). Boas and his followers also underestimated the importance of information that is now considered crucial to understanding Native American art and culture in both historical and contemporary contexts: the performative context of Native American oral art, its pedagogical and ceremonial functions, taboos governing its appropriate transmission, interactions between storyteller and listener, and the semiotic differences between oral and written language.[6] The omission of all of this information is indicative of the fact that ethnographers did not regard Native American cultures as living cultures-in-practice. Ethnographic narrative structure was similarly inflected with this trope of the disappearing Indian. It rhetorically situated Native American peoples on the outside in both spatial and temporal terms, representing them as exotic specimens on display for the curious gaze of the Anglo-American reader and locating them in a romanticized, distant past far removed from the implied reader's temporal and geographical location (H. Carr 162, 185; Clifford 112; Deloria 93–94). Although most ethnographers saw themselves as "friends of the Indian" and considered political advocacy for Indian rights as an important aspect of their work, few questioned the belief, though they may have lamented it, that American Indian cultures were dying (Deloria 84).

The "yellowback novels" read by the young Mourning Dove represented Indigenous people in active conflict with colonial powers and could be co-opted to resist ethnography's metanarrative of the disappearing "primitive." According to Clifford, ethnographic narrative rhetorically inscribed a spatial and temporal disjuncture between the "primitive" narrative object, suspended in an obsolete world of tradition and subsistence, and the "modern" historical present of both the observer-narrator and the reader. Especially when the object of representation was not historicized (as was the case in much early twentieth-century ethnography, which considered reservation life inauthentic and privileged "traditional" Indians), salvage ethnography portrayed "exotic societies in an 'ethnographic present' (which is always, in fact, a past). This synchronic suspension effectively textualizes the other, and gives the sense of a reality not in a temporal flux, not in the same ambiguous, moving *historical* present that includes and situates the other, the ethnographer, and the reader" (Clifford 111). The western, in contrast, allows for a more politically potent representation of Indigenous people in both temporal and spatial terms. Temporally, it depicts Indigenous people in the context of modernity, their struggle against colonialism ongoing and contingent. In spatial terms, the western's frontier location, as Louis Owens explains, "carries with it such a heavy burden of colonial discourse, it can only be conceived of as a space of extreme contestation" and is therefore "particularly apt" for representing the "transcultural zone of contact" between Native and Anglo-America (*Mixedblood Messages* 26). In a similar vein, Bernardin notes how the focus on mixed-blood figures in *Cogewea* counters the "elegiac mode" characteristic of narratives of the disappearing

Native (498). At the turn of the twentieth century, this distinction in temporal setting between the two genres made a significant difference insofar as ethnography proceeded from the premise that the struggle of the tribes was over. In this respect, popular western plots, despite their origins in the romantic tradition, were more representative of the contemporary social world in which most Native American people lived—in conflict and dialogue with Anglo-American interests and culture—than the supposedly "objective" discourse of ethnography, with its romantic nostalgia for the "pure" Indian of the distant past. *Cogewea* co-opts popular western conventions to represent aspects of early twentieth-century Native American life that were effectively silenced in ethnographic discourse, which represented conquest as a long-finished process and, as Renato Rosaldo has shown, effaced the colonial context in which fieldwork was typically carried out (91). Because the popular western's frontier setting made it possible to represent reservation life and politics, the interstitial perspective of Native people, their resistance to Anglo-American domination, and the ongoing relevance of ceremony in contemporary contexts, it could situate narratives about Native American people in the implied reader's social present, a formal characteristic that aligned the genre with realist modes of representation and moved away from ethnographic romanticism.

In addition to these formal and generic characteristics, popular westerns bore certain structural affinities with Native American storytelling practice because of the oral characteristics of popular writing. In his landmark study of orality, Walter J. Ong argues that there are fundamental differences between predominantly oral and predominantly literate cultures: In oral cultures, words are events; in literate cultures, words are things (31–33). In oral cultures, linguistic subjects do not experience the same separation between self and environment that they do in literate cultures. These and other distinctions arise from the materialization of the word that results from the development and widespread use of written alphabets: Sounds are broken down into discrete units and represented visually by material symbols external to the reading subject, as opposed to aural sounds internalized by the listening subject (71–74). Both Ruth Finnegan and Susan Brill de Ramírez have raised valid questions about Ong's contention that writing is a precondition for analytical thought and his tendency to draw broad divisions between oral and literate cultures (Finnegan 67–69; Brill de Ramírez 3); however, his argument that oral and graphic language have distinct structural and semiotic properties remains a useful model for analysis of oral aesthetics in written texts. Nevertheless, critiques of Ong, such as that of Finnegan, have rightly argued for a model that recognizes "the continuity of 'oral' and 'written' literature. There is no deep gulf between the two: they shade into each other both in the present and over many centuries of historical development" (quoted in Brill de Ramírez 11).[7]

On this continuum of oral/written narrative, the objectifying rhetoric of early twentieth-century ethnography was situated more closely to the written than popular narrative, which engaged several oral devices. Repetition, important in oral narrative as a mnemonic device (Ong 33–35), is a distinguishing feature of the popular novel, with its formulaic plots, stock characters, and recurring motifs. While repetition characterizes oral *story*, the *telling* of it varies from one occasion to the next depending upon such factors as the style of the particular storyteller, the response of the listener or listeners, and the social situation in which the story is told (Ong 57–67). Popular fiction similarly stresses variety of *telling* but repetition of *story* and adapts in response to changing social conditions—according to Ong, another characteristic of oral storytelling (66–67).

Early twentieth-century popular fiction was, in certain respects, a more conversive print form than ethnography. According to Brill de Ramírez, much Native American oral writing uses an intersubjective rhetorical structure that embeds it in oral storytelling practice, "in which the audience of listeners are present while the story is being told" and which "demonstrates a conversive interaction that continually, cyclically, and repetitively turns its focus from storyteller to story to listener to ancestors to descendants to other relatives and other persons, peoples, animals, things; and in this process, the listener's relationship to these 'others' is emphasized such that the listener becomes a part of the story herself" (31). According to Ong, "Oral communication unites people in groups. Writing and reading are solitary activities that throw the psyche back on itself" (69). Ong's binary definitions overlook the conversive aspects of reading, which have existed since antiquity (Manguel 42–45). These include the practice of reading aloud with a group, which was common in American homes before the advent of radio and television; group discussions of books at women's clubs; and, post-Internet, book clubs, blogs, and other digital book-discussion forums. In Mourning Dove's time, many popular fiction magazines used conversive strategies, particularly departments that published letters from readers, to construct communities of readers for their fiction. In her reading of "yellowback novels,"[8] described in her autobiography (186), Mourning Dove may have been exposed to some of the marketing strategies of early twentieth-century popular fiction serials such as *Popular* and *Adventure*, which included departments where readers and authors conversed about the stories published in the magazine and editorials that involved readers in its behind-the-scenes operations.[9] These conversive vehicles build collectivities, in a mass-market context, in a manner similar to that which Ong attributes to oral communication, sometimes enabling complete strangers to form strong social bonds on the basis of their affinity for a particular popular genre.

The moral didacticism of popular western plots could be adapted to resemble Native American lesson stories as described by the Abenaki storyteller and author Joseph Bruchac: "When children do wrong, rather than hitting them or physically abusing them, the first step toward correction is to tell a lesson story. Traditional stories . . . show the results of bad behavior and it is believed that such lessons remain in the child's heart, even though the child may not know it at the time" (44). As Dexter Fisher points out in her introduction to the reprint edition of *Cogewea*, the novel's plot is based on the Okanogan lesson story of Chipmunk (Kots-se-we-ah) and Owl Woman (xii). Similar to the way in which lesson stories both teach and entertain, early twentieth-century popular novels were regarded both as entertainment and, for better of worse, as powerful vehicles for the inculcation of values in the reader. *Cogewea* is a lesson story in written form, and the lesson it teaches is one of Native "survivance," to borrow Gerald Vizenor's term, rather than disappearance (53).

Whereas these features of popular narrative fit Ong's description of orality as "empathetic and participatory," traditional ethnographic narrative similarly fits his description of literacy as "objectively distanced" (45). Ethnographic narrative situated its representations at an objective distance from both the observing narrator and the passive, silent reader—a formal requirement that suppressed the fieldworker's intersubjective relationships with members of the community he or she studied—and addressed a passive reader far removed from the represented culture. The objectifying discourse of ethnography conflicted with Mourning Dove's goals for *Cogewea* as described in a 1916 newspaper interview given to promote the novel, in which she identifies *feeling* as precisely what is lacking in the Anglo-American understanding of Native American experience: "It is all wrong, this saying that Indians do not feel as deeply as whites. We do feel, and by and by some of us are going to be able to make our feelings appreciated, and then will the true Indian character be revealed" (quoted in Bernardin 490). Ethnographic discourse also objectified Native American cultures insofar as the performative context of Native American verbal art was not considered significant—a problem that, according to Vizenor, persisted in late twentieth-century anthologies of Native American writing.[10] Fieldworkers recorded relatively little information about storytelling practice and did not consider their acts of recording, transcribing, or translation to influence the meaning of stories they recorded (Murray 106). The assumption that the performative and oral contexts did not essentially matter was based upon and reinforced the belief that ethnographers were dealing with fossils of a dead culture rather than the practiced art of a living one and that written language was superior to and could transparently encompass oral language. Moreover, as Clifford has shown, ethnographic rhetoric figured writing itself as an objectifying process: Bringing oral culture into (Western) knowledge meant bringing it into writing, and bringing it into writing necessitated its death as an oral culture, much like pinning a butterfly to a card in order to understand how it flies (113).

It is precisely this interstitial perspective that is represented in *Cogewea*, the story of a mixed-blood woman who is pursued by two male rivals: Jim LaGrinder, an honorable mixed-blood cowboy, and Densmore, a white visitor from the East. The story is set on the Flathead Reservation in Montana during the period of the Dawes General Allotment Act of 1887, when Native reservations were being divided into small, individually owned tracts of land, a plan designed to assimilate Native people into mainstream white society by transforming them into yeoman farmers. When Densmore is tricked into believing that Cogewea's allotment is far larger than it really is, he conspires to seduce her in order to cheat her out of her land. Begging Cogewea to teach him about her culture and promising marriage and affluence in return, Densmore succeeds in convincing Cogewea to elope with him, but when Cogewea innocently discloses the fact that her allotment is worth very little, the infuriated Densmore beats her, ties her to a tree, and leaves her to die in the wilderness. Meanwhile, Cogewea's other suitor, the steadfast Jim LaGrinder, has learned of Densmore's plan and comes to Cogewea's rescue, and the novel concludes with the marriage of these two mixed-blood characters. The conventional frontier setting on the boundary between wilderness and civilization enables Mourning Dove to represent contemporary reservation life, pressing political and social issues, and the interstitial location of the main character, all of which would be regarded by ethnographers as signs of contamination but were well within popular western formal conventions—with the crucial difference that *Cogewea* represents the reservation and its inhabitants in the sympathetic position usually reserved for white homesteaders while its "savage" figure is a white visitor bent on learning Native American culture in order to acquire Native American land.

Cogewea challenges the authority and truth-value of ethnography at every opportunity. Interestingly, the name of its villain is the same as that of the prominent early twentieth-century ethnomusicologist Frances Densmore, who had worked in both Washington State, where Mourning Dove was born, and British Columbia, where her tribe's traditional fishing grounds were located (Hofman xi–xiii). *Cogewea* also contains a passage describing how Cogewea's friends "locoed" a folklore-collector:

> This here lady come up and begins askin' questions 'bout the buffaloes; and Injun names of flyin', walkin' and swimmin' things and a lot of bunk. Well, you know how the boys are. They sure locoed that there gal to a finish; and while she was a dashin' the information down in her little

tablet, we was a thinkin' up more lies to tell her. We didn't savey she was writing' a real book, or maybe we would a been more careful. (93–94)

Whether Frances Densmore was the target of this textual joke, or even the namesake for *Cogewea*'s villain, is a matter of speculation, but the above episode nevertheless satirizes ethnography of the kind that Densmore practiced by highlighting the ethnographer's predisposition to romantic fictions, as well as calling into question the higher truth-value of printed versions over their oral antecedents.[11] Indeed, as a folklore-collector herself, Mourning Dove knew from experience that the higher truth-value accorded to print culture was a sham, not only because of formal and contextual differences between written and oral versions but also because material relationships among collectors and between collectors and informants altered the written ethnographic record. In 1918 she wrote to McWhorter about her sources:

> They . . . are getting suspicious of my wanting folklores and if the Indians find out that their stories will reach print I am sure it will be hard for me to get any more legends without paying the hard cash for them. A Whiteman has spoiled my field of work. . . . This Mr. James Tait [actually James Teit, a student of Boas] has collected folklores among the Indians and has been paying five dollars apiece for good Indian legends and naturally that has spoiled the natives and of course they wish the same price from me whether the story is worth a nickel to me. A lot of times the same stories are told to me a little differently from one party and another will say, that is not the true fact. (quoted in Brown, "The Evolution" 167–68)

Mourning Dove's account of the folklore marketplace exposes the material relations masked by the ethnographer's objective posture. The commodity value of stories—ironically created when the oppression of Native American people leads to a perceived scarcity of their culture—constitutes a market for counterfeit stories. Hence ethnography is not only untruthful, it is produced within a system that is antithetical to truth. Mourning Dove invokes the same structure of economic interest masked by disinterested pursuit of cultural knowledge to represent her villain, Densmore.

Throughout the text, ideas associated with ethnography, such as belief in the inevitability of Native disappearance and the notion of pure "Indianness," are not only ridiculed but are identified with colonialism through the figure of Densmore, who voices the ethnographer's desire for cultural knowledge while concealing his colonial desire for Cogewea's land. Densmore is first identified with the colonizer's romantic visions of Indianness when he arrives at the reservation, where he expects to find "the painted and blanketed aborigine of history and romance" but instead encounters a "miniature group of half-bloods [Cogewea and her sister] and one ancient squaw [Cogewea's grandmother] and is disgusted by "the writers who had beguiled him to the 'wild and wooly'" (44). Densmore's romantic expectations immediately get him into all sorts of trouble, as is usually the case with the tenderfoot figure. In order to secure a job at Cogewea's ranch and experience the "wild and wooly," he falsely claims that he can ride a "bronc" (a term he misinterprets to mean "donkey"). Predictably, his first attempt at bronc riding ends in humiliation, but this tenderfoot is not an entirely benign victim of ridicule. He soon devises a plan to "court [Cogewea's] ideals . . . for a purpose. He would amass this [Cogewea's] fortune—transfer it to his own pocket—and then . . ." (84). Densmore seduces Cogewea by engaging her in long discussions about tribal values and rituals, replicating the relation between ethnographer and informant. They discuss hospitality, rules of governing the conduct of unmarried women, and courtship practices. Densmore persuades Cogewea to take him to her grandmother and listen to one of her stories, and he pretends to listen respectfully as Cogewea explains the ritual significance of tobacco. He eventually promises to "be Indian" if only Cogewea would marry him (162). His insidious intention to steal Cogewea's land under the guise of falling in love with both Cogewea and her culture exposes material relations that traditional ethnography erased; the latter, Rosaldo explains, rhetorically separated "the context of colonial domination from the production of ethnographic knowledge" (93). The figure of Densmore, whose ethnographic desire for knowledge about an alien culture conceals his hidden desire to possess its resources, exposes the ways in which the production of knowledge about Native American Indians was imbricated in their political subordination and economic exploitation—a connection denied by the ethnographic narrator's objective posture.

The villain of *Cogewea* is identified not only with ethnographic practice but also with the doctrine of Indian assimilation. Salvage ethnographers were mobilized by the belief that Native American peoples would naturally be assimilated by the "superior" Anglo-American culture—an assumption contradicted by the aggressive tactics used to help the process along. These included assimilationist policies that required Native American children to attend boarding schools where Native American languages and cultural practices were forbidden and which used literacy and vocational training to assimilate Native American children into Anglo-American culture and economy. This paternal approach was widely considered a progressive means by which to "marry" the two cultures and improve the economic conditions of Native American people, who, given that their parent cultures were presumed dead, were categorized as cultural orphans. As exemplified in the following exchange, Densmore's strategies of seduction vacillate between acquiring knowledge about Cogewea's culture and enticing her with the benefits of his, mirroring the symbiotic relationship between the ethnographic preservation of a "dead" culture and the paternalistic assimilation of its orphaned children:

> "Listen! My little Injun sweetheart! I have plenty, all that you could wish for. I want to share my wealth with you. . . . Suppose we form a partnership. . . . "
>
> "I would not sell myself!" was the scornful reply. "Money cannot bring happiness. Too often its heritage is one of unfathomed misery."
>
> Densmore realizing his mistake, retrenched hastily.
>
> "You misunderstood me. I am but endeavoring to show you that I care deeply and am anxious to be to you all that a husband should. If I could only hear you say that you care for me—that you love me ever so little."
>
> He was straining her to his breast and he felt her responsive form quiver. He attempted to lift her warm lips to his own, but she held aloof.
>
> "Cogewea!" he whispered, smoothing her raven tresses. "I love you to distraction! I am willing to meet you in every way that you desire. I will be Indian. Tell me more about your tribal customs. That marriage ceremony—" (162)

Densmore's promise to "be Indian" is similar to the ethnographic technique of "going native," whereby the observer becomes a participant in the "alien" culture with the ulterior motive of acquiring sacred knowledge (Murray 137). Densmore has ulterior motives as well: Since Native American marriage ceremonies were not binding under Anglo-American law, Densmore will be legally free to abandon Cogewea once he has secured her property. In the same way that Densmore promises on the one hand to give Cogewea access to the material benefits of this culture by assimilating her in marriage and on the other hand to honor and participate in her culture's marriage rituals, Anglo-American models of cultural exchange with Native American Indians (ostensibly) traded economic opportunity for Native American cultural knowledge. In both cases, this cultural economy is rooted in colonial interests in Native American land, a relationship exposed in *Cogewea* but repressed in colonial discourse. The Dawes Act promised to introduce Native American people to the opportunities of the Anglo-American economy and culture by encouraging individual ownership of property, but in practice, Native American land holdings diminished drastically under the Dawes Act, just as Cogewea's would have if Densmore's plan had succeeded.[12]

This critique of ethnographic discourse is accompanied by a subtle challenge to the identification between English literacy and assimilation, an identification that ideologically foreclosed the possibility of a Native American English literary tradition since English literacy signified the death of Native American culture. The primary vehicle for assimilating Native American children was the English literacy they acquired at boarding schools (attended both by Mourning Dove herself and her fictional character Cogewea). The view that English literacy was the best way to assimilate Native American people was predicated upon the binary opposition between oral and literate cultures. Not only did this construct overlook the long tradition of writing in Indigenous societies (Teuton 1–52), but it privileged literacy as both a natural and pivotal stage in cultural evolution: Once a culture became literate, its oral traditions were irretrievably lost (Clifford 113). Transforming Native Americans into Americans therefore combined English literacy training with strictly enforced rules against speaking Native languages. According to K. Tsianina Lomawaima, however, these schools "often strengthened rather than dissolved tribal identity" (quoted in Vizenor 59), contributing to what Louis Owens describes as the "subversive survival of indigenous Americans" (*Mixedblood Messages* 4). Thus Cogewea returns from boarding school with plans to use her Anglo-American education to advocate for her people, who "have suffered as much from the pen as from the bayonet of conquest" (*Cogewea* 92). According to her autobiography, Mourning Dove similarly regarded her education at a boarding school run by the Goodwin Catholic Mission near Kettle Falls, Washington, as a means of strengthening her tribal identity and empowering her to act on its behalf: "Both Catholicism and shamanism have been part of the beliefs and experiences of my entire life," she writes. "Together these were part of my childhood experiences and made me resolve to help my people record their traditions and gain all the rights they were entitled to" (*A Salishan Autobiography* 32).

Perhaps her strengthened tribal identity contributed as well to her choice of print medium. "Yellowback" novels were not part of the standard boarding school education, but they were the literature of the working classes, immigrants, and other low-income groups in the United States. An Irish American orphan named Jimmy Ryan, befriended by Mourning Dove's family, introduced Mourning Dove to the "yellowback novel," a genre that departed from the "native informant" model that McWhorter eventually persuaded Mourning Dove to adopt. Within the native informant model, Native autobiographers were valued because they could claim both intimate knowledge of the culture and the objective distance of a literate—and therefore assimilated—observer. In her autobiography, for example, Mourning Dove's writing self is sharply distinguished from her "Indian" self: She describes her traditional Okanogan education in detail but makes fewer references to her acquisition of English literacy, other than some passing references such as this one to her mother, who "would secretly scold me for being so interested in books" (*A Salishan Autobiography* 186). Implicit in Mourning Dove's autobiographical narration, then, is a distinction between the narrated "Indian self," who experiences a traditional Okanogan education, and the narrating, assimilated self, who no longer participates in the culture (since the culture is "dead") and can therefore report on it from an objective distance.

The omniscient narration of *Cogewea* sidesteps this negative relation between literacy and Native American identity. Furthermore, the frontispiece to the first edition of *Cogewea* does not figure its author as assimilated by virtue of her literacy:

> CO-GE-WE-A
> The Half-Blood
> A Depiction of the Great Montana Cattle Range
> By
> HUM-ISHU-MA
> "Mourning Dove"
> Author of "The Okanogan Sweat House"
> Honorary Member, Eastern Washington State Historical Society
> Life Member, Washington State Historical Society
>
> Given through SHO-POW-TAN
> With Notes and Biographical Sketch
> By Lucullus Virgil Mcwhorter
> Author of "The Crime Against the Yakimas,"
> "Border Settlers of Northwestern Virginia,"
> "The Discards," etc.

Here, the story Mourning Dove created is differentiated from its printed version, which is "given" by Sho-Pow-Tan (McWhorter's editorial persona). It is McWhorter who is represented as the assimilated, literate native informant, while Mourning Dove is rhetorically positioned inside the Native American culture from which the text of *Cogewea* has originated. At the same time, Mourning Dove derives literary authority from references to her other writings and membership in historical societies. The result is the representation of an authority that is at once Native American and literate.

The Mourning Dove/McWhorter correspondence, as discussed in detail by Brown, Bernardin, and others, suggests that McWhorter's editorial changes focused on the language of the novel rather than the plot, and it is the plot that improvises upon popular western conventions in ways that insist upon the ongoing power and relevance of Native American cultural practice, particularly oral practice.[13] Its courtship plot, culminating in the engagement of two mixed-blood characters, is particularly significant. In the popular western tradition, the boundaries of racial difference are variously transgressed or reinforced through the language of heterosexual attraction between men and women of different racial groups. This was a literary manifestation of nineteenth-century thought about racial difference, much of which was premised on the belief that patterns of sexual desire and repugnance between the races, the fertility rates of interracial unions, and the characteristics of the offspring operated according to the laws of "natural" racial difference (Young 14–16). In frontier fiction, the most familiar resolution to these love affairs is a tragic one, like the violent death of Cora and Uncas in Cooper's *Last of the Mohicans* (1826), which suggests that their interracial union can only occur in a platonic afterlife free from the constraints of the racialized body. When interracial marriage does occur, the union typically results in the disappearance of Native American culture. In Lydia Maria Child's *Hobomok* (1824), for example, little Hobomok grows up with no knowledge of his Native American ancestry, presumably because the strength of his mother's whiteness subsumes his Native American paternity. These two courtship plots thus have in common the fact that they resolve Native-white conflict through the disappearance of the Native, the only difference being whether this result is achieved through violent death or nonviolent marriage and assimilation. The marriage that concludes *Cogewea* departs from these models in ways that call into question the natural inevitability of white domination. Recall that Cogewea is rescued from the white seducer Densmore by a mixed-blood cowboy named Jim LaGrinder, whom Cogewea eventually marries. This marriage between two mixed-blood characters represents mixed-blood figures as fertile members of a reproductive culture, borrowing familiar conventions from the popular western but using them in an unconventional way: In the dominant western tradition, mixed-blood figures embody a phase in the inevitable process of assimilation and are either infertile, die tragically, or marry whites and produce white children.

    This position is quite clear in chapter 10 of *Cogewea,* which summarizes in detail the plot of Therese Broderick's *The Brand* (1909). Upon reading *The Brand*, Cogewea is so furious that she burns it—a clear a refusal to occupy the position of the silent, objectified reader. Cogewea is angered in particular by *The Brand*'s mixed-blood protagonist, whose love for a white woman is consummated only after both are able to "forget" his Native American ancestry. This is how Cogewea summarizes the plot:

> The scene opened on the Flathead [also the setting of *Cogewea*], where a half-blood "brave" is in love with a white girl; the heroine of the story. He dares not make a declaration of his affection because of his Indian blood. He curses his own mother for his heritage, hates his American parent for the sake of the girl of his heart. He deems himself beneath her; not good enough for her. But to cap the absurdity of the story, he weds the white "princess" and slaves for her the rest of his life. (91)

While this description of *The Brand* contains some exaggerations, its representation of the plot is fairly accurate: In *The Brand*, a mixed-blood ranch worker named Henry West falls in love with a white woman named Bess Fletcher. The complex plot revolves around the racial differences that keep the two lovers apart and is resolved when Bess Fletcher is able to "forget" Henry West's Native American ancestry, thereby assimilating him. The last lines of the novel celebrate Bess's act of forgetting: "Some-day," Henry begs her, "some-time, will you come back—when you can forget that tragedy—when you can forget—*that I am an Indian?*" (270). Bess relents in the novel's final passage. "I cannot go—I cannot leave all this. I cannot live without you now! Henry—Henry West! *I—have forgotten!*" (271). Bess's act of forgetting signals both the success of Henry West's assimilation and Beth's continued access to "all this"—namely, Native American land. Their marriage will be the vehicle by which the "superior" race will eventually dilute the "inferior" one until the latter simply "disappears," a common framework in the nineteenth century for understanding how assimilation would actually occur (Barnett 9–11). The same thinking later governed social-Darwinian ideas about the role of women in reproducing the so-called Anglo-Saxon race, exemplified in *The Virginian* by Molly Wood's instinctive attraction to the superior man (Slotkin, *Gunfighter Nation* 177). *The Brand* follows the same logic to signify Henry West's assimilation: Bess's capacity to "forget" Henry is Native signifies the "success" of the prior miscegenated marriage between Henry's white father and his mixed-blood mother. Otherwise, according to this logic, Bess's sexual nature would not allow her to form a union with a man too racially different from herself.

If Cogewea is particularly vehement in her criticism of *The Brand*, it is because the novel *Cogewea* is especially invested in exposing the sinister subtext of *The Brand's* position that the interracial "marriage" of cultures would naturally result in the "disappearance" of the Native. The language Densmore uses to court Cogewea is steeped in the benevolent paternalism typical of assimilationist arguments:

> The day has come when the Indian must desist from his wild, savage life. The Government is working hard for his betterment, and he should respond with a willingness to advance by adjusting himself to the new order of things. The opening of this reservation to settlement, tends to mingle him with his white brother, leading to an inter marriage of the two races. The tribesman will learn wisdom from his new neighbors, who will teach him how best to wrest his food supplies from the soil. The change was inevitable, and why should you go on the warpath? (143–44)

Densmore's rhetoric conceals his intention to murder Cogewea and steal her land just as a similar kind of masking underlined assimilationist policy, which was represented as a progressive departure from violent repression. Embodying this discourse in the figure of a murderous seducer, Mourning Dove represents assimilation as cultural violence, its hidden agenda identical to that of violent conquest: the acquisition of more territory for the colonizer and the further eradication of Native American people. The threat that Cogewea faces is synecdochic of the experience of Native Americans after the Dawes Act, which resulted in tremendous land losses because Native Americans were excluded from the cash economy and therefore could not pay property tax on their allotments, and which attempted to systematically dismantle Native American communities and cultures (R. White 115).

At the level of the plot, oral storytelling practice plays a crucial role in exposing and resisting death by assimilation. Suspicious of Densmore from the start, Cogewea's grandmother—the Stemteemä—recognizes his sinister intentions because of her knowledge of the oral tradition, in which the lessons of past conquests are remembered and transmitted. She attempts to teach its lessons to Cogewea through her storytelling, which recounts various phases in the history of conquest—

from the earliest prophesy of the arrival of "a pale-faced nation" to the arrival of the Lewis and Clark expedition. The Stemteemä immediately recognizes Densmore as an agent of colonization: "I do not like this Shoyahpee, who tries to steal my Cogewea from me and my people. I want her to marry someone of her own kind and class. I do not want the white man with his marked tongue. He will only cast her aside for one of his own race after he tires of her" (216). To warn Cogewea, the Stemteemä tells her "The Story of Green-Blanket Feet," a woman tricked into marrying a "Shoyahpee" and then brutally abused and abandoned by him. "The fate of *Green-Blanket Feet* is for you," she tells Cogewea, "unless you turn from [Densmore]" (176; italics in original). Cogewea replies that "the wisdom of the Stemteemä is of the past. She does not understand the waning of ancient ideas" (176). Cogewea's belief that the Stemteemä speaks for a dying culture is undercut by the omniscient narrator, who validates the Stemteemä's knowledge of Densmore's hidden intentions, providing what Bernardin describes as "an authoritative oral counter-narrative to the official histories of conquest voiced by Densmore" (501).

The lesson the Stemteemä attempts to teach Cogewea is mirrored in the lesson taught by the novel itself, a version of the Okanogan story of Chipmunk and Owl Woman (included in Mourning Dove's *Coyote Stories*), in which Chipmunk, despite her grandmother's efforts to protect her, is captured by Owl Woman, who eats her heart. After Meadow Lark brings Chipmunk back to life, Coyote plays a deadly trick on Owl Woman, killing her (Mourning Dove, *Coyote Stories* 51–59). I interpret Owl Woman as a version of the monster figures that, as Bruchac explains, are common in the lesson stories of many Native American Tribes and whose role is to warn listeners of the consequences of unwise choices (55). With Densmore as the Owl Woman figure (Bernardin 501), the plot of *Cogewea* puts the lesson story into practice in a modern, colonial context, not only teaching Anglo-American readers about the humanity of Native America peoples but also teaching Native American readers both to value their cultures and to recognize the many guises of colonization. Such interactions between the oral tradition and the history of colonization were properties regarded by ethnographers as "contamination," but they are compatible with the popular western's hybrid frontier setting, didactic conventions, and rescue plots.

It is particularly significant that Mourning Dove used a coming-back-to-life story as the basis for her novel because this story directly responds to the tendency of ethnography to represent oral practice as the artifact of a dead culture. Mourning Dove's western novel insists upon the vitality and relevance of Indigenous wisdom in a modern, colonial context. Indeed, Cogewea is rescued only after balance is restored between oral and graphic forms of knowledge. This balance, Teuton argues, is central to Indigenous philosophies of knowledge (xvii). The narrative structure of the novel signifies the authority of oral practice insofar as the Stemteemä's lesson stories warning Cogewea about Densmore, whom she suspects from the start, are validated by what the omniscient narrator reveals to be true. However, no action is taken to rescue Cogewea until written evidence surfaces in fragments of a letter that falls into Jim LaGrinder's possession, addressed to Densmore from an eastern lover. LaGrinder then learns that two of the cowboys at his ranch have deceived Densmore into believing that Cogewea is far wealthier than she really is. With this combination of oral and written evidence, LaGrinder realizes that Cogewea is in real danger, but he does not yet realize just how immediate the danger is: By this point in the novel, Cogewea, who has run away with Densmore, has been beaten and left for dead. This crucial information comes from the Stemteemä, who has seen "in vision the grandchild and . . . knew that something fearful was to happen. To me the spirits revealed Cogewea, child of my daughter, suspended over the dark swirl of wild rushing waters. She was struggling in the grasp of a frightful monster" (270–71). Acting upon the Stemteemä's vision, LaGrinder is able to find Cogewea, bound and unconscious, but still alive. The lesson implicit in this resolution is that literacy does not negate the power of oral knowledge—since the letter fragments provide only a partial picture of Densmore's plan—and that oral knowledge remains a powerful resource, since it not only saves Cogewea from dying but also leads to her marriage with LaGrinder, a union that signifies the reproductive power of modern Native American peoples.[14] Moreover, it is the interaction between oral and written sources that leads to the rescue of Cogewea. Both the content and structure of *Cogewea* are thus thoroughly steeped in an Indigenous philosophy of knowledge that seeks "the dynamic balance between oral and graphic discourses" (Teuton xviii).

That the ending was especially important to Mourning Dove is suggested by her correspondence with Lucullus McWhorter and by Mourning Dove's other writing, which indicates that McWhorter significantly altered the language of the text and added detailed ethnographic features (Brown, "Looking through the Glass Darkly" 280). While Mourning Dove accepted many of his editorial changes, describing them in one letter as "a tasty dressing like a cook would do with a fine meals" (quoted in Fisher xv), she strongly disagreed with his desire to change the ending, which McWhorter argued should better reflect what he regarded as the tragic reality of Native American history (Brown, "Legacy Profile" 53; Bernardin 502). That Mourning Dove would not concede on this particular point suggests that she refused to accept the disappearance of Native American culture as a foregone conclusion. Resisting models of the Native American writer as eyewitness to a dying oral culture, Mourning Dove found in the popular western a vehicle for inscribing living Indigenous cultural practices, both oral and written, into print.

5

Cattle Branding and the Traffic in Women

While early twentieth-century women's westerns put the genre to diverse uses, they show remarkably little interest in reinventing women in the cowboy hero's image à la Sharon Stone in Sam Raimi's 1995 film *The Quick and the Dead*. Instead, these texts are more interested in drawing analogies between women and cattle as objects of patriarchal exchange. Such tropes were also taken up by early twentieth-century feminist thinkers such as Charlotte Perkins Gilman and Emma Goldman, who used them to highlight the ways in which women's bodies were caught up in patriarchal relations of ownership, a departure from woman/slave analogies popular in nineteenth-century feminist rhetoric. In this chapter I argue that cattle and branding tropes link women's westerns to a broad and significant shift in American feminist discourse as it became disassociated from its nineteenth-century anti-slavery roots. My larger aim is to suggest that women's westerns are loosely linked by a set of shared concerns about women's position in postfrontier American society. The links are loose because women writers of popular westerns were not connected by the close-knit social networks that characterized the male-dominated frontier club. There is no evidence that Caroline Lockhart and B. M. Bower ever met, and Lockhart was greatly annoyed when an editor advised her to write more like Bower (Clayton 125). Curtis, McElrath, Bower, and Lockhart all worked in relative isolation from each other in a print culture that, broadly speaking, was structured by male-centered social networks. Mourning Dove's few contacts with broader print-culture networks consisted of her friendship with an Anglo-American orphan adopted by her family, who introduced her to pulp magazines, and her editor, whom she met by chance at a community event. That their westerns share a distinct figurative pattern despite their loose social and cultural affiliations makes this pattern all the more significant.

This pattern is exemplified in Frances McElrath's *The Rustler* when the orphaned teenager Mavvy is dragged to a local dance by her adoptive father, a notorious cattle rustler, who forces her to accept the sexual advances of another rustler. To Mavvy's rescue comes Horace Carew, fresh from rejection by his beloved, the genteel easterner Hazel Clifford. As these courtship dramas play out, the square-dance caller instructs the male dancers to "lock horns with your own heifers, and rassle 'em to their places" and to "corral the fillies, rope your own, and back to your claim with her!" (McElrath 63–64). The square-dance call aptly summarizes a powerful and reoccurring motif in women's westerns of the early twentieth century as well as marking a significant shift in mainstream American feminist discourse more broadly: Such analogies between cattle roundups and marriage markets resonate with analogies between patriarchy and slavery in feminist abolitionism and anticipate the argument of later feminist thinkers from Emma Goldman to Gayle Rubin that marriage enslaves, objectifies, and commodifies women.

A more well known model of feminist intervention in early twentieth-century popular western discourse is the liberal-feminist individualism of figures such as Annie Oakley, Elinore Pruitt Stewart, and the rodeo cowgirl. All are feminized versions of the western male hero: Oakley earned celebrity status as a sharpshooter with Buffalo Bill's Wild West Show, while taking great care to preserve her reputation as a respectable lady.[1] Stewart, who was renowned for the letters she published in the *Atlantic Monthly* detailing her experience, represented herself as the female version of the independent homesteader. Early twentieth-century rodeo cowgirls competed in the same events as men—although not against them—and were "the first significant group of professional women athletes in North America" (Savage 80).[2] The tradition continued with action-adventure film heroines such as *Lara Croft: Tomb Raider* (Simon West, director) and Sarah Connor of the *Terminator* film series (see Cameron, director, *The Terminator*) and is still prevalent in popular American film, television, and videogames. This liberal-feminist model empowers women insofar as they are able to emulate men while still maintaining their beauty or mothering characteristics as reassurance that equality will not unsex them.

In contrast, the westerns discussed in this chapter—McElrath's *The Rustler* (1902), B. M. Bower's *Lonesome Land* (1912), and Katharine Newlin Burt's *The Branding Iron* (1919)—engage a more radical, though still deeply problematic, feminism that challenges fundamental patriarchal structures. Indeed, they change our current understanding of the importance of western mythology in women's literary history, for they show that it was more than the repository of a conservative and limiting liberal feminist individualism or an exclusively patriarchal discourse that women write against.[3] Rather, these westerns participate in a shift in Anglo-American feminist discourse as American feminism decoupled from the abolition movement and became racially divided. While these texts criticize the deep patriarchal structures that commodify women, they also mark patriarchy as racially other, thereby supplanting one deep oppressive structure with another.

The decline of feminist abolitionism and the rise of social-Darwinian and eugenic feminisms left a rhetorical void in feminist discourse that the popular western could partially fill. While nineteenth-century feminist-abolitionists highlighted the similarities between slavery and patriarchy, by the turn of the century mainstream feminism aligned women's rights with social and evolutionary "progress." Louise Michele Newman has pointed out that this argument made it problematic for white feminists to criticize patriarchy within their own culture. According to the eugenic theories underpinning much early twentieth-century feminism, white women were more highly evolved than women of "inferior" cultures because civilized cultures are more protective of their women; hence white feminists were forced "to acknowledge that patriarchy had been key to their own racial advancement" (Newman 8). In this evolutionary model, the end of patriarchy was not the goal of feminism; rather, primitive and exploitative patriarchies must give way to the more advanced, protective version.

While the rhetorical power of the analogy between patriarchy and slavery had been undermined by the racialization of feminist ideology, the popular western contained tropes and conventions that allowed for modes of critique that were foreclosed elsewhere. Popular westerns by women drew analogies between the cattle roundup and the marriage market in order to expose the "protection" of white women in marriage as a disguised version of patriarchal ownership. They also invoked the myth of the western frontier as the origin of a uniquely American civilization to represent patriarchy as a mode of savagery still latent in Anglo-American culture. Furthermore, by depicting the West as a space in which patriarchy is exposed and feminist consciousness is raised, these texts satisfied an ideological need in the racialized feminisms that predominated in the early twentieth century. The West displaced abolitionism as the origin of American feminism, supporting the desire of Anglo-American feminists to distance themselves from their African American counterparts.

As Karen Sánchez-Eppler and others have shown, early nineteenth-century feminists regarded woman suffrage and the abolition of slavery as complementary causes because of the many similarities in the condition of women and African Americans (Andolsen 3–4; Sánchez-Eppler 14–49; Yellin 24–25). This relationship changed during debates leading to the passage of the Fifteenth Amendment in 1869, which extended the ballot to African American men but excluded woman suffrage because it was viewed as too radical a change (Yellin 5–10). Thereafter, Anglo-American suffrage leaders used more explicitly racist rhetoric, arguing, for example, that women should be given the vote because they were socially and intellectually superior to black men, who (in theory, at least) already had it (McPherson 358–60). According to Ann D. Gordon and Bettye Collier-Thomas, by the late nineteenth century the discourse of sisterhood had "virtually disappeared from what historians call 'the woman's movement'" (4). In its place were social-evolutionary discourses that differentiated white women from men and from women of more "primitive" races. White women's rights were more frequently justified on the basis of "racial commonalities" between white men and women and were interpreted as typifying the social advancement characteristic of "higher" (i.e., white) civilization (Newman 40, 22). Eugenic-feminist arguments were tied to the dominant narrative of national development, according to which the United States was a nation regenerated by its return to rugged, frontier conditions (Slotkin, *Gunfighter Nation* 11). Popular images of the West from this time display nostalgia for a passing frontier yet figure its disappearance as the inevitable outcome of Anglo-Saxon evolution toward a higher state of civilization (Nemerov 300–301). Anglo-American suffragists participated in this discourse by exploiting in their publicity early woman suffrage victories in several western states.[4] The January 1916 cover of the periodical the *Suffragist* proclaimed, "Ever farther and farther west men have migrated seeking freedom; it has been left for women to turn back to the East bringing the gift of freedom."[5]

Slavery was still commonly invoked in turn-of-the-century discourse concerning women's rights, but the abolitionist roots of American feminism were muted once patriarchy was redefined as a characteristic of "inferior" races. Antebellum analogies between slavery and patriarchy identified the tyrannical slave owner with the tyrannical husband. Conversely, late nineteenth-century women's rights discourse was more likely to attribute the existence of patriarchy in America to "alien" cultures. An example of this can be found in "A True Story," a pro-suffrage narrative about a Chinese American prostitute named Li Po Ton by suffrage activist Carrie Chapman Catt. According to Suzanne M. Marilley, Catt represents prostitution in America as a Chinese import, arguing that the lack of the vote does not *oppress* white women so much as it prevents them from helping disadvantaged women of color such as Li Po Ton (180–85). Although Catt and other feminists often described prostitution as a form of slavery, they abandoned the image of the supplicant African American slave woman as their slogan, which had once "signif[ied] both the situation of women in a patriarchal society and the situation of blacks in a slave society" (Yellin 171). Instead, they used references to biblical and classical slavery to illustrate white women's oppression. By the late nineteenth century, the twofold self-identification of anti-slavery feminists as both liberators of the slave and victims of slavery themselves gave way; instead, Anglo-American suffragists emphasized the liberator figure with imagery that featured strong, vigorous, white women (Yellin 171–75). African American suffragists continued to focus on how the vote would help African American women improve their own condition (Terborg-Penn 55), yet they were relegated to separate suffrage societies and excluded from the mainstream movement.

Formal histories of the American women's rights movement wrote abolition out more systematically. Opening with the assertion that "the prolonged slavery of woman is the darkest page in human history," *History of Woman Suffrage* (Stanton, Anthony, and Gage 13), nonetheless, largely ignores the achievements of African American woman suffragists (Terborg-Penn 110). Yet this work still stresses the importance of the abolition movement in mobilizing Anglo-American women politically and contributing to the ideas of early feminists such as Emily Collins, who recalls that "every work of denunciation of the wrongs of the Southern slave was, I felt, equally applicable to the wrongs of my sex" (quoted in Stanton, Anthony, and Gage 89). Almost twenty years later, Charlotte Perkins Gilman would characterize the enslavement of women as a primitive phase in the social evolution of human civilizations: "There seems to have come a time when it occurred to the dawning intelligence of [the] amiable savage that it was cheaper and easier to fight a little female, and have it done with, than to fight a big male every time. So he instituted the custom of enslaving the female" (*Women and Economics* 60). While Gilman sporadically refers to American slavery and abolition, she does not give either phenomenon a prominent place in her history of women's oppression and resistance. Carrie Chapman Catt and Nettie Rogers Shuler's 1926 post-mortem on the suffrage movement describes the "anti-slavery and anti-liquor movements" as "two great reforms" that "appealed strongly to the humanitarian sympathies of the better educated women." When "the majority of men not only did not want their help but expressed their antagonism in phrases and tones of bitter contempt," these women "chafed at the restraint of individual liberty, and the bravest boldly defended the right of any woman to give service to any cause and in any manner she chose" (Catt and Shuler 13). Despite language that identifies women as slaves who "chafed at the restraint of individual liberty," Catt and Shuler represent their abolitionist precursors as courageous rebels rather than subjugated victims. Stressing the racial difference between African American slaves and their white female rescuers, Catt disavows the ideological debt that American feminism owes to abolitionism—particularly for its concept of common humanity, which, As Ellen Carol Dubois has shown, early nineteenth-century feminists borrowed from Garrisonian abolitionism (*Woman Suffrage* 57).

Rather than liken patriarchy to the enslavement of humans, early twentieth-century westerns liken it to the commodification of livestock. Perhaps the most extended example of the "marriage roundup" is found in McElrath's *The Rustler*, which uses the Johnson County Rustler Wars as the backdrop for a feminist critique of women's status as commodities within a marital economy.[6] Its two main female characters are from different classes—Hazel Clifford is a genteel eastern visitor to Wyoming, while Mavvy is a poor orphan who has fallen into the hands of cattle rustlers—but both are vulnerable to the traffic in women. With no man's name to identify her and therefore no legitimate place in society, the orphan Mavvy (short for Maverick, an explicit reference to the maverick debate discussed in chapter 2) is at the mercy of whatever man happens to find her. Unfortunately, she is found by the cattle rustler Nathan Grimes, who uses her as a servant and for the sexual amusement of his rustler friends. Hazel's position is not as desperate, but it is not fundamentally different, either: Her father has died, leaving his estate in disarray. Hazel is therefore under economic pressure to marry one of two men who pursue her: Horace Carew, the gentleman rancher, and Jim, the working-class cowboy. Without the protection of patriarchal ownership, then, both women are identified with the maverick, or brandless, cattle that occasionally escape the roundup.

Both Hazel and Mavvy are "found brandless" at certain points in the text. As described by a minor character in the text, Mavvy's origin parallels that of the orphaned calves for which she is named: "She's the one that's called the Maverick. If she ever had another name I reckon they've forgot it. They [the Grimeses, a family of cattle rustlers] took her out of the poorhouse somewhere, and I don't guess she has a very good time with them two" (65). Similarly, Hazel is "found" by Jim on the open range when an injury to her horse leaves her stranded. Bitter because of the way Hazel rejected him, Jim kidnaps her.

Like *The Rustler*, Bower's *Lonesome Land* centers on a heroine who realizes that marriage exploits women rather than protects them; this understanding enables the protagonist to contemplate divorcing her abusive husband. American readers were not unreceptive to this message, for the novel was praised by critics and underwent numerous reprintings.[7] By that time, Bower was an extremely successful and prolific popular western novelist, able to take more risks with the conventions of the genre in this novel than in her earlier novels. The story begins with Val Peyson's arrival in the town of Hope, Montana, where she is to marry her lover, Manley Fleetwood, who has been preparing a home for her during their three-year separation. Val arrives in Hope with high expectations of the new life Manley's letters have promised, but she has been misled. Val expects their home to be "a picturesque little cottage" (59), but it is actually a run-down shack. Manley has also hidden from Val his weakness for alcohol. His vices are compounded throughout the novel until he eventually becomes a cattle rustler and physical abuser. As in *The Rustler*, Manley's activities as a rustler function as a metaphor for the mastery he claims over his wife.

Whereas Hazel is literally rustled by Jim, Val is figuratively rustled because her decision to marry Manley is based on lies and false promises, which, we are reminded throughout the novel, call into question the legitimacy of their marriage contract. The pivotal deception occurs in the novel's opening chapters, when Val arrives in Hope expecting Manley immediately to whisk her off to be married. Unfortunately, Manley is too drunk to meet her, so Val is greeted by Manley's friend Kent, whose excuses on Manley's behalf give Manley enough time to sober up. The marriage proceeds as planned, with Val none the wiser. Subsequently, Kent blames himself for Manley's abuse of Val, believing that she would not have married him had she, a strong believer in temperance, known about his alcoholism. The novel suggests that because Val was not fully informed when she entered the marriage contract, the marriage is as illegitimate as Manley's ownership of the rustled cattle—which, in case we miss the point, are branded with Val's initials.

In early twentieth-century popular westerns by women, the cattle roundup performs a rhetorical function similar, although not identical, to that which Sánchez-Eppler ascribes to certain analogies prevalent in antebellum abolitionist literature. In *Touching Liberty*, Sánchez-Eppler demonstrates that narratives depicting the sexual exploitation of African American slave women made it possible for white middle-class women to articulate anxieties about their own sexual victimization that were otherwise "unacknowledgeable" according to the conventions of true womanhood (36). However, abolitionist analogies emphasized the common humanity of Anglo- and African-American women, while branding analogies played up the difference between women and "chattel." These branding analogies, therefore, expose the crudities of patriarchy, which trades women as though they were cattle. The implied argument is thus slightly different from that of the abolitionist feminists, who maintained that common humanity overrides both race and gender and entitles *both* Anglo- and African American women to the same human rights. Branding tropes, in contrast, base their implied argument on the obvious difference between (white) women and racialized "chattel" and register the move away from the ideology of common humanity that had characterized abolitionist feminism. Nonetheless, they too enabled Anglo-American authors to represent taboo sexual content via displacement.

The Rustler implies that the unfortunate orphan Mavvy is a white slave, exploited for her sexuality just as cattle are. At the square dance described above, Mavvy's surrogate parents—the same people who found her "brandless" in the poorhouse—force her to accept the unwanted attention of a man named Bill Lowry:

> "Please don't," she pleaded, "I ain't a-goin' to dance."
> "Not with me?" cried Lowry.
> The Grimes woman prodded Mavvy in the side with her finger.
> "Go along, do it," she said.
> "I shan't,' said Mavvy.
> "Not a-goin' to dance? Not a-goin' to dance when I ask you?" shouted Lowry boozily. "Then I tell you what I'm goin' to do; I'm goin' to have a kiss from you for refusin'. Oh, jenks! I am!" (66)

We later learn that Bill Lowry is Grimes's partner in cattle rustling, a business relationship solidified through the gift exchange of Mavvy. The roundup metaphor thus signifies two classic functions of the sex/gender system: the control of female sexuality, and the gift exchange of women to solidify patriarchal kinship structures (G. Rubin 545–46).

In a highly suggestive episode in *Lonesome Land*, Manley's stolen cattle function as surrogates for Val, displacing onto the bodies of cattle the power Manley claims over Val's body and sexuality. Having returned to the ranch with several stolen calves, Manley orders Val to prepare the branding fire. Val, who does not yet know that Manley is a rustler, wonders why the rush, whereupon Manley snaps, "What the devil is it to you? . . . I want the fire, madam, and I want it *now*. I rather think I know when I want to brand without asking your advice" (240). This exchange, typical of how Manley speaks to Val at this late stage in their marriage, is reminiscent of the Lacanian model of patriarchy, which ascribes the authority of naming (or branding) to the male, while silencing the female. Having become "hardened" to being "brutalized" by Manley, Val "did not mind very much" (241). Immediately following this example of Manley's domination over Val, the narrative shifts to the plight of Manley's stolen calf. "He drove a big, line-backed heifer into a corner, roped and tied her down with surprising dexterity, and turned impatiently" to order Val around some more (241). Val responds with both obedience and sarcasm: "'Ere it is, sir—thank you, sir—'ope I 'aven't kep you wyting, sir,' she announced, after he fumed for two minutes inside the corral, and she had cynically hummed her way quite through the hymn which begins 'Blest be the tie that binds'" (242). This reference, which can be read ironically as referring to the bonds of marriage, reminds us of the bound heifer in the previous passage, highlighting the common plight of Val and the branded calves. As each calf is branded, Val hears, "with an inward quiver of pity and disgust, the spasmodic blat of the calf in the pen when the VP [branding iron] went searing into the hide on its ribs" (243). Here the calf's body performs a function similar to that of the African American slave woman's body in antebellum slave narratives described by Sánchez-Eppler. The master's sexual exploitation of the slave woman registers a critique of patriarchy but enables white women to remain "true women." Similarly, in this scene the power that Manley has over Val's body is displaced onto the body of the calf in order to represent a critique of patriarchy without compromising Val's role as the plucky western heroine, whose psyche, "hardened" to her husband's abuse, is contrasted with the calf's sensitive hide. Again, however, the abolitionist priority of expressing a common humanity across races is no longer a part of the discourse.

A particularly explicit inscription of the "marriage roundup" analogy appears in Katharine Newlin Burt's *The Branding Iron* (1919), one of some thirty novels Burt published between about 1911 and 1968. Born in New York, Burt (1887–1977) married the writer Maxwell Struthers Burt and with him founded the Bar BC Ranch, a cattle and dude ranch (now an historic site) near Jackson Hole, Wyoming. While *The Rustler* was an obscure and little-known novel and *Lonesome Land* enjoyed popular success, *The Branding Iron* was targeted by its publisher, Houghton Mifflin, as a likely bestseller, and appears to have fulfilled the company's desires: Writing in 1948, *Chicago Tribune* columnist Fanny Butcher remembered *The Branding Iron* as "one of the most sensational novels of its day. . . . It created a furore [*sic*], was made into a movie and Katharine Newlin Burt was considered one of the 'wilder' of the novelists about the wild west."[8] The novel's central message is the right of its heroine, Joan Landis, to belong "to her own self " (46). The novel takes its title from the incident that precipitates the main action, when Joan is branded—literally—by her jealous husband Pierre. Both Joan and Pierre are depicted as white savages; the branding of Joan is indeed a sign of the savage ways of the nameless "wild country" where they live (Burt 3). When Joan is introduced, her primitive nature is emphasized. Her face is "heavy" and "unlit from within, but built on lines of perfect animal beauty," while her body is "stretched there across the floor, heavily if not sluggishly built, dressed rudely in warm stuffs and clumsy boots" (4). This "animal beauty" compels male characters in the text to want to own and control her. In a chapter entitled "Pierre Takes Steps to Preserve His Property," Pierre violently brands Joan out of jealousy over the amount of time she spends with the local preacher. Whereas McElrath and Bower displace the physical dimension of patriarchal oppression onto the bodies of cattle, Burt literalizes the branding metaphor. Pierre tells Joan, "You belong to me an' not to [the preacher]" and compares her fate to that of "stock all over the country marked with them two bars. . . . The Two-Bar Brand, don't you fergit it!" (46–47). Then "[h]e lifted his brand and set it against the bare flesh of her shoulder" (48).

In the opening chapters of *The Branding Iron*, marriage is represented explicitly as patriarchal ownership, while in the earlier novels it is first disguised as chivalrous protection and then gradually unmasked. In *The Rustler*, Mavvy turns to the gentlemanly Horace for protection from the unwanted attentions of Lowry: "He made a drunken grab to catch her hands. The girl drew them away with a frightened scream.

Her terrified eyes instinctively crossed the room and begged protection from the gentleman in the doorway" (66). Horace rescues Mavvy from Lowry, strikes up a friendship with her, and eventually marries her. His intentions are not altogether pure, however, for initially he is drawn to Mavvy because she has information about the activities of the cattle rustlers. Mavvy also proves herself a better protector of Horace than the reverse, for when she learns of a plot to kill him, she intentionally rides his horse into the ambush and is shot in his place.

Hazel's plight, like Mavvy's, is compared to that of the unclaimed calf, particularly when an injury to her horse leaves her stranded alone on the open range. Just as Horace rescues Hazel from Lowry's attentions at the square dance, Jim makes a timely appearance and responds to Hazel's signals for help. As the scene progresses, however, Jim is slowly transformed from Hazel's protector into her master:

> "Thank you, Jim," she said, as she sprang onto Whitefoot. She reached out her hands for the reins, which Jim still held. "What are you going to do?" she asked, surprised and pleased at this show of courtesy.
>
> Without answering the question in words, Jim showed what he was going to do by springing onto the horse behind Hazel's saddle. He still retained the reins. He set spurs to the horse.
>
> It was done so very quickly, that, before Hazel recovered from her surprise sufficiently to speak, they had started off.
>
> "Oh!" she exclaimed. . . . "There's no use your fighting me, you've got to go with me," he muttered between his teeth; "don't scream unless you want something tied over your mouth." (93–94)

The above scene begins conventionally enough with the cowboy's rescue of a stranded lady traveler, but it ends when Hazel is literally "rustled" by Jim, whose dominance over her is identified with his spurring of the horse. Chivalric protection is unmasked as exploitative ownership.

Lonesome Land gives its heroine a potential savior in the person of Kent, the gentleman cowboy who befriends Val and does his best to protect her from Manley's abuse. However, eventually the novel forecloses the possibility of rescue. At first Kent's presence in the novel suggests that Manley's bad character, not the institution of marriage, is responsible for Val's plight, which would certainly be different if she had married a man like Kent. Nonetheless, while Kent is presented as a good man and a sympathetic character, he, too, eventually claims ownership of Val in the same way that Manley does. The comparison between these two men is reminiscent of Harriet Beecher Stowe's comparisons between "good" slave owners (Shelby) and "bad" ones (Legree) in *Uncle Tom's Cabin* (1852). Ultimately, the existence of "good" men who own slaves does not obviate the evils of the institution. Similarly, Kent's relationship with Val demonstrates that a "good" master is still a *master*, no matter how well intentioned.

Like McElrath, Bower devotes a full chapter to deconstructing the distinction between chivalrous protection and patriarchal ownership. Just as Jim "rescues" the stranded Hazel, Kent "rescues" Val from a grass fire that, owing partly to Manley's negligence, has encircled the ranch. In *The Rustler* it is the setting of Hazel's abduction—the unfenced range—that recalls the scene of branding and so identifies her with the rustled calf. Here the metaphor is established through the fire that surrounds Val, which, in addition to drawing from the classic literary association of fire with masculine sexuality, reminds Kent of the branding fire: "He untied his silk neckerchief, shook out the cinders, and pressed it against her closed eyes. 'Keep that over 'em,' he commanded, 'till we can do better. My eyes are more used to smoke than yours, I guess. Working around branding fires toughens 'em some'" (127–28). During the fire, Val is "branded" by a piece of burning debris: "A brand flew low over Val's head as she ran staggeringly. . . . A spark from the brand fell upon her hand, and she looked up stupidly, the heat and the smoke were choking her so that she could scarcely breathe" (126). Later, when the fire has been extinguished and Kent holds the fainting Val in his arms, he notices her "branded" hand: "His gaze traveled on down her slim figure to her ringed fingers lying loosely in her lap, a long, dry-looking blister upon one hand near the thumb; down to her slippers, showing beneath her scorched skirt. And he drew another long breath. He did not know why, but he had a strange, fleeting sense of possession" (129). By taking Manley's place as Val's protector and saving her from the fire, Kent has become a competitor with Manley for ownership of Val, a relation of which he is only dimly aware but one that is quite explicit in the above imagery. The metaphorical branding fire has left Kent's "brand" on Val's hand, in close proximity to the rings that mark Manley's competing claim. Kent exercises his own claim not only by carrying her inert body but also with his palpable, traveling gaze. By exposing Kent's protective impulses as a masked desire to own and control Val, the novel dismantles the myth that protecting women is an attribute of more advanced cultures, for the more "civilized" cowboy Kent proves to be no different than the dissolute Manley.

Kent's metaphoric rustling of Val during the prairie fire is mirrored in a later incident in which Kent alters the brand of one of Manley's rustled calves: "To heat the spur red-hot, draw it across the fresh VP again and again, and finally drag it crisscross once or twice to make assurance an absolute certainty, did not take long. Kent was particular about not wasting any seconds. The calf stopped its dismal blatting, and when Kent released it and coiled his rope, it jumped up and ran for its life, the cow [its mother] ambling solicitously at its heels" (274). The repetition of certain details identifies Kent with Manley, who, as I have described earlier, is also in a hurry to finish the task and makes his calves "blat" when he brands them. As a metaphor for Kent's relationship with Val, this act of brand altering can be read in two ways: It may signify either Kent's desire to undo Manley's claim and have Val for himself or his role in freeing Val from Manley so that, like the calf rejoining its mother, she can reunite with her family, a desire Val expresses more than once. The question looms throughout the novel: Is Kent a competitor with Manley for ownership of Val, or is he co-conspirator in Val's escape from Manley?

A fundamental premise of the feminist critique of patriarchy is that the recognition of the system *as such* is the first step toward dismantling it. All three of these novels describe female (and sometimes male) characters who undergo a shift in consciousness that enables them to disentangle themselves from patriarchal relations. After she is kidnapped, the formerly flirtatious Hazel becomes conscious of her status as an object of exchange, for in kidnapping her Jim shows Hazel her real standing as a commodity: "Jim has brought me here to show me my work and to punish me," she thinks (141). With this knowledge, Hazel is empowered to resist Jim's patriarchal rule. She does so by mothering the neglected children living in Jim's rustler hideaway. She nurses them, opens a school for them, and eventually earns the devotion of the whole rustler community. In so doing, Hazel literally reorganizes the social structure of the rustler community according to matriarchal rather than patriarchal principles. The text juxtaposes the authority Hazel derives from her motherly influence with the authority Jim derives from property ownership: "Jim had far exceeded his expectations. In money he was rich, and in position he was a robber baron. He maintained his place strenuously at the head of affairs, levying tribute from every one who came under the protection of the Hole-in-the-Wall" (153). Meanwhile, Hazel continues with her "gentle measures," which are "designed to frustrate the very work he was carrying on. He had brought her to the camp to witness with her own eyes his supremacy, and instead of bowing before it like the rest, she had quietly gone to work to undermine his power" (153). Hazel is not merely an annoyance to Jim; "She's dangerous," he thinks (153). Hazel is hazardous because of the structural relationship between Jim's authority and hers. Jim's patriarchal rule is signified by Hazel's passive subjection, so her refusal to perform in this role and her matriarchal reorganization of the rustler community amount to a breakdown in both the signification and structure of Jim's power.

Lonesome Land focuses as much attention on Kent's awakening to patriarchal relations as it does on Val's. Val has learned hard lessons from her marriage to Manley, and so she carefully negotiates her friendship with Kent. "I do so need a friend!" she tells him; someone "to whom I can talk when that is the only thing that will keep me sane" (213). She makes him "shake on it" and warns him not to make love to her: "I never did have much patience with the rule that a man must either be perfectly indifferent, or else make love. I'm so glad you—understand" (216, 217). With legal rituals and terms, Val defines their relationship as a contract that identifies Val as a person rather than chattel. However, Kent has difficulty finding nonpossessive ways to interact with Val. Val becomes an author to earn extra money and to gain psychic relief from her situation. Yet when she asks Kent's opinion of her work, he is too preoccupied with her physicality to pay much attention to her ideas: "Kent, perforce, listened to the story. Afterward, he assured her that it was outa sight. As a matter of fact, half the time he had not heard a word of what she was reading; he had been too busy just looking at her and being glad he was there" (237). Kent is unable to criticize Val's work objectively because he regards her as an ornamental object rather than a speaking subject. His role as protector also requires that he shield her from criticism.

The novel ultimately refuses Kent an outlet for his possessive/protective impulses, for he is denied an active role in the dramatic action sequence that concludes the narrative, which is set into motion when Val releases some of Manley's stolen calves. This action is reminiscent of Hazel's matriarchal undoing of Jim's authority in *The Rustler*, an act of matriarchal intervention in patriarchal systems of signification and possession. Hence the sight of Manley's VP-branded calves suckling mothers with different brands soon leads to Manley's undoing. In the pursuit that follows, Manley almost strangles Val to death, shoots a man, and steals Kent's horse; finally, the sheriff overpowers him. In an unusual departure from the conventions of the genre, the novel's cowboy hero is left out of the plot events that deliver justice to the antagonist. Instead, Kent remains with Val in her cabin as the resolution plays out. In a reversal of the grass-fire episode, in which Kent covers Val's eyes and assumes the power to see and act on her behalf, he now listens as Val describes Manley's violent demise, which she watches through a pair of field glasses: "'Why, your horse—' she gasped. 'Michael—he's got his feet straight up in the air—oh, Kent, he's rolling over and over! I can't see.' . . . She shivered and hid her face upon one upflung arm" (320). At first, Kent "gathered her in his arms," saying, "Don't cry—it's better this way" and other conventional words of comfort, but then "he realized suddenly that this was no way to comfort her, and stopped" (321). Convention dictates that when Manley dies, the good guy should get the girl, but Kent realizes that "this was not the time for love-making; and since he was denied that outlet for his feelings, he did not know what to do" (321). Kent has been left out of the events leading to Val's liberation from Manley, and the novel ends without the conventional transfer of Val's ownership from Manley to Kent. This ending fulfills a wish Val expresses earlier, "to solve my problem and—and leave you [Kent] out of it" (307). By leaving Kent out of the resolution of Val's problem, the novel transfers ownership of Val to Val herself.

All three novels use the "marriage roundup" metaphor to expose as false the distinction between "bad" patriarchy—the kind that enslaves and exploits women—and the benevolent protection of women that some eugenic theorists associated with the more "advanced" races. Furthermore, the western setting of these narratives encoded them as stories about racial progress, for American frontier mythology was deeply implicated in contemporary theories of whiteness as a racial identity. According to one such theory, white people in the United States could claim common racial ancestry as descendants of an ancient northern European race known as the Teutons, whose principles of organization were the prototype for American democracy. Manifest destiny, including the "settlement" of the American West, was the most recent phase in the global progress of the Teutonic people (Babb 38–40). Hence narratives about the American West, from the histories written by Frederick Jackson Turner and Theodore Roosevelt to the fictional stories of Owen Wister, were about the origins of *white* America.[9] At the same time, social-Darwinian thinking was also deeply entrenched (Cuddy and Roche 11). In the novels I am discussing, then, the most tyrannical patriarchs—the dissolute rustler Nathan Grimes and the drunken Manley Fleetwood—would also be read as the least evolved. To subject white women to the possessive instincts of such men would lead to racial regression; therefore, liberating female reproductive sexuality from the constraints of patriarchal ownership and control would result in *racial* progress, since the most primitive men would lose the basis of their power over women.

This argument is most explicit in *The Branding Iron*, a novel with pronounced differences from the other novels discussed in this chapter. Unlike *The Rustler* and *Lonesome Land*, *The Branding Iron* employs the branding metaphor in overt rather than covert terms and is also is an explicitly white-supremacist text, laying bare the racialism that informs but is not manifest in the other two texts. A significant part of the story takes place in the metropolitan East, which is represented as a racially mongrelized setting where the branding of women continues in a "civilized" guise. *The Branding Iron* explicitly links patriarchal critique and racial progress by introducing the figure of the racial other into its romantic plot through the figure of a Jewish character named Jasper Morena.

After Joan is branded by Pierre, she flees to New York City, where she meets Morena, a theater producer, and becomes an actress in one of his productions. At this point, a subplot develops in which Morena learns that his wife, Betty, is having an affair with his best friend. Responding with the same possessive jealousy that made Pierre brand Joan, Morena tells his wife, "You have been rash to pit yourself against me. You must have known that I would break you utterly. I will break you, my dear, and I will have you back, and I will be your master instead of your servant, and I will love you" (265). Morena's branding iron is public humiliation: He exposes Betty's affair, making it impossible for her to sue for divorce or seek refuge with her family, which has disowned her, leaving Betty with no option but to remain under Morena's control.

The similarity between the two brandings—one unfolding in a primitive, western environment, and the other in a civilized, eastern setting—invites us to figure out the difference, which is racial. Despite Jasper Morena's very successful negotiation of civilized society, he is represented as a savage at the core, and his savagery is connected to his Jewishness. Morena is at his most racialized and savage at those moments when he asserts his property rights over his wife to the other men who make claims upon her. To Betty's brother, he declares, "'I love my wife'—his voice was especially Hebraic and especially abhorrent . . . 'and as a husband I mean to keep her from the ruin this divorce would mean to her'" (244). His racial identity is similarly highlighted when he confronts his best friend about the affair: "'My friend,' he began, and the accentuation of the Hebraic quality of his voice had an instantaneous effect. . . . 'I thought I knew you fairly well'" (261). Another classic marker of savagery in the popular western is that the savage's conduct is controlled by instinct, not intellect.[10] Again, Morena displays this trait: "Jasper was perfectly conscious that his own gesture and speech . . . were too eager, too ingratiating, that they had a touch of servility. He hated them himself, but they were inherited with his blood, as instinctive as the wagging of a dog's tail" (239).

The apparently civilized Morena proves to be a savage at heart, while the apparently savage Pierre turns out to be capable of civilization. Having found religion, Pierre travels to New York to prove to Joan that he is a repentant man. Joan's natural attraction to Pierre is so intense that she forgives him and the couple reunites, despite his earlier brutal treatment of her. As the novel's final chapter plays out, Pierre shows Joan and the reader that he has learned to control his savage impulses, something that Jasper Morena, for all of his genteel cultivation, simply cannot do. Pierre demonstrates his strength of will, and therefore his racial superiority, in a confrontation with a rival for Joan's affection who had shot Pierre and left him for dead: "[Pierre's] own face was a mask of rage. . . . It was the Westerner's intention to kill. For a minute, no longer, he was a lightning channel of death. But Pierre, the Pierre shaped during the last four difficult years, turned upon his own writhing, savage soul and forced it to submit. . . . All the patience and the hunger and the beauty of his love possessed his face. There was simply no room in his heart for any lesser thing" (309). Rather than play out a conflict with his antagonist for ownership of Joan, Pierre politely asks the man "to leave [him] with [his] wife" (309).

That a Jewish figure is selected to represent the racial other is loaded with ideological meaning because race theories of the period categorized Jews as a primitive race of whites from which the more advanced Aryan race had evolved. Hence Jews were regarded by some race theorists as Caucasian and by others as "a denigrated racial other" (Young 84). *The Branding Iron* posits liberated female sexuality as a solution to the problem of determining the racial status of ambiguous figures such as Jasper Morena. Debates about women's political status were fraught with anxieties about the infiltration of American political society by the racial other, whose assimilation into the American "melting pot" made his presence harder to detect and extricate. Antiquated discourses of gender and race were resurrected to imagine a solution to this so-called problem of racial infiltration, namely, the white woman's instinctive attraction to men of her own race and aversion to the racial other (Young 107–9). Only white women had the instincts necessary to keep the race pure. Since liberating women from the political economy of sex meant liberating them from their role as the exchanged and allowing them control over their bodies and desires, empowering women would help reproduce white America. So, when Joan Landis is finally free to choose for herself, the man she chooses is the white one.

The novels I have been discussing have received very little scholarly attention, yet the themes they address are well known in the work of their more prominent contemporary Charlotte Perkins Gilman (1860–1935), whose importance in the history of American literary feminism is well established. Born in New England a member of the prestigious Beecher family, Gilman nonetheless grew up in poverty and had little formal education. A move West, to California, in her twenties proved pivotal in Gilman's personal and professional development. There, she recovered from the breakup of her first marriage and a likely case of severe postpartum depression, and she embarked on her career as a reformer and author.[11] As Jennifer Tuttle points out, Gilman may have rejected the rest cure that S. Weir Mitchell prescribed for nervous female patients, but she took seriously the "West cure" he prescribed for Owen Wister and claimed for herself the "healthful way of life in the West" that Mitchell considered appropriate only for men (Tuttle, "Rewriting the West Cure" 107). Dana Seitler demonstrates that Gilman was especially interested in applying the notion of the West as a regenerative space to the eugenic-feminist argument that strengthening women meant strengthening the white race ("Unnatural Selection" 65–66). Western and eugenic themes in Gilman's work have been interpreted as idiosyncratic rather than part of a more widely circulating feminist discourse, yet Gilman's use of livestock analogies performs rhetorical functions remarkably similar to those used in women's popular westerns. In *Women and Economics* (1898), Gilman uses livestock analogies to establish distinctions between nature and culture and to expose the crude economic underpinnings of patriarchal protectionism:

> The horse, in his present condition of slavery, is economically dependent. He gets his living at the hands of his master; and his exertions, though strenuous, bear no direct relation to his living. In fact, the horses who are the best fed and cared for and the horses who are the hardest worked are quite different animals. The horse works, it is true; but what he gets to eat depends on the power and will of his master. His living comes through another. He is economically dependent. So with the hard-worked savage or peasant women. Their labor is the property of another: they work under another will; and what they receive depends not on their labor, but on the power and will of another. They are economically dependent. This is true of the human female both individually and collectively. (7)

Elsewhere, Gilman equates the "over-sexing" of women—the excessive emphasis on their sexual difference, which she sees as a cultural weakness—with the over-sexing of milk cows. Just as the latter has become "a walking milk-machine, bred and tended to that express end," women's sex difference—her "comparative smallness and feebleness"—has been "carried to such an excess that women are commonly known as 'the weaker sex'" (*Women and Economics* 44–45).

Frontier mythology played a crucial role in Gilman's thinking about feminism and race. Using a social-Darwinian vocabulary that conflates the social category "race" with the biological category "species," Gilman argues in *Women and Economics* that the "sex-attributes" that differentiate men from women are unnaturally exaggerated in humans at the expense of their "race-attributes"—the qualities men and women have in common. Whereas the function of sex-attributes is reproduction, race-attributes are those that differentiate one species from another; hence the male-female difference is found in most species, while truly "human" traits are not: "All the varied activities of economic production and distribution, all our arts and industries, crafts and trades, all our growth in science, discovery, government, religion—these are along the line of self-preservation: these are, or should be common to both sexes . . . they are race-functions" (*Women and Economics* 52). The distinction between sex-functions and race-functions equates racial whiteness with personhood. To overcome the over-sexed state that oppresses them, women must cultivate their personhood—in other words, their racial identity. In her fiction, Gilman depicts the West as the ideal environment for doing so—in Seitler's terms, it is a "regenerative space" to which women travel so that they may forge a more progressive community" (Seitler, "Introduction" 9). In *The Crux*, Gilman depicts a community of single white women who emigrate to Wyoming, where they operate a successful boarding house. Eugenic marriage is a focal point of Gilman's vision for progressive gender relations. One of the women, Vivian, is romantically involved with a man, Morton, but when she discovers that he has syphilis, she rejects him, fearing that their marriage will produce unhealthy children. Vivian's racial characteristics are heightened at the moment she rejects Morton, who protests that Vivian is overestimating the importance of his illness: "It seems so terrible to you just because you're so pure and white." Morton despairs at her "white grace, her stately little ways, her delicate beauty, [which] had never seemed so desirable" (*The Crux* 143).

The "marriage roundup" analogy has left its traces on more recent feminist thought by way of Gayle Rubin's groundbreaking work of feminist anthropology, "The Traffic in Women" (1975). Branding tropes in early twentieth-century popular literature foreground the relations that Gayle Rubin would define as the "sex/gender system," the set of arrangements "by which a society transforms biological sexuality into products of human activity" (534). Elaborating on Claude Lévi-Strauss's theory that women are living representations of the kinship relation between different families or groups (201), Rubin argues that the social function of gender is to control reproductive sexuality in service of the kinship system (180). Anticipating Rubin's thought, the trope of cattle-branding highlights the ways in which female pleasure, sexuality, and maternity are co-opted into the service of a system that conflates patriarchal kinship with capitalist ownership. This trope draws the obvious analogy between the brand that marks a cow or horse as the property of a certain ranch and the status markers—single, married, divorced, widowed—that categorize women as belonging to a particular patriarch. Yet it also places the control of female reproduction at the heart of patriarchal kinship relations. The act of branding is itself the moment in which a patriarchal linguistic system akin to Jacques Lacan's Symbolic Order—complete with a phallus-wielding father figure—intervenes in the calf's natural, presocial bond with its mother.[12]

Popular westerns by women deserve a place in the history of feminist literature and thought because of these links to important nineteenth- and twentieth-century feminist discourses. They are also important literary examples of early twentieth-century eugenic feminism. Awareness of these texts changes our understanding of women's contribution to writing about the American West, which has been dominated by the assumption that women were not interested in and did not influence the production of popular western narratives. Read in a more critical light, these texts are also part of a discourse deployed to rewrite the history of American feminism by making the American West, and not the abolition movement, the origin of an American feminist consciousness. No longer regarding their cause as part of the broader human struggle for liberation, Anglo-American feminists and suffragists rewrote its history in terms of social-Darwinian narratives of racial progress. In so doing, they ignored or dismissed African American suffragists such as Mary Church Terrell, Coralie Franklin Cook, and Sylvanie Williams, all of whom urged their "sisters of the dominant race" not to exclude African American women from the movement (Terborg-Penn 66). As a poor substitute for earlier nineteenth-century slogans of sisterhood but a rich metaphor through which to unpack the complex workings of gender and patriarchy, the figure of the branded calf resonates with both the accomplishments and the blunders that are the legacy of Anglo-American feminist thought.

6

The Masculinization of the Western

The women writers I have discussed in previous chapters did not necessarily see themselves as infiltrating masculine terrain. True, B. M. Bower did write under a nom de plume and would retrospectively describe her writing as masculine, but, as I discussed in chapter 3, she did so under specific material conditions not shared by all women western novelists. Until the development of specialized western pulps for adults (as distinct from serial novels for juveniles) beginning in 1915, "quality" popular westerns were open to women writers and readers. Women's participation in the development of the popular western was erased after the fact, however, by gendered generic categories that developed after 1915 and that became entrenched in the 1920s, which structured masculinist approaches to the academic recovery of popular westerns in the late twentieth century. In this chapter, I trace the history of the masculinization of the twentieth-century popular western, which began in pulp magazines but profoundly influenced the ways in which the genre as a whole was both categorized and, later, studied. I begin by describing the pre-1915 general fiction pulps, which published western fiction along with other genres and targeted a general readership of both genders. After 1915, and especially in the 1920s, specialized pulp western magazines emerged and, as pulp publishers sought ever more targeted readerships, subdivided into the masculinized western and the feminized western romance. Despite the popularity and longevity of female-oriented pulp westerns, they were characterized by critics as a lesser imitation of the "real" masculine western. As scholars recovered the western and argued for its significance in the late twentieth century, a western canon emerged from which women writers were excluded.

The "Quality" General Fiction Pulps

Particularly after *The Virginian* became a bestseller in 1902, western fiction became a mainstay of the general fiction pulps. First appearing in the 1890s, this new class of what I call "respectable" cheap fiction magazines distinguished itself from dime and "yellowback" novels with claims of quality and originality despite the cheap price. These publications became important venues for professional writers who, thanks to recent copyright legislation, were able to capitalize on publishing the same work in multiple venues (Jaszi and Woodmansee 90–101). General fiction pulps moved away from the marketing strategies for which dime novels were known, including serial characters and "library" brand-name series that emphasized predictable subject matter (examples include Street & Smith's Buffalo Bill Stories, which featured stories about the famous scout, and the Bertha Clay Library, which featured woman-centered fiction).[1] Instead, general fiction pulps such as *Argosy* and *Ainslee's* embraced the traditional, noncommercial discourse of literary production that treated each story like an individual creation meant to appeal to the discriminating tastes of individual readers rather than to a mass audience. As Janice Radway has shown in her classic study of popular romances, these two imagined categories of readers—the individual reader of taste on the one hand and the predictable, mass readerships on the other, both of which oversimplify complex reading practices and communities—have been in tension in American publishing since the early nineteenth century (*Reading* 25).

General fiction pulps distanced themselves in particular from the dime novels that were widely disparaged as fodder for juvenile boys and an infantilized working class—the "mass mind" as Quentin Reynolds described it in his 1955 history of Street & Smith (102). According to the cultural discourse of the early twentieth century such primitive tastes were easily satisfied by the factory system of fiction production. "Respectable" fiction magazines, in contrast, depended upon the approbation of the female readers who were an influential component of the family-oriented, middle-class readership for "quality" fiction (Bold, *Frontier Club* 108–9). Street & Smith's *Popular* exemplifies this transition from an infantilized, low-income readership to a more respectable feminized one: It was initially marketed as "The Popular Magazine for Boys and 'Old Boys'" in an attempt to straddle both juvenile and adult markets, but it quickly changed its tack to "*The Popular*, a magazine for men, and the women who like to read about them" (G. Smith). Evident in this description is a sense that women, whether we like it or not, cannot be excluded from the respectable popular fiction marketplace, even for fiction magazines targeted primarily at men.

Although general pulp fiction magazines attempted to convey, primarily through the all-important cover image, a particular style of magazine, they all made tacit or explicit claims to quality, originality, and variety. The first of these, Frank Munsey's *Argosy* (founded in 1882), published "every genre imaginable," according to Nathan Madison. Its early covers eschewed the sensational visuals that dime novels were known for, consisting instead of the title and some text. The September 1904 cover, reading "Nearly 200 pages of Good Stories," is exemplary of the understated claims to quality made by *Argosy* to distinguish its quality content from its cheap price and from the sensationalism that other "cheap" fiction was known for. When Munsey began using cover illustrations in October 1904, these were again restrained in comparison to the sensational style of other cheap fiction covers and depicted a variety of subjects, from historical courtly drama to sea adventure (Stephensen-Payne, "Magazine Cover Images"). Competing general fiction pulps attempted to distinguish themselves from their rivals while similarly catering to a variety of tastes and emphasizing quality and originality. The *Blue Book*, for example, featured elegantly dressed stage actresses on its covers and promised "Always the Best Writers,"[2] while its competitor the *Popular* featured scenes of adventure and the outdoors interspersed with the occasional image of a pretty woman (The Pulp Magazines Project).

All adult general fiction magazines—even those, like *Argosy* and *Popular*, that cultivated a more rugged, outdoorsy, masculine image—took women readers into account and occasionally published women writers. Not only were women a powerful force in the literary marketplace, but the "genteel literary code" that emerged in the late nineteenth century, although contested by modernist magazines such as *Smart Set*, dictated that reading material had to be deemed fit to be read by the women and children who might come across it on a parlor table (Boyer 277–86). The western fiction appearing in general fiction magazines addressed a variety of themes and subjects befitting the diverse readers who were likely to encounter it (Ohmann 1–6). Hence B. M. Bower made a very good living from publishing a broad spectrum of western stories in the *Popular*, from serial cowboy stories featuring *The Happy Family*, a community of cowboys working at the fictional Flying U Ranch, to *Lonesome Land*, a novel about an emotionally and physically abused woman (discussed at length in chapter 5).[3]

Specialized Western Pulps

Beginning in 1915, general fiction pulps began to subdivide into distinct genres, including the western, the romance, the detective story, and many others. Among these was *Western Story*, the first "quality" all-western pulp magazine (Ashley). *Western Story* followed a literary fiction model by emphasizing quality and variety in plot, theme, and style. Subtitled "Good Clean Stories of Outdoor Life," *Western Story* aimed for respectable status by appealing to the family, which required at least some attention to woman-centered stories. As an example, *Western Story* 30, no. 4 (1922) led with Robert Adger Brown's "Crescent Moon," a story about a female ranch foreman known by the cowboys in her employ as Captain Nora. Collectively, the stories in this issue included a range of settings and situations. In Harley Lathrop's "The Horse and the Man," a Texas Ranger brings a Mexican outlaw and abuser of horses to justice. A store manager in a dingy mining town attempts to collect on a debt in "A Running Account," by Orville Leonard. A twelve-year-old boy orphaned in the wilderness is adopted by a family of bears in George Owen Baxter's "Wild Freedom." "Flapjack Meehan Rounds 'Em Up," by Frank Richardson Pierce, opens with an elderly prospector bursting into tears when he finally finds the gold that will enable him to support his wife in her old age. A. M. Chisolm's "A Thousand a Plate" follows the mishaps of two prospectors who try their hand at trapping. In Charles Reed Anderson's "Into the Unknown," explorers in Colorado discover, living in a secret underground complex, "a band of strange-looking white-haired men" (103). A newly wealthy investor in oil-rich Los Angeles gets his revenge on a crooked stockbroker in Raymond Ward Hofflund's "The Element of Chance."[4]

A 1922 issue of *Western Story* exemplifies its attention to woman-centered fiction. It includes a lead, eight-part serial novel by George Gilbert, creator of the above-mentioned Captain Nora, titled "Cow Woman."[5] In Orville Leonard's "The Lost Squaw Man," Ann Stedman and her husband search for Ann's missing brother, who is needed to help run the family ranch.[6] An outlaw gambles away a young woman's inheritance and then repents and falls in love with her, in Adolph Bennauer's "For the Girl He Left behind Him."[7] *Western Story* also included articles about women in its "filler" content, short anecdotes and articles on western topics. One of these announced the appointment of "The First Woman Sheriff of Michigan," while another declared, "Woman Sheriff Averts Lynching." Notable women's adventures included a horsewoman's twelve-hundred-mile journey on horseback from Oklahoma to California and a Colorado woman who killed a mountain lion after catching it eating her chickens.[8]

Assessing the proportion of this fiction that was authored by women is a task somewhat complicated by the widespread use of pseudonyms in cheap fiction publishing. In chapter 3 I demonstrate that women's western writers were not necessarily bound by male pseudonyms through the example of Caroline Lockhart, who used western travel writing to shed her pseudonymous identity as the popular journalist Suzette and to "come out" as Caroline Lockhart. Indeed, cross-gender pseudonyms were relatively uncommon. Pseudonyms had been used in cheap fiction production since the nineteenth century, performing two key functions for publishers. First, dime novel publishers used pseudonyms as brands that enabled them to streamline production of their most popular series; it was not uncommon for a given pseudonym to be the work of several different writers, as was the case for Bertha M. Clay (F. Carr). Second, pseudonyms enabled magazine publishers to exploit their most productive writers, who could write two or more stories for a single issue. For example, Muriel Newhall regularly contributed multiple stories under different signatures to the same issue of *Romantic Range*.[9] Pulp author Paul S. Powers also documented this practice in his memoir (Powers and Powers 163). Examples of pseudonyms used specifically to disguise an author's gender, however, are rare. B. M. Bower, whose gender-neutral signature was widely read as masculine, lamented the fact that she had been forbidden from publicizing herself, believing that this prevented her from reviving her career after the pulp market shrank in 1929. C. K. (Chloe Kathleen) Shaw also published westerns using a gender-neutral signature (The Fictionmags Index at Galactic Central), and Carmen Malone wrote cowboy poetry under the pseudonym "Pecos Pete."[10] However, there are more examples of women who published western fiction under their own names or feminine pseudonyms, including Vingie Roe, Lupe Loya (Lela Cole Kitson), and Cherry Wilson.[11] Conversely, men who produced love stories did not consistently conceal their gender. While Will F. Jenkins wrote for *Love Story Magazine* as Louisa Carter Lee, Charles Cannell wrote as Charles Vivian (The Fictionmags Index at Galactic Central). In sum, pseudonyms were used primarily for branding purposes, and rarely to disguise the gender of the author. This is true even of authors such as Muriel Newhall and Paul S. Powers, who used multiple pseudonyms. Thus, while the identities of many pulp authors remain unknown, it is reasonable to assume that author names appearing in the tables of contents of pulp fiction magazines do reflect the general gendered makeup of that magazine's authorship; pseudonyms that crossed genders were the exceptions, not the rule.

Although the content of *Western Story* was predominantly, but not exclusively, male authored and male centered during its early few years, the magazine was opening up to women writers just as the first romance western magazine appeared and constituted a feminized ghetto for women's westerns (a development I discuss in more detail below). Several of B. M. Bower's earlier stories were reprinted in *Western Story*, and new women writers emerged, including the prolific Cherry Wilson, creator of the serial character Comanche Kid. He is a redeemed outlaw forced to "turn bandit" by unlucky circumstances, who subsequently serves as a deputy in the fictional western town of Wyecat.[12] Lupe Loya also published frequently in *Western Story*. Her "Puncher vs Poet" depicts the puncher of the title staging a raid to win the esteem of his sweetheart from his rival, the "Poet."[13] The prolific Vingie E. Roe, who was already well established in general fiction pulps, also published several stories in *Western Story* (The Fictionmags Index at Galactic Central).

The demographics of pulp readerships are notoriously difficult to measure. Cheap fiction was associated with juvenile and working-class readers (Denning 30–82, E. Smith 16), yet pulp editor Harold Hersey, addressing the presumably middle-class readers of his memoir, insisted that pulp readers "are apt to be in your own family" (4) and included in that group professionals, office and factory workers, college-educated men and women, and even judges (4–11). Early twentieth-century educators like Edward N. Teall also knew that most readers were "omnivorous," with reading diets that transversed the cultural hierarchy (quoted in J. Rubin 511). Sociological researchers in the 1920s and 1930s challenged stereotypes about the lowbrow tastes of working-class readers by using library statistics to prove that they frequently checked out canonical literary fiction (J. Rubin 512–13). Pulp magazine editors themselves, never sure exactly who was reading their publications, constantly hedged their bets by spreading their overall production across several magazine titles and devising new titles or fine-tuning existing ones in hopes that one would be a "hit" (Hersey 39, 89). Unlike middle-class readerships of slick magazines, which had been commodified through targeted advertising by this time (Ohmann 25–29), pulp readers were believed by advertisers to be young, working-class individuals with little disposable income (Hersey 73). Because pulp income from advertising was insignificant and not carefully targeted, advertisements in pulps are not reliable indicators of audience. Ad space was sold in bulk, and the same ads were printed across a range of titles, some more relevant to the target market than others (Hersey 71). Most pulp advertising, which sold correspondence programs, medical cures, and cigarettes, addressed young working-class men, even ads appearing in *Love Story Magazine*.[14] More information about readers is contained in a publication's back pages, which featured "departments" of letters from readers.

If women appeared only occasionally as authors and characters in *Western Story*, their voices were frequent in the editorial section "The Round-Up" and the reader correspondence section "The Hollow Tree." Hersey describes such "departments" as "essential to the organic life of any periodical" in order to provide "the personal touch"

(87). Answering suspicions that much of this content was faked by editors, Hersey insisted that this practice was rare, used only in the case of new titles in order to "get the ball rolling" (24). Moreover, digitized census data has since made it possible to verify the identities of readers, whose hometowns and even complete addresses were usually included in their published letters. Despite the inevitable editorial influence upon the selection and content of reader letters, these letters still provide us with valuable insights into reader motivations, pleasures, and desires.

"The Roundup" was a regular column in which the editorial voice of the magazine interacted with reader letters about the magazine and the general topic of the American West. Readers relayed anecdotes about their own "real-life" western adventures or shared their knowledge about life in the West, especially with respect to guns and gun culture. Examples include a South Dakota man who shares his lengthy list of "old-time guns" and a "very, very old-timer[s]" recollections about "the cap-and-ball six shooter.[15] Another reader relates his inside knowledge about Steamboat, the famous Wyoming bucking horse.[16] The myth that horsehair lariats, laid around a campsite, can be used to repel snakes was challenged by one well-informed reader.[17] A little boosterism could also get a reader's name into print: A man calling himself "Zinza 'Slim' Halloway" from Idaho composed a poetic encomium to *Western Story* that was printed verbatim.[18] The editor would also occasionally provide sketches of the most popular authors, which included physical descriptions and biographical details, usually to authenticate the "westernness" of the magazine. For example, a biography of George Owen Baxter recounted how the early death of the author's father left him having to "get victuals and shelter for himself at once. He did it pronto, goin' to work on a big ranch."[19] By publishing readers' anecdotes and experiential knowledge of the West, "The Roundup" enabled readers to participate in the magazine's production of western representation and to corroborate its claims to western realism and authenticity.

Women were not equally represented with men in this department, but their letters were not uncommon and were not deemed out of place; insofar as *Western Story* positioned itself as family reading, women were integral to its imagined community even if they did not have an equal voice within it. The familial structure of its imagined readership is made particularly explicit in an edition focused exclusively on letters from people seeking lost friends and family members. The editor admonished its readers to write home to their mothers:

> Boys, remember each and every one of you, that your best friend, and the friend who deserves more from you than any other, is your mother. . . . On second thought, we guess the girls better step up here, too—the daughters. Although they are a whole lot better about writing home, perhaps they had better do it now, too.[20]

A few women vied with men for bragging rights as real life adventurers, including Mrs. Hazel Logan, who writes of her experiences in the "circus business" (128).[21] Others requested practical advice, such as Miss Ida May Switzer of Hamburg, Iowa, who wanted tips on the care of her pet wolf.[22]

Whereas "The Roundup" enabled readers to interact with the magazine, "The Hollow Tree," edited by Louise Rice, focused on readers' interactions with each other. As Kaestle and Radway point out, such community building was a key feature of print-culture expansion beginning in the late nineteenth century and profoundly reorganized American culture by challenging "the primacy of affiliation based solely on residence" ("A Framework" 21). "The Hollow Tree" facilitated contact between readers by publishing reader requests for "pen friends," as they were then called, for employment or investment opportunities in western-themed schemes such as ranching or mining, for advice, and for general companionship. Readers could also purchase buttons identifying themselves as members of "the Hollow Tree Gang" so they could recognize each other in other public contexts. This department created an imagined community of readers that traversed the vast distances—both social and geographic—that separated easterners and westerners, urban and rural inhabitants, factory workers and cowboys, stenographers and cowgirls. This point was made visually by the illustration accompanying every column, which depicted on the top left an office worker writing at his desk, on the top right a cowboy leaving a note in the aforesaid hollow tree. Most letter writers were, in one form or another, seeking community; for them, *Western Story* functioned as a means by which to find likeminded people as correspondents, business associates, employees, or benefactors. Through "The Hollow Tree" the *Western Story* readership was conceptualized as a family, bonded on the basis of the commonalities suggested by shared reading preferences. The metaphor of family included both men and women in the magazine's imagined community of readers: "There's a little news this week that will interest you all," editor Louise Rice reported in the August 5, 1922, issue. "It concerns the doings of some of the Treeites. Two of the brothers are sailing soon for South America where they will hunt for butterflies and birds for a museum, . . . having formed the partnership through the Hollow Tree. . . . Six different parties of girls and women are either hiking afoot, ahorseback, or in cars across the country this summer; the members of these parties met through the good offices of The Tree."[23] Even business propositions were couched in the terms of family and friendship: A "man of forty-five, with experience in the stock industry" wished to rent "a furnished-and-stocked ranch and manage same on the percentage basis." He writes that he is "looking for a new home and for a place where a good family would make friends, as much as for the actual business arrangement."[24] Another couple searches for "some old couple, who have a small place of about ten acres, to share their home with us, with the understanding that we are to be, as it were, their adopted children, and that we will take all work off their hands."[25]

Western Story readers unable to travel did so vicariously through "The Hollow Tree." Those seeking correspondents were often curious about western or "outdoor" life and frequently offered their own local knowledge in exchange for stories about the West: "I would like to hear from people who are interested in the out of doors. I will admit at present that I am not as wise on that subject as I hope to be, but, if any one would like some help on 'wireless,' I might be of assistance, as I have had quite a bit of experience in that line."[26] Many letters expressed interest in specific places: "Here's hoping that I may hear from some of the folks in Alaska, British Columbia, Maine, or any State or country where there is lumbering done."[27] Urban letter writers frequently wrote of their desire to escape the city if only vicariously in the fiction of *Western Story* or through correspondence with westerners: "Those who, like us, are shut up in the city, can at least hear from those who are not, through the good letters [in the Hollow Tree]."[28] Western letter writers offered anecdotes of their own western adventures; for example, two Wyoming cow punchers described sighting a mountain lion while on a hunting trip, while a writer calling himself "Lone Wolf" from El Mirasol Ranch in Geyserville, California, offered "information about this part of the world and ranching here" to interested correspondents.[29] Soldiers and sailors offered to share their travel experiences with *Western Story* readers: "I am lonely at present, due to a number of circumstances, and I would like to hear from any of The Gang. I was a soldier for five years and have been to Honolulu and to Manila, and during the war I was with the Twenty-seventh Infantry in Siberia."[30] Such readers capitalized on the commodification of adventure by trading their own adventures, not for money, but for companionship.

Within certain normative limits, "The Hollow Tree" supported "odd friendships" among its readers and included the marginalized within its community. The "odd friendships" included a research scientist who found temporary work as a beekeeper while he waited for his research to bear fruit,[31] and a "kid" from Seattle who asked Texans to send him "a couple of live horned toads." The marginalized and the lonely appeared frequently, including Clarence E. Beam, paralyzed from the waist down in an accident and in search of "a few good friends."[32] Single people wrote to "The Hollow Tree," attracted to its imaginary home space: "I am a bachelor without relatives, and I live alone. I have six rooms, but the only one that I occupy much is the kitchen, where the eats are cached." This bachelor's empty rooms suggest that a need for home and family lie behind his appeal to The Hollow Tree. He adds, "I would be tickled to hear from any of The Gang would care to write me, particularly anyone interested in dumb-bell and bar-bell lifting, as this is my favorite kind of exercise. Fraternally yours, L.A. Johnson.[33] Readers would sometimes describe their physical appearances in terms of hair and eye color, skin tone, and height, but the unspoken assumption was of a predominantly white community, with exceptions made for international readers, who provided the dominant readership with access to exotic adventure: "Kipling has said that 'East is East and West is West, and never the twain shall meet,' but around the Hollow Tree we manage to see that very thing done. We have a number of Hindus in the H. T. Gang, one Kongo African, a number of Japanese and Chinese, and some representatives of scattered nationalities such as Singhalese and Hawaiian and Filipino."[34] A few Native American readers capitalized on their insider status as western figures to seek inclusion in the "gang": "I am a Cherokee Indian from the West," one such letter, signed "Alaquah," reads, "but have lived in New York City for several years now.[35] One letter, though, suggests that the white hegemony conceals the actual diversity characterizing *Western Story* readers, who could identify themselves publicly by wearing Hollow Tree buttons:[36]

> In a town in the South where there is a great deal of that old-fashioned difference in the social life which used to be so strong down there, we have a number of gangsters [Hollow Tree readers], one of whom is an elderly and stately gentleman "of the old school." Another is the local bootblack, Italian by birth, but a perfectly good American; another, a bright young negro boy who is going to be a lawyer for the members of his own race; and another, a pretty and popular young social bud. Now all of those mentioned purchased buttons and in the course of time appeared with them on the streets. Can you fancy what a leveling process and what a fraternalizing element those buttons are?[37]

Women, whom Rice frequently addressed, as "Sisters of the Tree," were an integral part of the *Western Story* readership; their presence was indeed necessary to construct the intimate, familial bonds that defined the *Western Story* community of readers.[38] Women wrote to "The Hollow Tree" from a variety of motives: Some were, like many Hollow Tree correspondents, looking for companionship with likeminded people, such as J. Edna Ritchie of Daytona, Florida, who "would love to hear from some of The Gang who love the woods and the wild creatures."[39] Mrs. E. D. V. D. of Nevada sought domestic help, promising to provide in return "a good home, plenty of out-of-door life, and good remuneration."[40] Many women seeking companionship identified themselves as young married women. For twenty-three-year-old Mrs. W. V. Hewett, marriage had been an impediment to the way of life promoted in *Western Story*: "I want friends, and I hope that The Gang will take to me. . . . I would also like to hear from any one who has traveled. I have never been anywhere to speak of. I am twenty-three and married; was only sixteen when I made my leap."[41] Women's voices were included in the frequent letters from city dwellers and workers seeking the freedom of the West: "For years I have had the idea that I wanted to make the West my home," writes Miss J. V. Malden, "and now circumstances seem to say that I am free enough to put the dream into reality. I have worked for five years in a department store and four years in my present position with a large electrical concern. . . . Now, then, what I want is to hear from the sisters of The Tree who will advise me, from their experience and knowledge, as to whether I can put what I know to advantage out West."[42] Sometimes these were women in desperate straits looking for help. For example, an impoverished single mother asked for help finding adoptive parents for her baby.[43] A woman working in a southern cotton mill wrote a plea for a home where she could work for her room and board and go to school.[44]

These women saw themselves as legitimate members of "The Tree Gang" and the magazine as a legitimate vehicle by which to forge bonds with a community of women. "I would like to hear from a good, congenial woman or girl who would like to take up a homestead with me—one who has some interest in chickens and similar tastes. Also would be glad to hear from any sisters of the Tree Gang."[45] Young women living on western ranches were particularly sought-after correspondents: Miss Romona Baker of Petaluma was described by the "Hollow Tree" editor as "the real outdoor girl that so many of the sisters want to hear from." "I am a California girl," wrote Baker, "but I spent a great many of my younger years in Mexico; am sixteen and live on a chicken ranch, which seems very different from the cattle ranges to which I have been accustomed. I can ride almost any kind of horse, and I was what you might say raised in a saddle."[46] These women were not unaware, nor uncritical, of the fact that men still dominated the Hollow Tree's imagined community. Hazel Brink playfully admonished male readers to make more room for women's voices: "Some of you hombres push over and let an old woman of sixty set a spell and fry her bacon alongside yourn." Brink goes on to describe how her "wanderlust" had taken her to fifteen western and midwestern states, not to mention Canada and the American South.[47] Mrs. Ernest B. Harmon asked, in a postscript, "Why not put a woman's picture seated at the desk on our page, instead of a man?"[48] Such critiques were always lighthearted, in keeping with the seemly congenial, familial culture of the *Western Story* readership.

There were limits to "The Hollow Tree's" tolerance for difference. Most notably, this department upheld a heteronormative regime through its warning to readers that letters would be exchanged "only between men and men, boys and boys, women and women, girls and girls."[49] Prohibitions against intergenerational exchange would protect impressionable children from unknown and potentially dangerous influences, while gender segregation both assumed and policed a heteronormative social structure. Nonetheless, many different kinds of readers "fried their bacon" in the pages of "The Hollow Tree": men, women, adults, juveniles, seniors, people of color, people with disabilities, single men and women, and urban and rural readers from diverse geographic locations. With the advent of gendered pulp westerns in 1924 this diversity would diminish, and pulp magazines would emphasize heteronormativity far more emphatically in both their fiction and reader departments.

Gendered Pulp Western Magazines

Male and female-oriented western fiction emerged virtually simultaneously as general western fiction branched off into gendered subcategories. Pulp editor and writer Harold Brainerd Hersey credited himself with inventing the first western love story pulp, Clayton Magazines' *Ranch Romances*, which began publication in 1924 and was both an immediate and long-lived success. In an effort to create more targeted publications, Hersey, who worked for the pulp publisher Clayton at the time, analyzed Clayton's general-adventure pulp *Ace-High*, identifying sub-categories that could be the basis for new, specialized publications. This process led to the creation of two new magazines, *Ranch Romances* and *Cowboy Stories* (89). "Instead of the Cowboy hero," Hersey claimed of *Ranch Romances*, "we offered the cowgirl heroine" (170). Thus, the female-centered *Ranch Romances* was not a later imitation of the male-centered western but emerged simultaneously with it. Interestingly, it was *Ranch Romances* rather than *Cowboy Stories* that Hersey considered his greatest hit (119). B. M. Bower's publisher Street & Smith introduced its own western love story magazine

Romantic Range in 1935[50] as the pulp market recovered from the 1929 crash (Ashley). Western romances featured woman-centered western fiction and became a significant, if denigrated, venue for women's popular writing about the West after World War I. As feminized publications they were lower in status than the general fiction magazines but created opportunities for an emerging generation of women writers who accepted their relatively confining generic categories and, after the 1929 crash, low pay of one to one-and-a-half cents a word.[51]

Western love stories explicitly targeted the women who already constituted significant proportion of the readership for "respectable" western fiction in the early twentieth century. Significant numbers of women wrote for western love story magazines, many of them as lead authors, including Mona Farnsworth (pen name for Muriel Newhall), Anita Allen (who also used the pen name Marion O'Hearn), and Agnes Best—just a few examples of the scores of women writers whose recovery is finally possible thanks to emerging digital tools.[52] Western love stories followed a relatively narrow set of generic conventions, including the requirement that stories feature a heterosexual love story and end with marriage or at the very least an avowal of heterosexual love. The new, feminized western thus functioned to discipline and streamline women's westerns, which had formerly circulated primarily in general fiction pulps or in "quality" novel form.

The experience of B. M. Bower negotiating a changed market for western fiction in the late 1930s suggests the costs to women writers of these shifts. By now Street & Smith had slashed its payments to authors while simultaneously, in a steady stream of new, specialized titles including *Romantic Range*, offering a new generation of emerging authors a relatively precarious livelihood provided they were willing to accept the low pay. Even as it created a market explicitly for women writers of the West, *Romantic Range* narrowly defined the roles of the women it represented in its magazine. B. M. Bower did not even consider it a potential venue when she tried to revive her career in the late 1930s. Writing to literary agent Edith Burrows in an attempt to place her work in the prestigious "smooth" or "slick" magazines (a category that included *The Saturday Evening Post* and *Life*, which were printed on high-quality paper), Bower described how the post-1929 popular fiction marketplace had affected her livelihood:

> In the beginning—about thirty-five years ago—I sent my first long story, "Chip, of the Flying U," to Ainslee's magazine. They used it as a circulation builder for their new Popular Magazine—and they informed me that it had done the work with a bang, so to speak. After that they put me under contract to write exclusively for Popular and Ainslee's. . . . They took everything I wrote, as fast as I could write it. . . . I had a large following [in *Popular*] and with [the pulp magazine] Short Stories. At the time [1929] of . . . the crash in the magazine market I was getting from six cents to eight cents a word for my stuff.
>
> But the smooth paper magazines did not know me—my market absorbed everything as fast as I could turn it out, and I fear I followed the line of least resistance.
>
> After the debacle in the magazine world my market was pretty well shot.[53]

Bower did not even consider the romance pulps a potential venue for her work, quite possibly because of the lower status, increasing creative constraints, and decreasing pay that these venues offered.

Pulp romance westerns provided readers with a narrower range of fiction—and fictional roles for women—than their general-western predecessors. Although Hersey implied that the western romance replaced male with female adventure heroes, few covers of *Romantic Range* depicted women in the context of action or adventure. Covers commonly depicted a man and woman riding horseback together in a suitably western landscape, smiling congenially (see fig. 1). Covers depicting a man and woman kissing showed the woman in either a yielding posture or struggling against the more powerful male.[54] When *Romantic Range* switched, during and after World War II, from custom illustrations of its content to generic photographs, it often featured pretty western girls in pastoral outdoor settings, smiling in the company of a man, as caregivers posing with horses or baby animals, or in chaste pin-up style poses.[55] Only in rare cases did *Romantic Range* covers depict women alone or in positions of agency, such as one cover that showed a woman actively embracing and kissing a surprised-looking cowboy (see fig. 2).

Images within the magazine, which illustrated select scenes from its fiction, more often included women in the context of western adven-

Fig. 1. A typical cover image from Street & Smith's *Romantic Range*. Illustrator unknown. From *Romantic Range* 4, no. 2 (June 1937). *Romantic Range* is © and ™ Condé Nast. Used with permission.

ture, but still in a heterosexual romantic context. Like the covers, internal illustrations frequently depicted the heroine riding side-by-side with the cowboy hero. These scenes of relative equality between hero and heroine were usually countered, however, by internal illustrations of action scenes depicting the heroine as victim or in need of male protection (see figs. 3 and 4).

Fiction in *Romantic Range* mapped love stories onto conventional adventure plots, such as conflicts over property or resources. In "The Last Ride," by Carmony Cove, the heroine is the feisty daughter of a rancher, but she is in love with her father's rival, an advocate of fenc-

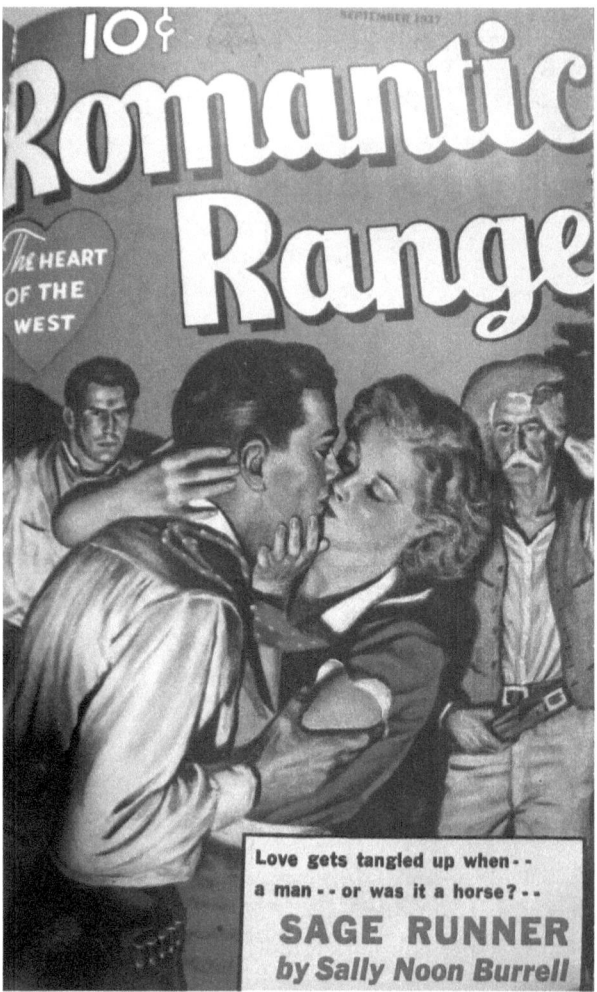

FIG. 2. This *Romantic Range* cover image depicting a woman's active embrace of the cowboy departs from the cover-heroine's usual passive pose. Illustrator unknown. From *Romantic Range* 4, no. 5 (September 1937). *Romantic Range* is © and ™ Condé Nast. Used with permission.

ing the open range.[56] Other heroines fall in love with the hero in the course of some western adventure, as is the case when the heroine of Paul Randall Morrisson's "The Lemon and the Lioness," an eastern woman who inherits a ranch, travels west to confront her ranch foreman, who she feels is being insubordinate. Instead of asserting

Judith sprang to the front, reached for the whip, and sent the frightened team racing toward the pass.

FIG. 3. *Romantic Range* occasionally depicted women as agents of adventure in its internal illustrations. Illustrator unknown. From *Romantic Range* 1, no. 2 (December 1935): 93. *Romantic Range* is © and ™ Condé Nast. Used with permission.

her authority over him, she finds herself depending on his protection during a violent confrontation with rustlers, and the two fall in love.[57] Heroines are not always participants in adventure, nor are they always feisty and independent. In Muriel Newhall's "To a Girl's Heart," published under the pseudonym Regina Bailey,[58] the hero falsely believes that he needs wealth to impress his lover and risks his

FIG. 4. Women in *Romantic Range* were most frequently depicted in the context of rescue by the cowboy hero, although in this image, the female figure's assertive gaze contradicts other signifiers of her dependency. Illustrator unknown. From *Romantic Range* 1, no. 2 (December 1935): 69. *Romantic Range* is © and ™ Condé Nast. Used with permission.

life and ranch for a gold strike to do so while she remains in the background as an observer.[59] In Jack Bechdolt's "Desert Rose" the passive and submissive heroine finds herself under the protection of a prospector who appears indifferent to her until she stumbles upon a rich lode of silver.[60] Whether or not the heroine is submissive or rebellious, the plot resolves with marriage or at least an avowal of love between hero and heroine, together with the promise of patriarchal protection for the latter.

Western love stories emphasize the fact that the heroine is alone and vulnerable in the West. Often, she is trying to defend her property, usually inherited from her father. These figures are heroic insofar as they have been thrust into playing a man's role. In Muriel Ives's "Ransom Oil" (as Edna T. Green),[61] bandits kidnap the heroine and try to force her to sign over her ranch to them.[62] In Stella Spencer's "Fugitive's Daughter" the heroine's father is wrongly accused of a crime by men with designs on his property, and she must protect him and look after the ranch.[63] Some heroines love heroically, choosing good men who are misunderstood by the broader society or who are off limits because they come from a rival family. In Carmony Cove's "The Last Ride," a rancher's daughter loves a man who stands for fencing the open range and is thus resented by her rancher community.[64] Rebellious heroines can scorn the authority of the hero only provisionally, as does the western-bred heroine of "singed romance" until he proves his mettle by saving them both from a sabotaged mine.[65] In Sally Noon Burrell's "The Man from Cloud Peak" the rebellious heroine orchestrates her own kidnapping to teach her father a lesson, but when the kidnapping becomes real, she is confronted with her real state of dependency.[66] Not all heroines are western born. Occasional stories feature eastern women who travel, alone, to the West, where they become embroiled in western adventure. In Edith M. Noy's "Cupid and the Camp Wagon" a stenographer on vacation becomes entangled in a war between a sheepherder and powerful cattlemen.[67] In Aline Ballard's "Chorus Girl," a stage performer falls for a western man who rebuffs her. When he is stabbed, she saves his life by rushing him to a doctor and is rewarded with his love.[68] Whether western or eastern born, the outcome for the heroine is almost always the same.

The self-reliant woman of the West was a mainstay of *Romantic Range*. Stories often introduced these heroines as lone figures in the wilderness, sometimes engaged in feats of heroic action. The reader is soon reassured, however, that a "true woman" lies beneath these masculine appearances. Stella Spencer's "Fugitive's Daughter" begins with the image of a woman riding her pony on a rocky slope. Suddenly the pony slips and falls, breaking its leg. Distressed at her pony's plight, the woman nonetheless does not hesitate to shoot him. Despite her willingness to kill when necessary, the story drops hints that she is a true woman at her core: "Not even the worn boots, patched overalls and faded waist could hide the supple loveliness of her slender, rounded figure."[69] We soon learn that she is actually a dutiful daughter on a secret visit to her fugitive—and wrongly accused—father's hideout. Sometimes these self-reliant women are initially mistaken for men. In Robert Henry Hall's "A Cache for Landon," a ranch owner named Landon turns out to be a woman.[70] In M. A. Cameron's "Heart Brand," a cowboy roping a wild horse is, on closer inspection, a woman.[71] In both stories, we are again reassured that the heroines, despite an initial masculine appearance, are "real" women. The former is threatened by an unwanted marriage, decreed in her dead father's will, and ultimately depends on the hero to protect her. The latter is acting out of daughterly duty, trying to capture a sought-after stallion so that she can use the reward money to save her father's ranch. Acts of independence paradoxically serve to remind us how powerfully "feminine" these women actually are. The more they wear rough clothes and perform feats of heroism, the more womanly they ultimately prove to be.

Heroines in *Romantic Range* are always young and white and rarely have significant relationships with other women. While father figures are ubiquitous, mothers are rare, despite the frequent references to women's natural roles as caregivers. If a mother figure is mentioned, as is the case in Stella Spencer's "Fugitive's Daughter," she is either long dead or ensconced in the domestic sphere far from the action.[72] Occasionally secondary female characters function as romantic rivals to the heroine, foils to her ideal qualities. In Jack Bechdolt's "Desert Rose," the shy and submissive heroine wrongly believes that the hero is in love with a vivacious blond neighbor whose vanity casts her humility and selflessness in stark relief.[73] In "Range Secret," the hero, a film star on a western trip to recover his health, is caught between two daughters of rival families and must determine whose motives are pure. The scheming and jealous Milly immediately fawns over the hero's status as a movie star, but the hero is attracted to the aloof Cynthia. The possessive Milly plots Cynthia's kidnapping, the hero comes to her rescue, and Cynthia admits her love for him. Milly's selfish attraction to the hero is proven superficially based on his film-star status, while the heroine loves him for his heroic deeds.[74]

There were exceptions to the above patterns, but even these did not radically disrupt conventions. One of the most popular and prolific authors to appear in *Romantic Range* was also one of the most innovative. Muriel Newhall wrote hundreds of stories for *Romantic Range* and other pulps under several pseudonyms, including her most common pseudonym, Mona Farnsworth. In some issues, Newhall published three or more stories under different pseudonyms.[75] Newhall regularly toyed with convention in her western love stories. She was one of the few *Romantic Range* authors to include older female characters in her stories,[76] and she frequently found ways to subvert or play with convention. In "Memory Trail" (written under the pseudonym Mona Farnsworth) the heroic acts are performed by an eighty-year-old backwoodsman.[77] In "Range Secret" (written under the pseudonym Edna T. Green), the metafictional hero is an actor who plays western heroes but has never actually traveled West.[78] Newhall's most striking creation is a series about Sheriff Minnie written under the pseudonym Muriel Ives. Illustrations depict Minnie as a middle-aged, sturdily built woman who wears the traditional sheriff's uniform of hat, chaps, spurs, boots, guns, and badge (see fig. 5). She is a vocal critic of romance and of young, pretty, defenseless women: "You nincompoops make me sick! You sigh and you cry and you get red noses, but you ain't got the guts to up and get what you want!"[79] Such women are usually the first to be suspected of the crime. To persuade them to tell the truth, Minnie often feigns sympathy. One such victim of Minnie's tactics accuses her of setting a trap, to which Minnie replies, "Shucks. . . . I'm the sheriff ain't I? Whatcha expect me to do, play mumbletypeg?"[80] Despite her impatience with female helplessness, Minnie ultimately exonerates these women from guilt. In "You Never Can Tell," Minnie prevents a range war over a single woman who rents her land out to farmers, angering the cattlemen who want her land for grazing.[81] In "Look Who's Here," Minnie exonerates a dance-hall girl suspected of gunning down her husband's murderer at the dance hall.[82] She solves these crimes primarily with her wits, about which she brags regularly: "I'm so damned smart . . . I ain't got breath left to admire myself."[83]

Fig. 5. Muriel Ives's cross-dressing series character Sheriff Minnie. Illustration by William Timmons. From *Romantic Range* 12, no. 2 (June 1941): 41. *Romantic Range* is © and ™ Condé Nast. Used with permission.

In keeping with the economy of subversion governing virtually all *Romantic Range* fiction, these stories conclude in ways that restore the heteronormative regime. The beneficiaries of Minnie's crime fighting are usually young heterosexual couples who marry in the end. The reader is also reassured that Sheriff Minnie is still a "real" woman by her romance and eventual marriage to Peter Whittlesley. At first Minnie rebuffs his advances because, we are told, she loves her job as sheriff more than she loves Whittlesley; however, Whittlesley plays as much a disciplinary as a romantic function, lurking in the background of every story to remind readers that Minnie's queer gender performance is provisional and temporary. Eventually, Minnie does marry Peter, but her story does not end here. Subsequent stories follow Minnie's efforts to remain sheriff despite pressure from Peter, who seems to think that marriage will magically transform her into his cook and housekeeper. In "A Woman's Place," Minnie runs for reelection as sheriff against a pretty young woman named Trixie, using a sexist platform: "Don't Put a Girl Who Should Be Married in Public Office! Woman's Place Is in the Home!"[84] Minnie forgets, however, that voters might see her the same way, and both women lose the election to the male candidate. Minnie gets her job back in the next installment, but also settles into the routine of preparing Peter's dinner, which she manages to do in between investigating crimes.[85] Sheriff Minnie remained a regular feature in *Romantic Range*, even through the World War II years when content was severely reduced. The last Sheriff Minnie story appeared in November 1946, just two months before *Romantic Range* ceased publication. In "Will and Testament," Minnie helps save a young woman from marriage to an abuser and clears the way for her to marry the man she really loves.[86] Throughout the series, Minnie's position as sheriff is represented as an exceptional case rather than a precedent that other women might follow. Still, Minnie is queer. She behaves as though the categories "girl" and "woman" do not apply to her and, in so doing, calls their very meaning into question. Even within the generic limitations of the romance western, possibilities for gender trouble, to borrow Judith Butler's famous phrase, exist.

Men as well as women read *Romantic Range*, or at least the editors of the reader-letters sections, which were evenly split between letters from men and women, wanted to make it look this way.[87] Some content of *Romantic Range* also appears to address heterosexual men. Whereas Janice Radway argues of paperback romances targeting exclusively female readerships that their plots attempt to recuperate patriarchy for (heterosexual) female readers (*Reading* 157), much fiction in *Romantic Range* is equally concerned with reassuring men that they are adequate patriarchs, countering pulp magazine advertising that exploited male anxieties about economic status and body image. For example, in Newhall's "To a Girl's Heart," written under the pseudonym Regina Bailey, a cowboy overhears a wealthy, effete man propose to his sweetheart and assumes that he will need to become wealthy to compete for her hand. He risks his life for a gold strike, only to find out that his sweetheart had turned down his rival and is, moreover, deeply insulted by his assumption that she would marry exclusively for money.[88] This message is quite the inverse of pulp ads for correspondence schools and body-building programs, which warned men that they needed well-paying jobs and muscular bodies to attract women, but the implied reader in both cases is the young, low-income male.

The readers' sections in the back pages of *Romantic Range* enabled readers to interact respectively with each other and with the magazine, but they also suggest a more homogenous readership than that of *Western Story*, made up largely of young, single men and women. In "Around the Double R Corral" readers shared personal experiences of the West or asked questions about western life, much as they did in the comparable section in *Western Story*. "Pony Express" (later renamed "Overland Mail") provided readers with a forum for exchanging letters with each other. These sections performed many functions comparable to those in *Western Story*: They enabled readers to participate in the construction of western representation and to form communities based on shared bonds of reading. Readers continued to seek letters from particular types of people, often people of the West, and to trade accounts of specific places in contracts of mutual entertainment. However, *Romantic Range* letter writers were less diverse, most between the ages of eighteen and twenty-six. They were evenly split between male and female readers, and letters tended to follow a narrow formula: Writers described themselves as new or longtime readers of the magazine, praised its quality (but without going into much detail about its strengths), described their hobbies and personal appearance, and explained the type of person they wished to correspond with. Readers often desired to correspond with westerners or "cowboys and cowgirls," offering in return to share information about their own homes, particularly if they lived somewhere exotic. While *Western Story*, in keeping with its self-image as a "clean" family-oriented publication, prohibited romance (while reinforcing heteronormativity) by facilitating exchange only between people of the same sex, *Romantic Range* permitted its readers to seek correspondents of the opposite sex; indeed, its erotically charged, heteronormative content encouraged such liaisons. As an aside, prohibitions against heterosexual romance did not prevent readers from using reader departments to pursue same-sex relationships. Queer sexuality was of course well underground in the 1930s and 1940s, but pulp editors undoubtedly knew about its existence. Hersey insisted that editors did not cater to "abnormal" readers—men who read romances, and women who read science fiction (7), giving us a rare glimpse of a subversive, queer pulp readership.

The Ghettoization of Women's Westerns

The western romance certainly opened new publishing opportunities for women, although these were already starting to expand in the general western pulps before they became further specialized. In the first two years of *Western Story*, only two to three of the weekly issues contained women writers, but beginning in 1921, woman-authored content became more significant. Between 1921 and 1924, fourteen to seventeen issues contained one or two short or serialized stories by women (The Fictionmags Index at Galactic Central). The bulk of this fiction was written by just a few writers: Cherry Wilson, Lupe Loya, B. M. Bower, and Mary Imlay Taylor. Their writing varied in theme, style, and subject and could quite explicitly assert feminist goals. Lupe Loya's "Clementine," published in 1921, satirically deploys the first-person voice of a misogynist "old-timer" who offers his tale as an object lesson in the pitfalls of woman suffrage (which had become law the previous year). "Lovely woman has got a certain speer, so long as she stays in that speer minding her own business she's all right; but just you let her get out of it once—and everything is upset right then and there," he warns.[89] To prove his point, he tells the story of a young woman who, upon returning home after a long absence, helps her remarried mother take control of her assets from her exploitative and controlling husband. The naïve narrator does not realize that his story is actually an indictment of patriarchy and argument for the education and liberation of women.[90] Cherry Wilson's "Valley of Sinister Blossoms" resembles the love stories that would become a staple of the romance western, although it develops the motif of the "sinister blossom" to an extent that would be rare in the more plot-driven romance westerns.[91] In 1924, the year *Ranch Romances* appeared, women-authored content in *Western Story* dropped off significantly: Only six weekly issues contained fiction by women, almost all of it written by Cherry Wilson, who was already a well-established contributor to *Western Story* (The Fictionmags Index at Galactic Central). Meanwhile, the monthly *Ranch Romances*, although still dominated by male writers, became a significant venue for women's western fiction, publishing one to two women authors per monthly issue (The Fictionmags Index at Galactic Central). While Cherry Wilson continued to write for *Western Story*, Lupe Loya began publishing most of her work in *Ranch Romances*. Bower, who at this point was still widely believed to be a male writer, continued to appear, mainly in reprint form, in the assortment of western publications that appeared as the number of pulp titles proliferated in the late 1920s (The Fictionmags Index at Galactic Central). Taylor, who was well established in the general fiction magazine *Ainslee's*, continued to publish in that venue (The Fictionmags Index at Galactic Central).

Male authors contributed significantly to the content of western romance fiction magazines. In the early years of *Ranch Romances*, about 80 percent of its content was male-authored. By the mid-1930s *Romantic Range* was written predominantly by women but still published male authors in virtually every issue. The pulp-writing profession was male dominated in general, and as professionals, pulp writers were expected to be able to write fiction to order that satisfied the criteria of a given publication regardless of an author's personal preferences (Bold, *Selling* 2–6). It did not necessarily demean the pulp writer to produce content for women—indeed, it could be seen as a virtue in a writer to be able to produce content that had little to do with his personal identity or experiences. Part of the professional's job was the dispassionate ability to perform a task regardless of his personal desires (C. Wilson 6). Hence male writers continued to contribute for *Ranch Romances* as they did earlier western publications. Moreover, the term "romance" was still commonly used to describe idealized adventure narratives as well as love stories; the latter usage of the term began in the twentieth century, whereas the former dates back several centuries.[92] Hence titles like *Ranch Romances* and *Romantic Range* did not necessarily exclude male readers and indeed might attract those looking to meet young women, as many *Romantic Range* readers, according to their letters, hoped to do.

The Masculinization of the Western

In the male-dominated pulp fiction market, western romance magazines became the first western form written primarily for women. While this development provided women writers with professional opportunities as authors of western fiction, it paradoxically helped seal the fate of the western as a masculine genre: Once women were removed to their own feminized western ghetto, the "real" western became masculine by default, instantiating what has become a pervasive myth about the western: that it was a genre created exclusively by and for male readers, foreign to women's experience. Gendered categories first developed by pulp magazine publishers in order to subdivide general fiction pulp readers by gender were later adopted by pulp fiction historians and critics as spontaneous, natural categories. For example, John Dinan wrote in 1983 that "the bulk of Western pulp fiction was written by males for males. . . . The so-called 'romance-Westerns' were the exceptions to the rule" (13–14). The fact that, as Dinan points out, a romance western title, *Ranch Romances*, would outlast all other western pulps and was ranked by Dinan's own sources as among the top three western pulps in quality (Nolan; Dinan 14), did not, in Dinan's view, contradict this obvious truth. Subsequent recuperations of the popular western by John G. Cawelti, Robert Murray Davis, and others, also focused on the male-authored, action-adventure tradition. Efforts to form a literary western canon were similarly male centered.[93]

In fact, women readers and authors have played a substantial role in the history of the genre. Western fiction gained respectability in the early twentieth century largely through its circulation in novel form, a form that was still deeply marked by its nineteenth-century feminized roots and in which both men and women participated. The general fiction pulps that popularized western fiction in the early twentieth century, and the first all-western pulp magazine *Western Story* that followed, also built their reputations by catering to a "respectable" readership that by definition included women. But just as the numbers of women published in *Western Story* began to increase after 1921, the appearance of *Ranch Romances* in 1924 seems to have initiated a rapid decline. At least one regular contributor to *Western Story*, Lupe Loya, began to publish primarily in *Ranch Romances* (The Fictionmags Index at Galactic Central), and surely other women were encouraged to place their work in the newly created ghetto for women's western writing or were even actively excluded from the "general" western field as the genre was redefined as a masculine one. Still, within the confined generic space of the romance western, authors like Muriel Newhall continued to represent acts of gender insubordination, just as an earlier generation of novelists such as Emma Ghent Curtis, Frances McElrath, and B. M. Bower had done. They did so, however, within a cultural field that had changed dramatically. As opposed to the contested space in which women challenged some of the foundational concepts organizing their lives—including marriage, femininity, and domesticity—the romance western categorized and commodified the woman's western, redefining it as an inferior copy of a masculine original and severely curtailing the political and rhetorical goals that were central to earlier women's westerns.

Conclusion

In addition to offering detailed historical readings of forgotten woman's texts, I suggest that incorporating women writers into the debate about the popular western tradition requires that we rethink the terms in which this tradition is understood. The current study of the popular western is structured by gendered generic categories that obscure the actual complexity of popular westerns as a cultural form in which both men and women have participated throughout the history of the genre. Indeed, the absence of women writers from the field of the popular western has been actively and repeatedly reconstructed at virtually every major juncture in the history of the genre.

While James Fenimore Cooper's Leatherstocking novels were collectively canonized as the progenitors of the modern western by Cawelti and others (186), many women's texts were excluded from these accounts, including Lydia Maria Child's *Hobomok* (1824), Catharine Maria Sedgwick's *Hope Leslie* (1827), and Ann S. Stephens's *Malaeska* (1839).[1] All of these texts were considered popular successes in their own day. *Malaeska*, for example, was selected to launch Beadle & Adams's new dime novel venture in 1860 (Bold, "Malaeska's Revenge" 23). As Bold observes, Beadle & Adams eventually threw their marketing efforts behind the male-centered *Seth Jones*, by Edward S. Ellis, which established the dominant formula (24).

When "quality" publishers set out to redeem the West from the dime novel ghetto, women were again written out. Although Owen Wister admired his female contemporary Mary Hallock Foote (Johnson 157), who was also the more prolific author of middlebrow novels set in the West, Wister's debt to Foote remains unexplored, while Foote is, thanks largely to Christine Hill Smith, only beginning to receive attention commensurate with her considerable literary activity. Bower's immense popularity had to be reckoned with by Etulain and Marsden in their 1974 recuperation of the popular western, but that volume's essay on Bower reads her difference from a male-authored standard as a missed opportunity, an evasion, and a "failure to come to grips with" themes that animate *The Virginian* (Meyer 26). Subsequent works reproduced this construct, including Stephen McVeigh's *The American Western* (2007). While McVeigh acknowledges B. M. Bower as "perhaps the first to stake a claim to [the] post-*Virginian* literary territory," he dismisses her work as "melodramatic" in comparison to the male authors he discusses at much greater length, including Zane Grey, well known for his own purple prose (46–47). Fortunately, scholars now have a valuable tool for the recovery of women writers in Nina Baym's comprehensive survey, *Woman Writers of the American West 1833–1927* (2011), which includes several authors of popular westerns.

The masculinist critical paradigms that prevailed during the scholarly recuperation of the western only partially explain the invisibility of women's popular westerns. The endurance of male-authored texts is also a product of the assumptions and practices of cultural gatekeepers including publishers, editors, and booksellers. The publication of *The Rustler* is a case in point. Both Owen Wister and Francis McElrath had social connections that supported their aspirations as novelists. McElrath was a member of a prominent New York newspaper family,[2] while Owen Wister was well connected to the New York publishing scene (Bold, *Frontier Club* 82–83). However, the similarity ends there: Whereas *The Virginian* was supported by an aggressive marketing campaign (Bold, *Frontier Club* 88), *The Rustler* was marked as an ephemeral text from the very moment of its production, receiving little attention either from its own publisher, Funk & Wagnalls, or from the broader publishing community. Its debut was announced in *Publishers' Weekly* on March 15, 1902, along with Funk & Wagnalls's other spring titles, but it was not singled out for special promotion.[3] Funk & Wagnalls allotted two novels, Israel Putnam's historical novel *Daniel Everton, Volunteer Regular* and Michael Davitt's history *The Boer Fight for*

Freedom, full-page advertisements in *Publishers' Weekly* on May 3 and 24, 1902, respectively.[4] *The Rustler* was among a list of titles publicized on May 31 as "Novels for the Vacation Outfit." The copy constructs the novel as light reading: "A STORY OF LIFE AMONG COWBOYS: Every reader who delights in a tale full of dash and adventure, love, and breathless suspense will revel in this story of the adventures of a spirited Eastern girl in the recent "Rustler" uprising of outlaw cattlemen in Wyoming."[5] The novel received no further publicity in *Publishers' Weekly*, and no additional editions were produced. Funk & Wagnalls positioned the novel, then, as recreational reading, the value of which did not transcend its commodity function or fundamentally distinguish it from other offerings in this category. The legacy of *The Rustler* in American literary history fulfilled the ephemeral status originally assigned by its publisher.

A further contributor to female erasure are sociological structures that support men more than women, enabling male writers to concentrate on their craft while women have had to negotiate multiple demands on their time and resources. Both Owen Wister and Zane Grey had wives who managed the family household and supported them professionally, freeing them to devote more time to their writing, not to mention the hunting and fishing trips that both men enjoyed (Bold, *Frontier Club* 111–17; Kant 2). There are no comparable cases, with respect to popular westerns at least, of women writers whose careers were supported to the same extent by family members behind the scenes. Indeed, they are more likely to be caregivers as well as authors, as was the case for Emma Ghent Curtis and, in her early years, B. M. Bower, both of whom began their writing careers while looking after small children.[6] In her later life Bower supported her adult children and their families and saw her third husband, Bud Cowan, through illness while trying to sustain her own declining career (BMB). Mourning Dove grappled with poverty and low-wage work while pursuing activist work and a writing career (Miller). While Wister and Grey left their families for months at a time (Bold, *Frontier Club* 113; Kant 2), B. M. Bower could expect criticism for sending her daughter to boarding school so she could focus on her writing (Bower and Doke).

After their deaths, Wister's and Grey's legacies were well managed, again by female family members: Wister's daughter, Fanny

Kemble Wister, edited his western journals and diaries, taking care to protect his reputation as creator of the lone frontiersman (Bold, *Frontier Club* 110–11). Dolly Grey saw some twenty completed manuscripts through publication and made twenty-three film deals (Kant 401). The labor of women thus helped sustain the respective reputations of Wister and Grey throughout their lives and well after their deaths. For the most part there were no such caretakers of the legacies of the women in this study. The one exception is B. M. Bower, whose daughter and granddaughter both attempted to publish her biography but did not succeed. Unlike Fanny Kemble Wister and Dolly Grey, Bower's daughter Dele Newman Doke did not have the benefit of a large inheritance to support her so that she could focus on the project. By the time she was able to submit a partial manuscript to Little, Brown in 1968, Bower's former book publisher felt that there was insufficient interest in the work.[7] Dele's daughter, Kate Baird Anderson, resumed the project but died before she could complete it (BMB). The fate of Bower's biography is a long-term but direct consequence of conditions in her lifetime (discussed above and in chapter 3), which left her less able than Wister or Grey to withstand the post-1929 collapse of the pulp fiction market.

When scholarship ignores or downplays the role that these material relations play in the production of culture, it reinforces, passively or otherwise, the ideological, material, and institutional obstacles that exclude women from a given cultural field, making the effects of these obstacles appear natural. In an attempt to arrest this cycle, I have embedded my readings of popular westerns by women in the context of the power relations that relegated their contributions to ephemeral or subgeneric status or simply erased them. Nonetheless, it is important not to mistake a lack of power and resources for a lack of importance, influence, or impact upon the genre, although the systemic erasure of women writers from dominant accounts of the genre makes their contributions difficult to track. Perhaps most telling among the invisible contributions that women have made to the western literary tradition is the example of Wallace Stegner's Pulitzer Prize–winning *Angle of Repose* (1971), which, as Mary Ellen Williams Walsh has shown, borrows extensively, sometimes quoting verbatim, from Mary Hallock Foote's autobiography, *A Victorian Gentlewoman in the Far West*, without appropriate citation or acknowledgement. Indeed, the relationship between Stegner and Foote works well as an allegory of the broader relationship between women writers and the western.

Some of the women in this study were clearly successful professional authors who have had an impact on the genre. Indeed, many texts now considered landmarks of the western can be shown to have women-authored precedents. The darkly inclined Caroline Lockhart fashioned western antiheros in *Me—Smith* (1911) and *The Lady Doc* (1912) well before the rise of the "revisionist" westerns of the 1960s. Muriel Newhall attracted pulp readers while reframing the western from the "outside" perspective of a butch woman sheriff—a move that makes Newhall a pioneer of the "postwestern" (Campbell 4). The 1939 film *Destry Rides Again* has been selected for preservation by the Library of Congress's National Film Preservation Board and is known for its unlikely western hero: a milk-drinking, pacifist Sheriff played by Jimmy Stewart. Audiences for this film, however, would have been familiar with similar figures from Bower's books, which regularly toyed with the rugged masculine code that her chief rival, Zane Grey, was known for. One such example is the cowboy Andy Green, the best rider at the Flying U ranch who harbors a secret past as a circus rider. Bower's introduction to Andy in her short story collection *The Happy Family* is worth quoting at length:

> Andy was one of those mild-mannered men whose genius runs to riding horses which object violently to being ridden; one of those lucky fellows who never seems to get his neck broken, however much he may jeopardize it; and, moreover, he was that rare genius, who can make a "pretty" ride where other broncho-fighters resemble nothing so much as a scarecrow in a cyclone. Andy not only could ride—he could ride gracefully. And the reason for that, not many knew: Andy, in the years before he wandered to the range, had danced, in spangled tights, upon the broad rump of a big gray horse which galloped around a saw-dust ring with the regularity of movement that suggested a machine, while a sober-clothed man in the center cracked a whip and yelped commands. Andy had jumped through blazing hoops and over sagging bunting while he rode—and he was just a trifle ashamed of the fact. Also—though it does not particularly matter—he had, later in the performance, gone hurtling around the

big tent dressed in the garb of an ancient Roman and driving four deep-chested bays abreast. As has been explained, he never boasted of his circus experience; though his days in spangled tights probably had much to do with the inimitable grace of him in the saddle. (120–21)

Bower established a tradition of satirical and humanized treatments of the masculine code that continued to resonate after her death in 1940, in films such as *True Grit* (1969) and *Unforgiven* (1991).

Other writers in this study were less interested in cultivating professional identities as western authors than in the political uses of the western. The novels of Emma Ghent Curtis, Francis McElrath, and Mourning Dove address specific, localized debates (woman suffrage in Colorado, the "rustler wars" of Wyoming, Indigenous rights in the Pacific Northwest) and, in the case of Curtis and Mourning Dove at least, were written in the context of the authors' other activist work. Their novels shed important light on the diverse ways in which the genre could be put to rhetorical use, as well as on its influence in shaping perceptions of American history, society, and culture. The fact that three authors working in relative isolation from each other all saw in the popular western a similar vehicle for socially and politically engaged storytelling suggests that their works are not anomalous or accidental but are representative of a rich and flexible discourse. Whether as ambitious and prolific professionals, or as part-time authors who wrote fiction as part of a larger program of social and political engagement, the women in this study represent the undeniably reality that women were active and important participants in the origins of the popular western as we now know it.

Notes

Abbreviations

APS   American Periodicals Series
BMB   B. M. Bower Papers
CHNC Colorado Historic Newspapers Collection
LB   Little, Brown & Company Records
PHN   Proquest Historical Newspapers

Introduction

1. See Kolodny, *Land before Her*; Lee and Lewis, *Women, Women Writers, and the West*; and Stauffer and Rosowski, *Women and Western American Literature*. For a full discussion of early efforts to recover women writers of the West, see Lamont, "Big Books Wanted."

2. For readings of domesticity and marriage in male-authored westerns, see Graulich, "What If Wister Were a Woman?"; Halverson, "Violent Housekeepers"; and Handley, *Marriage, Violence, and the Nation*.

1. Western Violence and the Limits of Sentimental Power

1. U.S. Bureau of the Census, 1860 U.S. Federal Census, Clinton Township, Jackson County, Indiana (Washington DC: National Archives and Records Administration, 1860), roll M653_250, 30; Colorado State Archives, 1885 Colorado State Census, Fremont County (Denver: Colorado State Archives, 1885); U.S. Bureau of the Census, 1900 U.S. Federal Census, Fruitmere, Fremont County, Colorado (Washington DC: National Archives and Records Administration, 1900), roll 123, 9B; "The Funeral of Mrs. Curtis Held Monday Afternoon," *Canon City Canon*, February 28, 1918, 1, History Colorado.

2. *Colorado Transcript*, May 16, 1894, n.p., CHNC; "Colorado Populists Meet," *New York Times*, October, 5 1898, n.p., PHN; "Femininities," *Chicago Daily Tribune*, April 1, 1894, 29, PHN; "The Month's Magazines," *Los Angeles Times*, July 7, 1907, section 6, 14, PHN; "The Funeral of Mrs. Curtis Held Monday Afternoon," *Canon City Canon*, February 28, 1918, 1, CHNC.

3. *Alamosa Journal*, December 11, 1884, 1, CHNC.

4. "Characteristics of the Cowboy," *Castle Rock Journal*, November 24, 1886, 4, CHNC.

5. *Aspen Times*, December 13, 1884, 2, CHNC.

6. *Aspen Times*, May 20, 1882, 1, CHNC.
7. *Aspen Weekly Times*, August 22, 1885, 2, CHNC.
8. *Aspen Weekly Times*, August 22, 1886, 3, CHNC.
9. *Fort Collins Courier*, May 20, 1886, 6, CHNC.
10. *Alamosa Journal*, December 11, 1884, 1, CHNC.
11. "A Mule That Defied Arrest," *Fort Collins Courier*, May 24, 1888, 6, CHNC.
12. "The Late Indian Fight," *Leadville Herald*, August 10, 1884, 4, CHNC.
13. "Tit for Tat," *Delores News*, August 23, 1884, 3, CHNC.
14. *Colorado Transcript*, September 1, 1886, 4, CHNC.
15. *Aspen Weekly Times*, October 15, 1887, 1, CHNC.
16. *Aspen Morning Chronicle*, February 28, 1889, 1, CHNC.
17. *Aspen Daily Chronicle*, May 1, 1889, 1, CHNC.
18. *Avalanche*, July 20, 1889, 1, CHNC.
19. *Aspen Daily Chronicle*, March 5, 1890, 1, CHNC.
20. "Just as He Is," *Carbonate Chronicle*, November 18, 1889, 1, CHNC.
21. *Aspen Daily Chronicle*, September 6, 1890, 2, CHNC.
22. *Aspen Daily Chronicle*, October 9, 1890, 2, CHNC.

2. Domestic Politics and Cattle Rustling

1. See, e.g., "The Trouble in Wyoming," *New York Times*, April 14, 1892, 1, PHN.
2. Histories of the Johnson County War consulted to formulate this sketch of the maverick dispute include Baber and Walker, *Longest Rope*; Flagg, *Review of the Cattle Business*; Gage, *Johnson County War*; Mercer, *Banditti of the Plains*; and Helena Huntington Smith, *War on Powder River*. Much of this history is conflicting, and the exact details of many key incidents are in dispute. I have found Smith's book *War on Powder River* especially helpful for sorting through this material because hers is the only text to supply thorough documentation and more rigorous critical analysis of the social conditions underlining the dispute.
3. On the cultural representation of labor unrest through frontier metaphors in the late nineteenth century, see Slotkin, *Fatal Environment*, 477–98.
4. For a full discussion of court cases and vigilantism, see Smith, *War on Powder River*, 116–68. Suspicion of Barber's involvement is based on an order that he issues shortly before the invasion that effectively prevented the sheriff of Johnson County from summoning the militia to intervene. See Helena Huntington Smith, *War on Powder River*, 193; and Mercer, *Banditti of the Plains*, 40–45.
5. Barber's telegraph did not mention the murders of Champion and Ray or the premeditated invasion, again suggesting that Barber had been involved in the plot and was subsequently protecting his colleagues. The telegraph correspondence between Barber, the president, and the military has been collected in Heald, *Wyoming Flames*.
6. See Baker, "Domestication of Politics," 90–93; and Dubois, *Feminism and Suffrage*, 40–52.
7. The perceived importance of the frontier to American democracy was aptly captured by the journalist Charles Nordoff in 1875: "It is plain that the knowledge that any one may [take up land in the public domain] makes those who do not more contented with their lot, which they thus feel to be one of choice and not of compulsion" (quoted in Wrobel, *End of American Exceptionalism*, 10).

3. Women's Westerns and the Myth of the Pseudonym

1. The classic text on this subject is G. Edward White's *The Eastern Establishment and the Western Experience*.

2. For an example, see Bower's satirical depiction of a popular western author in *The Phantom Herd* (1916).

3. Dele Newman Doke, "Break Your Own Trail" (unpublished biography of B. M. Bower), ca. 1968, 44, BMB. This is one of two unfinished biographies of Bower, both written by descendants. While reliable in certain ways, both biographies are problematic in their representation of Bower's troubled marital history. "Break Your Own Trail" misrepresents and/or obscures details relating to Bower's first two marriages and her relationships with her children by Clayton Bower, which Dele believed Bower would prefer to remain private. Doke abandoned the biography when the unfinished draft she submitted to Little, Brown was rejected. Her daughter, Kate Baird Anderson, revived the biography project in the 1990s and wrote more openly about Bower's marital history; however, Anderson's more graphic account of domestic abuse in Bower's first marriage is largely based on Bower's novel *Lonesome Land*, which she read as an autobiography despite the fact that Bower herself insisted that she was first and foremost a fiction writer. Anderson also takes liberties in her depiction of Bower's motives and state of mind, which are not always documented or corroborated by other sources. I use these biographies as sources for general biographical details that are corroborated by the historical record, other materials in the Bower archive, or conversations with Bower's living descendants. My account of Bower's marriages is based on analysis of all relevant documents in the Bower archive.

4. Kate Baird Anderson, *Skeleton in the Closet*, unpublished biography of B. M. Bower, 1999, 14–15, BMB.

5. Interview with Bill Bower and Reed Doke, April 10, 2008. Bower herself never mentioned the abuse unless she did so in documents that have since been destroyed. However, she depicts domestic violence in her semi-autobiographical novel *Lonesome Land*, discussed in chapter 5. Bower's granddaughter, Kate Baird Anderson, wrote in private correspondence that Clayton had "attacked [Bower] with intent to kill," evidently basing her claim on *Lonesome Land* (letter to Betty Ulrich, August 14, 1997, BMB); however, Clayton's grandson, Bill Bower, believes that this claim is exaggerated and that there was perhaps one isolated event in which Clayton lost his temper (interview with Bower and Doke). Aside from *Lonesome Land*, the earliest recorded evidence that abuse took place is a 1972 letter from Ivan Ross to Dele Doke. Ross was the nephew of Bertrand Sinclair, Bower's second husband, who had known Bower during her first marriage. According to Ross, Sinclair had told him the details of "what happened to your mother and Bower," strongly implying that Clayton had been violent enough with Bertha to send Sinclair "into a cold, towering rage" (Ivan Ross, letter to Dele Doke, November 9, 1972, BMB).

6. Reed Doke, "BMB Timeline," 1, BMB.

7. For an example, see *Authors Magazine*, December 1902.

8. Dele Doke, "Break Your Own Trail," 102, BMB.

9. Bower's publication history is documented in her manuscript record books, BMB.

10. Baird Anderson, *Skeleton in the Closet*, 10, BMB.

11. Dele Doke, "Break Your Own Trail," 94–95, BMB. See also Keller, *Pender Harbour Cowboy*, 29.

12. B. M. Bower (as Bertha May Happ), "The Strike of the Dishpan Brigade," unspecified Minnesota journal, n.d., BMB; Baird Anderson, *Skeleton in the Closet*, 16, BMB.

13. In 1903 Bower published at least two stories as "Bertha Muzzy Bower": "Guileful Peppajee Jim," *Argonaut* (San Francisco), August 24, 1902, 116; and "The Maid and the Money," *Ainslee's*, October 1903.

14. Bower, letter to Little, Brown, February 23, 1912, BMB.
15. Bower, letter to Byron Crane, March 1, 1937, BMB.
16. Bower, letter to Edith Burrows, August 30, 1938, BMB.
17. Bower, letter to Little, Brown, October 21, 1912, BMB; advertisement for "Good Indian" in the *Bookman*, February 1913, 705, APS.
18. Bower, letter to Alfred R. McIntyre, April 12, 1922, LB.
19. Alfred R. McIntyre, letter to Bower, April 18, 1922, LB.
20. Bower, letter to Alfred R. McIntyre, April 27, 1922, LB
21. Bower, letter, to Alfred R. McIntyre, April 27, 1922, LB.
22. Edith Anderson, letter to Little, Brown, January 10, 1922, LB.
23. Little, Brown [Alfred R. McIntyre], letter to Bower, May 31, 1922, LB.
24. Little, Brown, letter to Curtis Brown, June 1, 1920, LB.
25. Little, Brown, letter to Bower, February 3, 1921, LB.
26. Bower, letter to Edith Burrows, August 30, 1938, BMB.
27. All biographical information about Lockhart is based on John Clayton's excellent biography.

4. Why Mourning Dove Wrote a Western

1. Although the first draft of *Cogewea* was completed by 1914, numerous delays, including a long editorial process, difficulties securing a publisher, and interruptions in American book production during World War I, prevented its publication until 1927. See Fisher, "Introduction," xiv–xv.

2. For a range of essays on issues of representation in Native American texts, see Bataille, *Native American Representations*. For a thorough history and analysis of the "editorialized" Mourning Dove, see Brown, "Looking through the Glass Darkly." For an excellent analysis of the production of *Cogewea*, see. Bernardin, "Mixed Messages," 487–95. In contrast to criticism of McWhorter as an overly dominant editor, Godfrey, in "Mourning Dove's Textual Frontier," sees his contribution in a positive light, suggesting that he and Mourning Dove contribute different but equally important, perspectives and skills to the text.

3. See Allen, *Blood Narrative*, 127–59; Lisa Brooks, "The Constitution of the White Earth Nation"; Justice, *Our Fire Survives the Storm*; Teuton, *Deep Waters*.

4. Shortly after *Cogewea* first appeared in print, an Indian agent accused McWhorter of writing the entire novel (Fisher xvi). Since then, its status as a Native American text has been debated. Positions on this question have ranged from Elizabeth Ammons's contention that Mourning Dove cannot be considered the author of *Cogewea* to Alanna Kathleen Brown's use of archival sources to recover Mourning Dove's voice. See Ammons, *Conflicting Stories*, 138; and Brown, "Mourning Dove's Voice in *Cogewea*." For additional responses to debates about the authenticity of *Cogewea*, see Gunn Allen, *The Sacred Hoop*, 85; and Larson, *American Indian Fiction*, 173–80.

5. For a history of ethnographic methods in nineteenth- and early twentieth-century America, see Helen Carr, *Inventing the American Primitive*, 197–256.

6. On Boas's ethnographic method, see Murray, *Forked Tongues*, 105–8. For a broader discussion of ethnographic approaches to representing performance, see Clements, *Native American Verbal Art*, 31–52. For a comparative semiotic analysis of orality and literacy, see Ong, *Orality and Literacy*. For an application of Ong's theories to the study of Native American verbal art, see Clements, *Native American Verbal Art*, 6–7. On the material practice of storytelling in Native American culture, see Bruchac, *Roots of Survival*. For discussions of how contempo-

rary Native American writing is informed by oral practice, see Blaeser, *Gerald Vizenor*, 18–37. See also Brill de Ramírez, *Contemporary American Indian Literatures*.

7. Such continuity is demonstrated in Fiske's *Television Culture*. Arguing that television culture is "a popular culture in which orality plays a central role, "Fiske rejects identifications between literacy and technology and between orality and "the primitive" (105).

8. "Yellowback" was a term that, in the mid- to late nineteenth-century United States and Britain, referred to mass-produced novels and magazines. The term may have originated from the yellowish color of cheap paper used to make these books and/or the common use of the attention-getting color yellow by publishers of sensation fiction. See "Yellow-back," *Oxford English Dictionary Online*, www.oed.com, accessed July 22, 2014.

9. *Adventure Magazine's* "Camp-fire" section, in which were printed letters from readers and authors, is mentioned in Engen, *Writer of the Plains*, 48–52. The campfire motif is an especially illustrative example of how "letters" sections mimicked oral storytelling situations. The following quotation from a letter to *Popular* is exemplary of the kinds of conversations that this popular fiction publisher encouraged in its letters section: "The winter is on here now and the work consists of riding fence and 'riding a fork handle,' so your magazine is eagerly looked forward to." The letter is signed not by an individual reader, but by a collective readership consisting of Calvin M. West, Alex Kimbrough, and Tom Lawdon, who identify themselves as belonging to the 7-L Ranch in Chinook, Montana. Readers of popular magazines thus imagined their reading as a communal activity reminiscent of aural reception ("Letter to the Editor," *Popular Magazine*, April 1, 1910).

10. For a full-length discussion of methodological approaches to recording verbal art, see Clements, *Native American Verbal Art*.

11. On Frances Densmore's ethnographic approach, see Helen Carr, *Inventing the American Primitive*, 186–97.

12. According to Richard White, Native American land holdings were reduced by approximately 50 percent between 1881 and 1900 (*It's Your Misfortune and None of My Own*, 115).

13. See Bernardin, "Mixed Messages," 487–95; and Brown, "The Evolution," 125–80, and "Looking through the Glass Darkly."

14. In this respect, my interpretation of the ending is slightly different from that of Susan K. Bernardin, who, in her brilliant reading of discourses in *Cogewea*, argues that the marriage "gestures to the unhealed rifts between Native Americans and Euro-America" rather than the "renewed social order" signified by marriages in conventional westerns (503). I find that, when read as a response to *The Brand*, the ending of *Cogewea* generates a more optimistic vision of the future of Native American people than *The Brand's* assimilating marriage.

5. Cattle Branding and the Traffic in Women

1. One "behind-the-scenes" publicity photo, taken in 1893, depicts Oakley in her tent, seated in a rocking chair, reading. Her modest Victorian dress and well-appointed living quarters portray her as a model Victorian American lady (Savage, *Cowgirls*, 46).

2. Beginning in 1929, women were banned from competing in the most dangerous events and redirected to safer sports, such as barrel racing. For a history of the rodeo cowgirl, see Savage, *Cowgirls*.

3. Scholarship about women's western fiction has emphasized authors who write against popular conventions rather than from within them. An early and classic example is Annette Kolodny's *The Land before Her*. Susan Rosowski, in *Birthing a Nation*, has emphasized the use of

birth metaphors as opposed to violence in women's writing about the West. See also my discussion of Jane Tompkins in the introduction.

4. Wyoming Territory granted women the vote in 1869, taking advantage of the more relaxed laws regulating territories. By 1911, Wyoming, Idaho, Utah, Colorado, Washington, and California were suffrage states.

5. This caption accompanies an illustration of Liberty striding eastward across a map of the United States. Her torch lights up the suffrage states, while the remaining states are depicted in darkness; however, Liberty's purposeful stride implies that it is only a matter of time before enlightenment reaches the East as well.

6. See chapter 2.

7. According to my 1912 edition, published by Little, Brown, the novel had been reprinted at least three times.

8. "The Literary Spotlight," *Chicago Tribune*, June 13, 1948, part 4, 4. Published accounts of Burt's biography are sketchy. My brief biography is based on that provided by the American Heritage Center's inventory of the Burt Family Papers. While I have not been able to find precise sales figures for *The Branding Iron*, there is evidence that Houghton Mifflin invested substantially in its promotion and that it sold exceptionally well. Their records show several mail outs to "special buyers," bookstores, and "the trade," and promotional material for Burt's subsequent books refers to the success of *The Branding Iron* (Houghton Mifflin Company Records). The film version of *The Branding Iron* (Reginald Barker, director) was released by Goldwyn in 1920.

9. For Turner, the transformational effects of the American frontier were limited to Europeans: "Our early history is the study of European germs developing in an American environment. . . . Little by little [the colonist] transforms the wilderness, but the outcome is not the old Europe, not simply the development of Germanic germs . . . the fact is, that here is a new product that is American" (2). In the first volume of *Winning of the West*, Roosevelt claimed that Americans were the descendants of ancient "Germanic peoples," who were able to resist absorption into the Roman Empire and subsequently "went forth from their marshy forests conquering and to conquer. . . . [With] the discovery of America, a new period of even vaster race expansion began" (18–21). For a discussion of Owen Wister's construction of an indigenous white identity in *The Virginian* (1902), see Tuttle, "Indigenous Whiteness."

10. This passage from Thomas Jefferson's *Writings* invokes both of these ubiquitous stereotypes: "[American Indian] women are submitted to unjust drudgery. This I believe is the case with every barbarous people. With such, force is law. The stronger sex imposes the weaker. It is civilization alone which replaces women in the enjoyment of their natural equality. That first teaches us to subdue selfish passions and to respect those rights in others which we value in ourselves" (quoted in Pearce, *The Savages of America*, 93).

11. Charlotte Perkins Gilman Society, "About Charlotte Perkins Gilman."

12. On the semiotics of branding, see Allmendinger, *The Cowboy*, 15–47. Allmendinger does not focus on how female sexuality figures in the semiotics of branding but does lay the groundwork for thinking about branding as a significant trope in western American literature.

6. The Masculinization of the Western

1. On general fiction pulps, see Mott, *History of American Magazines*, 114; On "libraries," see Mott, *History of American Magazines*, 118; "New Buffalo Bill Weekly," Stanford University; F. Carr, "Bertha M. Clay."

2. Stephensen-Payne, "Magazine Cover Images." Also see the August 16, 1904, cover of the *Blue Book* in The Pulp Magazines Project.

3. See BMB.
4. *Western Story* 30, no. 4 (November 25, 1922).
5. *Western Story* 23, no. 2–24, no. 3 (January–March 1922).
6. *Western Story* 27, no. 6 (August 5, 1922): 45–60.
7. *Western Story* 28, no. 5 (September 9, 1922): 58–62.
8. *Western Story* 28, no. 2 (August 19, 1922): 88; 19, no. 1 (July 30, 1921): 54; 28, no. 3 (August 26, 1922): 28; 18, no. 5 (16 July 1921): 100.
9. See tables of contents and manuscript vouchers for *Romantic Range* (Street & Smith Records).
10. See manuscript vouchers for *Romantic Range* (Street & Smith Records).
11. Oklahoma State University Library, "Vingie E. Roe"; *Wikipedia*, "Lela Cole Kitson"; *Spokesman-Review*, "Republic Woman Writer Scores."
12. *Western Story* 26, no. 5 (June 17, 1922): 29.
13. *Western Story* 26, no. 6 (June 24 1922): 45–54.
14. See, e.g., *Love Story Magazine* 105, no. 5 (March 10, 1934): advertising section, in The Pulp Magazines Project.
15. *Western Story* 28, no. 2 (August 19, 1922): 131; 28, no. 5 (September 9, 1922): 131.
16. *Western Story* 28, no. 3 (August 26, 1922): 133.
17. *Western Story* 28, no. 3 (August 26, 1922): 133.
18. *Western Story* 28, no. 3 (August 26, 1922): 133.
19. *Western Story* 18, no. 4 (July 9, 1921): 133.
20. *Western Story* 28, no. 6 (September 16, 1922): 132.
21. *Western Story* 28, no. 6 (September 16, 1922): 128.
22. *Western Story* 28, no. 1 (August 12, 1922): 129.
23. *Western Story* 27, no. 6 (August 5, 1922): 138.
24. *Western Story* 28, no. 3 (August 26, 1922): 138.
25. *Western Story* 28, no. 1 (August 12, 1922): 135.
26. *Western Story* 18, no. 3 (July 2, 1921): 139.
27. *Western Story* 18, no. 6 (September 16, 1922): 137.
28. *Western Story* 18, no. 6 (September 16, 1922): 137.
29. *Western Story* 28, no. 1 (August 12, 1922): 137; 28, no. 2 (August 19, 1922): 137.
30. *Western Story* 18, no. 6 (September 16, 1922): 138.
31. *Western Story* 28, no. 1 (August 12, 1922): 135–36.
32. *Western Story* 28, no. 1 (August 12, 1922); 138.
33. *Western Story* 28, no. 6 (September 16, 1922): 138.
34. *Western Story* 29, no. 6 (October 28, 1922): 138.
35. *Western Story* 27, no. 4 (July 22, 1922): 139.
36. *Western Story* 29, no. 3 (October 7, 1922): 139.
37. *Western Story* 27, no. 4 (July 22, 1922): 136.
38. *Western Story* 19, no. 2 (August 6, 1921): 137.
39. *Western Story* 28, no. 3 (August 26, 1922): 139.
40. *Western Story* 18, no. 4 (July 9, 1921): 138.
41. *Western Story* 18, no. 6 (September 16, 1922): 138.
42. *Western Story* 19, no. 2 (August 6, 1921): 136.
43. *Western Story* 28, no. 1 (August 12, 1922): 136.
44. *Western Story* 28, no. 2 (August 19, 1922): 138.
45. *Western Story* 18, no. 4 (July 9, 1921): 138.

46. *Western Story* 19, no. 1 (July 30, 1921): 141.
47. *Western Story* 28, no. 2 (August 19, 1922): 138.
48. *Western Story* 19, no. 2 (August 6, 1921): 136.
49. *Western Story* 28, no. 1 (August 12, 1922): 137.
50. *Romantic Range* 1, no. 1, appeared in November 1935.
51. *Romantic Range* manuscript purchase cards, 1935–38, Street & Smith Records. On the denigration of romances see Bacon, *Love Story Writer*, 5–6.
52. For example, see The Fictionmags Index at Galactic Central.
53. B. M. Bower, letter to Edith Burrows, August 30, 1938, BMB.
54. *Romantic Range* 5, no. 3 (January 1938).
55. *Romantic Range* 15, no. 6 (April 1943).
56. *Romantic Range* 1, no. 2 (December 1935): 33–44.
57. *Romantic Range* 1, no. 6 (April 1936): 73–82.
58. Street & Smith Manuscript Purchase Cards, 1935–38 (Street & Smith Records). I have used manuscript purchase cards, which were used to keep track of payments to authors, to identify the authors behind certain pseudonyms.
59. *Romantic Range* 1, no. 5 (March 1936): 93–99.
60. *Romantic Range* 1, no. 4 (February 1936): 8–30.
61. Street & Smith Manuscript Purchase Cards, 1935–38 (Street & Smith Records).
62. *Romantic Range* 1, no. 6 (April 1936): 33–40.
63. *Romantic Range* 1, no. 2 (December 1935): 74–83.
64. *Romantic Range* 1, no. 2 (December 1935): 33–44.
65. *Romantic Range* 1, no. 1 (November 1935): 114–26.
66. *Romantic Range* 1, no. 6 (March 1935): 70–92.
67. *Romantic Range* 1, no. 1 (November 1935): 29–40.
68. *Romantic Range* 1, no. 5 (March 1936): 12–30.
69. *Romantic Range* 1, no. 2 (December 1935): 77.
70. *Romantic Range* 1, no. 1 (November 1935): 64–100.
71. *Romantic Range* 1, no. 1 (November 1935): 100–113.
72. *Romantic Range* 1, no. 2 (December 1935): 75–83.
73. *Romantic Range* 1, no. 4 (February 1936): 8–30.
74. *Romantic Range* 1, no. 5 (March 1936): 101–17.
75. For example, three Newhall stories appeared in the March 1936 issue (1, no. 3) under the pseudonyms Mona Farnsworth, Edna T. Green, and Regina Bailey. See tables of contents for *Romantic Range* (Street & Smith Records).
76. For example, see Muriel Newhall (as Mona Farnsworth), "Silver Mine Love," *Romantic Range* 1, no. 4 (February 1936): 58–66.
77. *Romantic Range* 1, no. 5 (March 1936): 36–47.
78. *Romantic Range* 1, no. 5 (March 1936): 101–17.
79. "Salt Beef," *Romantic Range* 9, no. 3 (January 1940): 32.
80. "Look Who's Here," *Romantic Range* 8, no. 6 (October 1939): 72.
81. *Romantic Range* 8, no. 5 (September 1939): 89–94.
82. *Romantic Range* 8, no. 6 (October 1939): 64–72.
83. "You Never Can Tell," *Romantic Range* 8, no. 5 (September 1939): 115.
84. *Romantic Range* 13, no. 6 (April 1942): 43.
85. *Romantic Range* 14, no. 6 (October 1942): 117–26.
86. *Romantic Range* 23, no. 1 (November 1946): 106–21.

87. This analysis is based on analysis of randomly selected issues, one per year, from the twelve-year print run of the magazine.

88. *Romantic Range* 1, no. 5 (March 1936): 93–99.

89. *Western Story* 14, no. 4 (April 16, 1921): 119.

90. *Western Story* 14, no. 4 (April 16, 1921): 119–27.

91. *Western Story* 19, no. 5 (August 27, 1921): 118–29.

92. *Oxford English Dictionary*, s.v. "romance," www.oed.com, accessed July 8, 2014.

93. Examples include Estleman, *The Wister Trace*; and Bredahl, *New Ground*. For a full discussion of western canon formation, see Lamont, "Big Books Wanted."

Conclusion

1. On the connections among Cooper, Child, and Sedgwick, see Opfermann, "Lydia Marie Child."

2. "The Lounger," *Critic*, July 1902, 3, APS.

3. Funk & Wagnalls, "Spring Publications" (advertisement), *Publishers' Weekly*, March 15, 1902, 760.

4. Funk & Wagnalls, "The Boer Fight for Freedom" (advertisement), *Publishers' Weekly*, May 24, 1902, 1189; "Daniel Everton" (advertisement), *Publishers' Weekly*, May 3, 1902, 1067.

5. Funk & Wagnalls, "Novels for the Vacation Outfit" (advertisement), *Publishers' Weekly*, May 31, 1902, 1285.

6. See chapters 1 and 3.

7. Molly Batchelder, letter to Dele Newman Doke, January 30, 1968, BMB.

Bibliography

Archival Collections, Digital Archives, and Digital Indexes

American Heritage Center
  Burt Family Papers. http://rmoa.unm.edu/docviewer.php?docId=wyu-ah07570.xml.
American Periodicals Series Online
American Women's Dime Novel Project. http://chnm.gmu.edu/dimenovels.
Colorado State Library and History Colorado (Denver)
  Colorado Historic Newspapers Collection. Colorado newspapers from 1880 to 1890. www.coloradohistoricnewspapers.org.
Galactic Central (magazine database). www.philsp.com.
  The Fictionmags Index. Edited by William G. Contento. www.philsp.com/homeville/fmi/0start.htm.
Houghton Library, Harvard University
  Houghton Mifflin Company Records. MS Am 2030–2030.4.
  Little, Brown & Company Records. 1905–1997, 97M-45.
Oklahoma State University Library
  Vingie E. Roe Collection
Proquest Historical Newspapers. Historical articles from major newspapers including the *New York Times*, the *Chicago Daily Tribune*, and the *Los Angeles Times*. http://www.proquest.com/products-services/pq-hist-news.html.
The Pulp Magazines Project. Sponsored by Patrick Scott Belk. 2010–2013. www.pulpmags.org.
Stanford University Libraries
  Dime Novels and Penny Dreadfuls Collection. http://web.stanford.edu/dept/SUL/library/prod/depts/dp/pennies/home.html.
Syracuse University Libraries
  Street & Smith Records. Special Collections Research Center.
University of Oklahoma Library

B. M. Bower Papers. The papers at the University of Oklahoma are copies of the originals, which were in the private collection of Reed Doke, Fayetteville, Arkansas, but are now housed at History Colorado, Denver (the Colorado historical society).

Published Works, Films, Online Sources, and Interviews

Allen, Chadwick. *Blood Narrative: Indigenous Identity in American Indian and Maori Literary and Activist Texts.* Durham NC: Duke University Press, 2002. Print.

Allmendinger, Blake. *The Cowboy: Representations of Labor in an American Work Culture.* New York: Oxford University Press, 1992. Print.

Ammons, Elizabeth. *Conflicting Stories: American Women Writers at the Turn into the Twentieth Century.* New York: Oxford University Press, 1991. Print.

Andolsen, Barbara Hilkert. *"Daughters of Jefferson, Daughters of Bootblacks": Racism and American Feminism.* Macon GA: Mercer University Press, 1986. Print.

Ashley, Mike. "The Golden Age of Pulp Fiction." Accessed at The Pulp Magazines Project, November 28, 2013. Web.

Babb, Valerie Melissa. *Whiteness Visible: The Meaning of Whiteness in American Literature and Culture.* New York: New York University Press, 1998. Print.

Baber, D. F., and William Walker. *The Longest Rope: The Truth about the Johnson County Cattle War.* Caldwell ID: Caxton, 1940. Print.

Bacon, Daisy. *Love Story Writer.* New York: Hermitage House, 1954. Print.

Baker, Paula. "The Domestication of Politics: Women and American Political Society, 1780–1920." In *Unequal Sisters: A Multi-cultural Reader in U.S. Women's History*, edited by Vicki Ruiz and Ellen Carol DuBois, 85–110. New York: Routledge, 1994. Print.

Barker, Reginald, director. *The Branding Iron.* With performances by Barbara Castleton, James Kirkwood, and Russell Simpson. Goldwyn Studio, 1920. Film.

Barnett, Louise K. *The Ignoble Savage: American Literary Racism, 1790–1890.* Westport CT: Greenwood, 1975. Print.

Bataille, Gretchen M., ed. *Native American Representations: First Encounters, Distorted Images, and Literary Appropriations.* Lincoln: University of Nebraska Press, 2001. Print.

Baym, Nina. *Women Writers of the American West, 1833–1927.* Urbana: University of Illinois Press, 2011. Print.

Bernardin, Susan K. "Mixed Messages: Authority and Authorship in Mourning Dove's *Cogewea, the Half-Blood*: A Depiction of the Great Montana Cattle Range." In *American Literature: A Journal of Literary History, Criticism, and Bibliography* 67, no. 3 (1995): 487–509. Print.

Blaeser, Kimberly M. *Gerald Vizenor: Writing in the Oral Tradition.* Norman: University of Oklahoma Press, 1996. Print.

Bold, Christine. *The Frontier Club: Popular Westerns and Cultural Power, 1880–1924.* New York: Oxford University Press, 2013. Print.

———. "Malaeska's Revenge; or, The Dime Novel Tradition in Popular Fiction." In *Wanted Dead or Alive: The American West in Popular Culture*, edited by Richard Aquila, 21–42. Urbana: University of Illinois Press, 1996. Print.

———. *Selling the Wild West: Popular Western Fiction, 1860–1960.* Bloomington: Indiana University Press, 1987. Print.

Bourdieu, Pierre. *The Field of Cultural Production: Essays on Art and Literature.* Translated by Randall Johnson. New York: Columbia University Press, 1993. Print.

Bower, B. M. "The Backsliding of Sister Stewart." *Authors Magazine*, February 1902, n.p. Print.
———. *Chip, of the Flying U.* New York: G. W. Dillingham, 1904; reprint, Lincoln: University of Nebraska Press, 1995. Print.
———. *Cow Country.* Boston: Little, Brown, 1921. Print.
———. *Good Indian.* Boston: Little, Brown, 1912. Print.
———. *The Happy Family.* New York: G. W. Dillingham, 1907; reprint, Lincoln: University of Nebraska Press, 1996. Print.
———. *Lonesome Land.* Boston: Little, Brown, 1912; reprint, Lincoln: University of Nebraska Press, 1997. Print.
———. "The Maid and the Money." *Ainslee's,* October 1903, 145–49. Print.
———. *The Phantom Herd.* Boston: Little, Brown, 1916. Print.
Bower, Bill, and Reed Doke. Interview with the author. April 10, 2008.
Boyer, Paul S. "Gilded-Age Consensus, Repressive Campaigns, and Gradual Liberalization: The Shifting Rhythms of Book Censorship." In *Print in Motion: The Expansion of Publishing and Reading in the United States, 1880–1940,* edited by Carl F. Kaestle and Janice A. Radway, 276–98. Chapel Hill: University of North Carolina Press, 2008. Print.
Bredahl, Carl. *New Ground: Western American Narrative and the Literary Canon.* Chapel Hill: University of North Carolina Press, 1989. Print.
Brill de Ramirez, Susan Berry. *Contemporary American Indian Literatures and the Oral Tradition.* Tucson: University of Arizona Press, 1999. Print.
Brisbin, James S. *The Beef Bonanza; Or, How to Get Rich on the Plains.* Philadelphia: Lippincott, 1881. Print.
Broderick, Therese. *The Brand: A Tale of the Flathead Reservation.* Seattle: Alice Harriman, 1909. Print.
Brooks, Joanna. "Sacajawea, Meet *Cogewea*: A Red Progressive Revision of Frontier Romance." In *Lewis and Clark: Legacies, Memories, and New Perspectives,* edited by Kris Fresonke and Mark Spence, 184–97. Berkeley: University of California Press, 2004. Print.
Brooks, Lisa. "The Constitution of the White Earth Nation: A New Innovation in a Longstanding Indigenous Literary Tradition." *Studies in American Indian Literatures* 23, no. 4 (2011): 48–76. Web.
Brown, Alanna Kathleen. "The Evolution of Mourning Dove's Coyote Stories." *Studies in American Indian Literatures* 4, no. 2–3 (1992): 161–80. Print.
———. "Legacy Profile: Mourning Dove (Humishuma) (1880–1936)." *Legacy: A Journal of American Women Writers* 6, no. 1 (1989): 51–58. Print.
———. "Looking through the Glass Darkly: The Editorialized Mourning Dove." In *New Voices in Native American Literary Criticism,* edited by Arnold Krupat, 274–90. Washington DC: Smithsonian Institution Press, 1993. Print.
———. "Mourning Dove (Humishuma)." In *American Women Prose Writers, 1870–1920,* edited by Sharon M. Harris, Heidi L. M. Jacobs, and Jennifer Putzi, 284–93. Detroit: Gale, 2000. Print.
———. "Mourning Dove's Voice in *Cogewea.*" *Wicazo Sa Review* 4, no. 2 (1989): 2–15. Print.
Bruchac, Joseph. *Roots of Survival: Native American Storytelling and the Sacred.* Golden CO: Fulcrum, 1996. Print.
Burt, Katharine Newlin. *The Branding Iron.* Boston: Houghton Mifflin, 1919. Print.
Calder, Alison. "Getting the Real Story: Implications of the Demand for Authenticity in Writings from the Canadian West." In *True West: Authenticity and the American West,* edited

by William R. Handley and Nathaniel Lewis, 56–71. Lincoln: University of Nebraska Press, 2004. Print.

Cameron, James, director. *The Terminator.* Orion, 1984. Film.

Campbell, Neil. *Post-westerns: Cinema, Region, West.* Lincoln: University of Nebraska Press, 2013. Print.

Carr, Felicia L. "Bertha M. Clay." Accessed at American Women's Dime Novel Project, n.d., Web. December 4, 2013.

Carr, Helen. *Inventing the American Primitive: Politics, Gender, and the Representation of Native American Literary Traditions, 1789–1936.* New York: New York University Press, 1996. Print.

Catt, Carrie Chapman. "A True Story." *Woman's Journal* 4, no. 11 (1891): 304. Print.

Catt, Carrie Chapman, and Nettie Rogers Shuler, eds. *Woman Suffrage and Politics: The Inner Story of the Suffrage Movement.* New York: Charles Scribner's Sons, 1923; reprint, Seattle: University of Washington Press, 1969. Print.

Cawelti, John G. *Six-Gun Mystique Sequel.* Bowling Green OH: Bowling Green State University Popular Press, 1999. Print.

Chapman, Mary, and Angela Mills. "Introduction." In *Treacherous Texts: U.S. Suffrage Literature, 1846–1946,* edited by Mary Chapman and Angela Mills, 1–7. New Brunswick NJ: Rutgers University Press, 2011. Print.

———. "Introduction to Part 1." In *Treacherous Texts: U.S. Suffrage Literature, 1846–1946,* edited by Mary Chapman and Angela Mills, 10–17. New Brunswick NJ: Rutgers University Press, 2011. Print.

Charlotte Perkins Gilman Society. "About Charlotte Perkins Gilman." n.d. Web. https://sites.google.com/site/gilmansociety//about-charlotte-perkins-gilman, accessed Mar 21, 2015.

Child, Lydia Maria. *Hobomok* (originally published 1824). In *Hobomok and Other Writings on Indians,* edited by Carolyn L. Karcher, 1–152. New Brunswick NJ: Rutgers University Press, 1986. Print.

Clayton, John. *The Cowboy Girl: The Life of Caroline Lockhart.* Lincoln: University of Nebraska Press, 2007. Print.

Clements, William. *Native American Verbal Art: Texts and Contexts.* Tucson: University of Arizona Press, 1996. Print.

Clifford, James. "On the Ethnographic Allegory." In *Writing Culture: The Poetics and Politics of Ethnography,* edited by James Clifford and George E. Marcus, 98–121. Berkeley: University of California Press, 1986. Print.

Clifford, James, and George E. Marcus, eds. *Writing Culture: The Poetics and Politics of Ethnography.* Berkeley: University of California Press, 1986. Print.

Cooper, James Fenimore. *The Last of the Mohicans.* Philadelphia: H. C. Cary & I. Lea, 1826; reprint, New York: Penguin, 2014. Print.

Cott, Nancy F. "Giving Character to Our Whole Civil Polity: Marriage and the Public Order in the Late Nineteenth Century." In *U.S. History as Women's History: New Feminist Essays,* edited by Linda K. Kerber, Alice Kressle-Harris, and Katheryn Kish Sklar, 107–21. Chapel Hill: University of North Carolina Press, 1995. Print.

Cuddy, Lois A., and Claire M. Roche, eds. *Evolution and Eugenics in American Literature and Culture, 1880–1940: Essays on Ideological Conflict and Complicity.* Lewisburg PA: Bucknell University Press, 2003. Print.

———. "Introduction." In *Evolution and Eugenics in American Literature and Culture, 1880–1940: Essays on Ideological Conflict and Complicity,* edited by Lois A. Cuddy and Claire M. Roche, 9–53. Lewisburg PA: Bucknell University Press, 2003. Print.

Curtis, Emma Ghent. *The Administratrix*. New York: John B. Alden, 1889. Print.
———. *The Fate of a Fool*. New York: John A. Berry, 1888. Print.
———. "Woman on the Ranch." *Farmer's Wife* 1, no. 2 (August 1891): 1. Print.
Davis, Robert Murray. *Playing Cowboys: Low Culture and High Art in the Western*. Norman: University of Oklahoma Press, 1992. Print.
Dean, Janet. "Searching for the New Western Literary Criticism." *Modern Fiction Studies* 46, no. 4 (Winter 2000): 949–58. Print.
Deloria, Philip. *Playing Indian*. New Haven CT: Yale University Press, 1998. Print.
Denning, Michael. *Mechanic Accents: Dime Novels and Working Class Culture in America*. London: Verso, 1998. Print.
Diggs, Annie L. "The Women in the Alliance Movement." *Arena* 6 (July 1892): 161–79.
Dinan, John. *The Pulp Western: A Popular History of the Western Fiction Magazine in America*. San Bernardino CA: Borgo, 1983. Print.
Dubois, Ellen Carol. *Feminism and Suffrage: The Emergence of an Independent Women's Movement in America, 1848–1869*. Ithaca NY: Cornell University Press, 1978. Print.
———. *Woman Suffrage and Women's Rights*. New York: New York University Press, 1998. Print.
Dymond, Justine. "Modernism(s) Inside Out: History, Space, and Modern American Indian Subjectivity in *Cogewea, the Half-Blood*." In *Geomodernisms: Race, Modernism, Modernity*, edited by Laura Doyle and Laura Winkiel, 297–312. Bloomington: Indiana University Press, 2005. Print.
Eagleton, Mary. Introduction to *Feminist Literary Theory: A Reader*. 3rd ed., edited by Mary Eagleton, 1–8. Malden MA: Wiley-Blackwell, 2011. Print.
Edwards, Rebecca. *Angels in the Machinery: Gender in American Party Politics from the Civil War to the Progressive Era*. New York: Oxford University Press, 1997. Print.
Engen, Orrin A. *Writer of the Plains: A Biography of B. M. Bower*. Culver City CA: Pontine, 1973. Print.
Estleman, Loren D. *The Wister Trace: Classic Novels of the American Frontier*. Ottawa IL: Jameson, 1987. Print.
Etulain, Richard W., and Michael T. Marsden. *Popular Western: Essays toward a Definition*. Bowling Green OH: Bowling Green University Popular Press, 1974. Print.
Fetterley, Judith, and Marjorie Pryse. *Writing out of Place: Regionalism, Women, and American Literary Culture*. Urbana: University of Illinois Press, 2003. Print.
Finnegan, Ruth. *Literacy and Orality*. Oxford: Blackwell, 1988. Print.
Fisher, Dexter. "Introduction." In *Cogewea, the Half-Blood* by Mourning Dove, v–xxix. Lincoln: University of Nebraska Press, 1981. Print.
Fiske, John. *Television Culture*. London: Methuen, 1987. Print.
Flagg, Oscar H. *A Review of the Cattle Business in Johnson County, Wyoming, since 1892 and the Causes that Led to the Recent Invasion*. New York: Arno, 1969. Originally published in 1892 as a series of articles in the *Buffalo (Wyoming) Bulletin*, 1892. Print.
Frantz, Joe B., and Julian E. Choate. *The American Cowboy: The Myth and the Reality*. Norman: University of Oklahoma Press, 1955. Print.
French, Warren. "The Cowboy in the Dime Novel." *University of Texas Studies in English* 30 (1951): 219–34. Print.
Gage, Jack R. *The Johnson County War*. Cheyenne WY: Flintlock, 1967. Print.
Georgi-Findlay, Brigitte. *Frontiers of Women's Writing: Women's Narratives and the Rhetoric of Westward Expansion*. Tucson: University of Arizona Press, 1996. Print.
Gilman, Charlotte Perkins. *The Crux*. New York: Charlton, 1911; reprint, Durham NC: Duke University Press, 2003. Print.

———. *Women and Economics.* Boston: Small, Maynard, 1898; reprint, New York: Source Book, 1970. Print.

Glazer, Penina Migdal, and Miriam Slater. *Unequal Colleagues: The Entrance of Women into the Professions, 1890–1940.* New Brunswick NJ: Rutgers University Press, 1987. Print.

Godfrey, Laura G. "Mourning Dove's Textual Frontier." *Arizona Quarterly: A Journal of American Literature, Culture, and Theory* 62, no. 1 (2006): 65–83. Print.

Goldman, Emma. "The Traffic in Women." In *Red Emma Speaks: Selected Writings and Speeches*, edited by Alix Kates Shulman, 143–57. New York: Random House, 1972. Print.

Gordon, Ann D., and Bettye Collier-Thomas. *African American Women and the Vote, 1837–1965.* Amherst: University of Massachusetts Press, 1997. Print.

Graulich, Melody. "What If Wister Were a Woman?" In *Reading "The Virginian" in the New West*, edited by Melody Graulich and Stephen Tatum, 198–212. Lincoln: University of Nebraska Press, 2003. Print.

Graulich, Melody, and Stephen Tatum, eds. *Reading "The Virginian" in the New West.* Lincoln: University of Nebraska Press, 2003. Print.

Gunn Allen, Paula. *The Sacred Hoop: Recovering the Feminine in American Indian Tradition.* 2nd ed. Boston: Beacon, 1986. Print.

Halverson, Cathryn. "Violent Housekeepers: Rewriting Domesticity." *Riders of the Purple Sage: Rocky Mountain Review of Language and Literature* 56, no. 1 (2002): 37–53. Print.

Hammill, Faye. *Women, Celebrity, and Literary Culture between the Wars.* Austin: University of Texas Press, 2007. Print.

Handley, William R. *Marriage, Violence, and the Nation in the American Literary West.* New York: Cambridge University Press, 2002. Print.

Handley, William R., and Nathaniel Lewis, eds. *True West: Authenticity and the American West.* Lincoln: University of Nebraska Press, 2004. Print.

———. "Introduction." In *True West: Authenticity and the American West*, edited by William R. Handley and Nathaniel Lewis, 1–19. Lincoln: University of Nebraska Press, 2004. Print.

Heald, George D., ed. *Wyoming Flames of '92: Official Communications during the Johnson County Cattle War.* Oshoto WY: Self-published, 1972. Print.

Hersey, Harold Brainerd. *Pulpwood Editor: The Fabulous World of the Thriller Magazines Revealed by a Veteran Editor and Publisher.* New York: Frederick A. Stokes, 1937; reprint, Westport CT: Greenwood, 1974. Print.

Hewitt, Nancy A. "Beyond the Search for Sisterhood: American Women's History in the 1980s." In *Unequal Sisters: A Multi-cultural Reader in U.S. Women's History*, edited by Vicki Ruiz and Ellen Carol Dubois, 1–19. New York: Routledge, 1994. Print.

Hofman, Charles, Ed. *Frances Densmore and American Indian Music.* New York: Museum of the American Indian, Heye Foundation, 1968. Print.

Hubbard, Alice. "Head, Heart, and Hand." *Fra: A Journal of Affirmation* 5, no. 4 (July 1910): 127. Print.

Hulan, Renee, ed. *Native North America.* Toronto: ECW, 1999. Print.

Jackson, Brenda K. *Domesticating the West: The Re-creation of the Nineteenth-Century American Middle Class.* Lincoln: University of Nebraska Press, 2005. Print.

Jaskoski, Helen, ed. *Early Native American Writing: New Critical Essays.* Cambridge: Cambridge University Press, 1996. Print.

Jaszi, Peter, and Martha Woodmansee. "Copyright in Transition." In *Print in Motion: The Expansion of Publishing and Reading in the United States, 1880–1940*, edited by Carl F. Kaestle and Janice A. Radway, 90–101. Chapel Hill: University of North Carolina Press, 2008. Print.

Johnson, Lee Ann. *Mary Hallock Foote*. Boston: Twayne, 1980. Print.
Justice, Daniel Heath. *Our Fire Survives the Storm: A Cherokee Literary History*. Minneapolis: University of Minnesota Press, 2006. Print.
Kaestle, Carl F., and Janice A. Radway, eds. *Print in Motion: The Expansion of Publishing and Reading in the United States, 1880–1940*. Chapel Hill: University of North Carolina Press, 2008. Print.
———. "A Framework for the History of Publishing and Reading in the United States, 1889–1940." In *Print in Motion: The Expansion of Publishing and Reading in the United States, 1880–1940*, edited by Carl F. Kaestle and Janice A. Radway, 7–21. Chapel Hill: University of North Carolina Press, 2008. Print.
Kant, Candace C. Introduction to *Dolly and Zane Grey: Letters from a Marriage* by Zane Grey, Lina Elise Grey, and Candace C. Kant, 1–10. Reno: University of Nevada Press, 2008. Print.
Kaplan, Amy. "Manifest Domesticity." In *No More Separate Spheres! A Next Wave American Studies Reader*, edited by Cathy N. Davidson and Jessamyn Hatcher, 183–207. Durham NC: Duke University Press, 2002. Print.
Keller, Betty. *Pender Harbour Cowboy: The Many Lives of Bertrand Sinclair*. Victoria, BC: Touchwood, 2000. Print.
Kent, Alicia. "Mourning Dove's *Cogewea*: Writing Her Way into Modernity." *melus* 24, no. 3 (1999): 39–66. Print.
Kolodny, Annette. *The Land before Her: Fantasy and Experience of the American Frontiers, 1630–1860*. Chapel Hill: University of North Carolina Press, 1984. Print.
Lamont, Victoria. "Big Books Wanted: Women and Western American Literature in the Twenty-First Century." *Legacy: A Journal of American Women Writers* 31, no. 2 (2014): 311–26. Print.
Larson, Charles A. *American Indian Fiction*. Albuquerque: University of New Mexico Press, 1978. Print.
Lee, L. L., and Merrill Lewis. *Women, Women Writers, and the West*. Troy NY: Whitston, 1980. Print.
Lewis, Nathaniel. *Unsettling the Literary West: Authenticity and Authorship*. Lincoln: University of Nebraska Press, 2003. Print.
Lockhart, Caroline. "A Girl in the Rockies." *Lippincott's Monthly Magazine*, August 1902, n.p. Print.
———. *The Lady Doc*. Philadelphia: J. B. Lippincott, 1912. Print.
———. *Me—Smith*. Philadelphia: J. B. Lippincott, 1911. Print.
MacKell, Jan. *Brothels, Bordellos, and Bad Girls: Prostitution in Colorado, 1860–1930*. Albuquerque: University of New Mexico Press, 2004. Print.
Madison, Nathan Vernon. "The Argosy." Accessed at The Pulp Magazines Project, November 28, 2013. Web.
Manguel, Alberto. *A History of Reading*. Toronto: Alfred A. Knopf Canada, 1996. Print.
Marilley, Suzanne M. *Woman Suffrage and the Origins of Liberal Feminism in the United States, 1820–1920*. Cambridge MA: Harvard University Press, 1996. Print.
McElrath, Frances. *The Rustler: A Tale of Love and War in Wyoming*. New York: Funk & Wagnalls, 1902; reprint, Lincoln: University of Nebraska Press, 2002. Print.
McPherson, James M. "Abolitionists, Woman Suffrage, and the Negro, 1865–1869." In *Abolitionism and Issues of Race and Gender*, edited by John R. McKivigan, 354–62. New York: Garland, 1999. Print.
McVeigh, Steven. *The American Western*. Edinburgh: Edinburgh University Press, 2007. Print.
Mead, Rebecca. *How the Vote Was Won: Woman Suffrage in the Western United States, 1868–1914*. New York: New York University Press, 2004. Print.

Mercer, A. S. *The Banditti of the Plains; Or, the Cattlemen's Invasion of Wyoming in 1892: The Crowning Infamy of the Ages.* [Denver: A. S. Mercer], 1894; reprint, Norman: University of Oklahoma Press, 1954. Print.

Meyer, Roy W. "B. M. Bower: The Poor Man's Wister." In *Popular Western: Essays toward a Definition*, edited by Richard W. Etulain and Michael T. Marsden, 25–38. Bowling Green OH: Bowling Green University Popular Press, 1974. Print.

Miller, Jay. "Mourning Dove." In *American National Biography Online*. Oxford University Press, 2000. Web. http://www.anb.org/login.html?url=%2Farticles%2Fhome.html&ip=70.49.20.110&nocookie=0, accessed June 4, 2015.

Moore, Jacqueline M. *Cow Boys and Cattle Men: Class and Masculinities on the Texas Frontier, 1865–1900.* New York: New York University Press, 2010. Print.

Mott, Frank Luther. *History of American Magazines.* Cambridge MA: Belknap Press of Harvard University Press, 1930. Print.

Mourning Dove. *Cogewea, the Half Blood.* Boston: Four Seas Company, 1927; reprint, Lincoln: University of Nebraska Press, 1981. Print.

———. *Coyote Stories.* Edited by Hester Dean Guie. 1933. Lincoln: University of Nebraska Press, 1990. Print.

———. *A Salishan Autobiography.* Lincoln: University of Nebraska Press, 1990. Print.

Murray, David. *Forked Tongues: Speech, Writing, and Representation in North American Indian Texts.* Bloomington: Indiana University Press, 1991. Print.

Library of Congress, National Film Preservation Board. "Complete National Film Registry Listing." n.d. Web. https://www.loc.gov/programs/national-film-preservation-board/film-registry/complete-national-film-registry-listing, accessed June 4, 2015.

Nemerov, Alex. "Doing the 'Old America': The Image of the American West, 1880–1920." In *The West as America: Reinterpreting Images of the Frontier, 1820–1920*, edited by William H. Truettner, 285–344. Washington: Smithsonian Institution Press, 1991. Print.

Newman, Louise Michele. *White Women's Rights: The Racial Origins of Feminism in the United States.* New York: Oxford University Press, 1999. Print.

Nolan, Michelle. "Ranch Romances: The Last of the Original Pulps." Accessed at The Pulp Magazines Project, November 4, 2013. Web.

Ohmann, Richard M. *Selling Culture: Magazines, Markets, and Class at the Turn of the Century.* London: Verso, 1996. Print.

Oklahoma State University Library. "Vingie E. Roe" (biography). Vingie E. Roe Collection. September 6, 2013. Web. http://info.library.okstate.edu/c.php?g=151956&p=997938, accessed December 5, 2013.

Ong, Walter J. *Orality and Literacy: The Technologizing of the Word.* London: Routledge, 1982. Print.

Opfermann, Susanne. "Lydia Maria Child, James Fenimore Cooper, and Catharine Maria Sedgwick: A Dialogue on Race, Culture, and Gender." In *Soft Canons: American Women Writers and Masculine Tradition*, edited by Karen L. Kilcup, 27–47. Iowa City: University of Iowa Press, 1999. Print.

Owens, Louis. "As If an Indian Were Really an Indian: Native American Voices and Postcolonial Theory." In *Native American Representations: First Encounters, Distorted Images, and Literary Appropriations*, edited by Gretchen M. Bataille, 11–24. Lincoln: University of Nebraska Press, 2001. Print.

———. *Mixedblood Messages: Literature, Film, Family, Place.* Norman: University of Oklahoma Press, 1998. Print.

Pearce, Roy Harvey. *The Savages of America; a Study of the Indian and the Idea of Civilization.* Baltimore: Johns Hopkins University Press, 1965. Print.
Powers, Paul S., and Laurie Powers. *Pulp Writer: Twenty Years in the American Grub Street.* Lincoln: University of Nebraska Press, 2007. Print.
Radway, Janice. *A Feeling for Books: The Book-of-the-Month Club, Literary Taste, and Middle-Class Desire.* Chapel Hill: University of North Carolina Press, 1997. Print.
———. *Reading the Romance: Women, Patriarchy, and Popular Literature.* 2nd ed. Chapel Hill: University of North Carolina Press, 1991. Print.
Raimi, Sam, director. *The Quick and the Dead.* Sony/Columbia, 1995. Film.
Reddin, Paul. *Wild West Shows.* Urbana: University of Illinois Press, 1999. Print.
Reynolds, Quentin. *The Fiction Factory; Or, From Pulp Row to Quality Street.* New York: Random House, 1955. Print.
Riley, Glenda. *Building and Breaking Families in the American West.* Albuquerque: University of New Mexico Press, 1996. Print.
———. *The Female Frontier: A Comparative View of Women on the Prairie and the Plains.* Lawrence: University Press of Kansas, 1988. Print.
Roosevelt, Theodore. *The Winning of the West.* Vol. 1. New York: Putnam, 1889. Print.
Rosaldo, Renato. "From the Door of His Tent: The Fieldworker and the Inquisitor." In *Writing Culture: The Poetics and Politics of Ethnography,* edited by James Clifford and George E. Marcus, 77–97. Berkeley: University of California Press, 1986. Print.
Rosowski, Susan J. *Birthing a Nation: Gender, Creativity, and the West in American Literature.* Lincoln: University of Nebraska Press, 1999. Print.
Rubin, Gayle. "The Traffic in Women: Notes on the 'Political Economy' of Sex." In *Literary Theory: An Anthology,* edited by Julie Rivkin and Michael Ryan, 533–60. Maldin MA: Blackwell, 1998. Print.
Rubin, Joan Shelley. "Making Meaning: Analysis and Affect in the Study and Practice of Reading." In *Print in Motion: The Expansion of Publishing and Reading in the United States, 1880–1940,* edited by Carl F. Kaestle and Janice A. Radway, 511–27. Chapel Hill: University of North Carolina Press, 2008. Print.
Ruiz, Vicki, and Ellen Carol DuBois, eds. *Unequal Sisters: A Multi-cultural Reader in U.S. Women's History.* 2nd ed. New York: Routledge, 1994. Print.
Sánchez-Eppler, Karen. *Touching Liberty: Abolition, Feminism, and the Politics of the Body.* Berkeley: University of California Press, 1993. Print.
Savage, Candace Sherk. *Cowgirls.* Berkeley CA: Ten Speed, 1996. Print.
Sedgwick, Catharine Maria. *Hope Leslie.* New York: White, Gallaher, & White, 1827; reprint, New Brunswick NJ: Rutgers University Press, 1987. Print.
Seitler, Dana, ed. "Introduction." In *The Crux* by Charlotte Perkins Gilman, 1–19. Durham NC: Duke University Press, 2003. Print.
———. "Unnatural Selection: Mothers, Eugenic Feminism, and Charlotte Perkins Gilman's Regeneration Narratives." *American Quarterly* 55 (2003): 61–88. Print.
Silko, Leslie Marmon. *Storyteller.* New York: Seaver, 1981. Print.
Slotkin, Richard. *The Fatal Environment: The Myth of the Frontier in the Age of Industrialization, 1800–1890.* New York: Atheneum, 1985. Print.
———. *Gunfighter Nation: The Myth of the Frontier in Twentieth-Century America.* Norman: University of Oklahoma Press, 1998. Print.
Smith, Christine Hill. *Social Class in the Writings of Mary Hallock Foote.* Reno: University of Nevada Press, 2009. Print.

Smith, Erin A. *Hardboiled: Working-Class Readers and Pulp Magazines*. Philadelphia: Temple University Press, 2000. Print.

Smith, Georgia Clarkson. "*The Popular* Magazine." n.d. Web. http://www.pulpmags.org/data base_pages/popular.html, accessed at The Pulp Magazines Project, November 28, 2013.

Smith, Helena Huntington. *The War on Powder River*. Lincoln: University of Nebraska Press, 1967. Print.

Spokesman-Review. "Republic Woman Writer Scores." January 22, 1924, 11. Print.

Stanford University. "New Buffalo Bill Weekly." n.d. Web. Accessed at the Dime Novels and Penny Dreadfuls Collection, December 4, 2014.

Stanton, Elizabeth Cady, Susan B. Anthony, and Matilda Joslyn Gage. *History of Woman Suffrage*. Vol 1. New York: Fowler & Wells, 1881; reprint, New York: Arno, 1969. Print.

Stauffer, Helen Winter, and Susan J. Rosowski. *Women and Western American Literature*. Troy NY: Witston, 1982. Print.

Stephens, Anne S. *Malaeska, the Indian Wife of the White Hunter*. New York: Beadle & Adams, 1860. Print.

Stephensen-Payne, Phil. "Western Fiction Index." n.d. Web. http://www.philsp.com/wfil .html, accessed at Galactic Central, November 1 and 28, 2013.

———. "Magazine Cover Images." n.d. Web. http://www.philsp.com/lists/ii_magazines .html, accessed at Galactic Central, November 1 and 28, 2013.

Stewart, Elinore Pruitt. 1914. *Letters of a Woman Homesteader*. Lincoln: University of Nebraska Press, 1961. Print.

Stowe, Harriet Beecher. *Uncle Tom's Cabin*. Boston: John P. Jewett, 1852; reprint, New York: Norton, 1994. Print.

Terborg-Penn, Rosalyn. *African American Women in the Struggle for the Vote, 1850–1920*. Bloomington: Indiana University Press, 1998. Print.

Teuton, Christopher B. *Deep Waters: The Textual Continuum in American Indian Literature*. Lincoln: University of Nebraska Press, 2010. Print.

Tompkins, Jane P. *Sensational Designs: The Cultural Work of American Fiction*. New York: Oxford University Press, 1985. Print.

———. *West of Everything: The Inner Life of Westerns*. New York: Oxford University Press, 1992. Print.

Turner, Frederick Jackson. *The Turner Thesis concerning the Role of the Frontier in American History*, edited by George Roger Taylor. Boston: Heath, 1956. Print. Originally delivered as a speech in 1893.

Tuttle, Jennifer. "Rewriting the West Cure: Charlotte Perkins Gilman, Owen Wister, and the Sexual Politics of Neurasthenia." In *The Mixed Legacy of Charlotte Perkins Gilman*, edited by Catherine J. Golden and Joanna Schneider Zangrando, 103–21. Newark: University of Delaware Press, 2000. Print.

———. "Indigenous Whiteness and Wister's Invisible Indians." In *Reading "The Virginian" in the New West*, edited by Melody Graulich and Stephen Tatum, 89–111. Lincoln: University of Nebraska Press, 2003. Print.

Viehmann, Martha L. "'My People . . . My Kind': Mourning Dove's *Cogewea, the Half-Blood*, as a Narrative of Mixed Descent." In *Early Native American Writing: New Critical Essays*, edited by Helen Jaskoski, 204–21. Cambridge: Cambridge University Press, 1996. Print.

Vizenor, Gerald. "Native American Indian Literatures: Narratives of Survivance." In *Native North America*, edited by Renee Hulan, 47–63. Toronto: ECW, 1999. Print.

Walsh, Mary Ellen Williams. "*Angle of Repose* and the Writings of Mary Hallock Foote: A Source Study." In *Critical Essays on Wallace Stegner*, edited by Anthony Arthur, 184–209. Boston: G. K. Hall, 1982. Print.

Washburn, Albina L. "Woman Suffrage Items." *Woman's Journal* 23 (1892): 276. Print.

Welter, Barbara. *Dimity Convictions: The American Woman in the Nineteenth Century*. Athens: Ohio University Press, 1976. Print.

West, Simon, director. *Lara Croft: Tomb Raider*. Paramount, 2001. Film.

White, G. Edward. *The Eastern Establishment and the Western Experience: The West of Frederic Remington, Theodore Roosevelt, and Owen Wister*. New Haven CT: Yale University Press, 1968. Print.

White, Richard. *It's Your Misfortune and None of My Own: A History of the American West*. Norman: University of Oklahoma Press, 1991. Print.

Wikipedia. "Lela Cole Kitson." May 17, 2013. Web. https://en.wikipedia.org/wiki/Lela_Cole_Kitson, accessed December 5, 2013.

Wilson, Christopher. *The Labor of Words: Literary Professionalism in the Progressive Era*. Athens: University of Georgia Press, 1985. Print.

Wilson, Michael. "Writing a Friendship Dance: Orality in Mourning Dove's *Cogewea*." *American Indian Culture and Research Journal* 20, no. 1 (1996): 27–41. Print.

Wister, Owen. *The Virginian*. New York: Macmillan, 1902; reprint, New York: Penguin, 1988. Print.

Womack, Craig S. *Red on Red: Native American Literary Separatism*. Minneapolis: University of Minnesota Press, 1999. Print.

Wrobel, David M. *End of American Exceptionalism: Frontier Anxiety from the Old West to the New Deal*. Lawrence: University Press of Kansas, 1993. Print.

Yates, Norris Wilson. *Gender and Genre: An Introduction to Women Writers of Formula Westerns, 1900–1950*. Albuquerque: University of New Mexico Press, 1995. Print.

Yellin, Jean Fagan. *Women and Sisters: The Antislavery Feminists in American Culture*. New Haven CT: Yale University Press, 1989. Print.

Young, Robert J. C. *Colonial Desire: Hybridity in Theory, Culture, and Race*. London: Routledge, 1995. Print.

Žižek, Slavoj. *The Sublime Object of Ideology*. London: Verso, 1989. Print.

Index

Abenaki Indians, 85. *See also* Native Americans
Ace-High, 138
The Administratrix (Curtis): moral reform in, 15, 23–29; political themes of, 12, 15, 21–23; publication of, 13–14, 19; western image in, 5, 20–21, 75
Adventure, 85
adventure stories: in magazines, 129, 132, 133, 135, 138, 140–41, *143*; romance in, 141–46, 148, 152; westerns as, 8, 153
African Americans: as cowboys, 3; and suffrage, 14–15, 105–6, 123; as westerners, 56–57; white feminists on, 104, 105, 108–10. *See also* race; slavery
Ainslee's, 59, 65, 126, 140, 152
Alamosa Journal, 16, 17
Albuquerque NM, 17
alcohol, 46, 60, 106, 108. *See also* Woman's Christian Temperance Union
Alice Harriman, 76
Allen, Anita, 139
Allen, Paula Gunn, 77
Allmendinger, Blake, 39, 166n12
American Heritage Center, 166n8
The American Western (McVeigh), 156
Ammons, Elizabeth, 164n4
Anderson, Charles Reed, 128–29
Anderson, Kate Baird, 57, 158, 163n3, 163n5

Angle of Repose (Stegner), 158–59
Argosy, 3, 53, 126, 127
"Around the Double R Corral," 150
Aspen Daily Chronicle, 19
Aspen Morning Chronicle, 19
Aspen Times, 17
Aspen Weekly Times, 17, 18
assimilation. *See* Native Americans, colonization of
Atlantic Monthly, 102
Austin, Mary, 13
Authors Magazine, 58, 59
autochthonous theory of regional writing, 56
Averell, James, 38
"The Backsliding of Sister Stewart" (Bower), 58–59
Bailey, Regina. *See* Newhall, Muriel
Ballard, Aline, 145
Bar BC Ranch, 111
Barber, Amos, 38, 41, 162nn4–5
Baxter, George Owen, 128, 132
Baym, Nina, 156
Beadle & Adams, 155
Beam, Clarence E., 135
Bechdolt, Jack, 144, 146
Beecher family, 120
The Beef Bonanza (Brisbin), 36
Bennauer, Adolph, 129

Bernardin, Susan, 77, 82–83, 93–94, 97, 165n14
Bertha Clay Library, 126
Best, Agnes, 139
Birthing a Nation (Rosowski), 165n3
Blaeser, Kimberly, 78–79
Blue Book, 127
boarding schools, 91–92. *See also* teachers
Boas, Franz, 80, 81, 88
The Boer Fight for Freedom (Davitt), 156–57
Bold, Christine, 5, 11, 16, 42, 75, 77
Bookman, 64
Boston, 36, 57, 61, 68
Bourdieu, Pierre, 4, 63
Bower, Bill, 163n5
Bower, B. M. (Bertha Muzzy): authenticity of, 7, 54, 55, 56, 59–60; background of, 57–59; biography of, 57, 158, 163n3, 163n5; career of, 1, 58–59, 61, 64–67, 101, 128, 130, 138–40, 151, 152, 154, 156, 157; Caroline Lockhart compared with, 7, 67–68, 74; death of, 64, 67; and frontier club, 6, 8, 75; *Lonesome Land*, 103, 107–8, 111, 113; and masculinity, 125, 159–60; nom de plume of, 53, 57, 61, 64–67, 125, 130
Bower, Clayton, 57–59, 61, 163n3, 163n5
Bower, Grace, 57
Bower, Harry, 57
Bower, Roy, 57, 58
The Brand (Broderick), 76, 94–96, 165n14
The Branding Iron (film), 166n8
The Branding Iron (Burt), 103, 110–11, 116–19, 166n8
"Break Your Own Trail," 163n3
Bredahl, Carl, 169n93
Brill de Ramírez, Susan Berry, 79, 83–84
Brisbin, James S., 36
British Columbia, 87
Brock, J. Elmer, 37
Broderick, Therese, 76, 94–95
Brooks, Joanna, 77
Brown, Alanna Kathleen, 93–94, 164n4
Brown, Robert Adger, 128
Bruchac, Joseph, 85, 97
Buffalo WY, 41
Buffalo Bill series, 3, 15, 76, 126

Buffalo Bill's Wild West Show, 18–19, 31, 102. *See also* wild west shows
Burrell, Sally Noon, 145
Burrows, Edith, 64, 139
Burt, Katharine Newlin, 8, 103, 110–11, 166n8
Burt, Maxwell Struthers, 111
Butcher, Fanny, 111
Butler, Judith, 149
"A Cache for Landon" (Hall), 146
Calder, Alison, 56
California, 61, 65, 120, 129, 135, 137, 166n4
Cameron, M. A., 146
Canadian Rockies, 69–70
Cannell, Charles, 130
Canon City CO, 12, 13
Captain Nora, 128, 129
Carbonate Chronicle, 19
Carr, F. *See* Clay, Bertha M.
Casper WY, 41
Castle Rock Journal, 16–17
Cather, Willa, 2
Catt, Carrie Chapman, 105, 106
cattle: branding of, 32–33, 36–40, 43, 45, 49–50, 101, 107–14, 116–19, 122, 123, 166n12; cowboys' handling of, 19, 40, 60; symbolism of, 8, 40, 48–50, 62, 101, 102, 104, 107–14, 116–23, 166n12. *See also* mavericks
cattlemen: in *The Administratrix*, 15; cowboys' confrontations with, 18; in love stories, 145; Owen Wister with, 56, 59; and range wars, 31–42, 44; in Sheriff Minnie story, 147; social class of, 11, 16, 46, 62, 63, 75. *See also* cattle ranching, open; elite class; ranchers
cattle ranching, open: and cowboy image, 11–12; in love stories, 145; as subject, 3, 5, 31; wealth from, 35–39. *See also* cattlemen; ranchers
cattle rustlers. *See* rustlers
Cawelti, John G., 153, 155
Century, 13
Champion, Nate, 32, 33, 38, 41, 44, 162n5
Chicago, 36, 61
Chicago Tribune, 111

Child, Lydia Maria, 94, 155
Chinese, 56–57, 105, 136. *See also* immigrants
Chinook MT, 165n9
Chip, of the Flying U (Bower), 7, 59, 61–64, 71, 140
Chipmunk (Native American legend), 85, 97
Chisholm, A. M., 128
"Chorus Girl" (Ballard), 145
Christianity, 21, 23–24
Civil War, 23, 67–68
Clay, Bertha M., 129
Clayton, John, 69, 71
Clayton Magazines, 138
"Clementine" (Loya), 151
Cleveland MN, 57
Clifford, James, 76–77, 82, 86
Cody, Buffalo Bill, 72
Cody WY, 70–73
Cody Stampede, 72
Cogewea, the Half-Blood (Mourning Dove): authenticity of, 77, 80, 83, 164n4; on class tensions, 6, 96–97; plot of, 86–89, 93–94, 97–98, 165n14; publication of, 75–77, 164n1; race in, 94–96; significance of, 77, 78; style of, 93–94, 98–99
Collier-Thomas, Bettye, 104
Collins, Emily, 106
colonialism: and Native culture, 82, 89, 91, 96–98; in West, 6, 76, 117, 166n9; of western authors, 75
Colorado: cowboys in, 16–20; moral reform in, 21–22, 25; representation of, 56, 75, 128–29; suffrage in, 12–15, 19–21, 160, 166n4; women's situations in, 26–29
Colorado Industrial School for Boys, 13
Colorado People's Party, 13, 14
Colville reservation, 76
Comanche Kid, 130
Confederated Tribes of the Colville Reservation, 6. *See also* Native Americans
Connor, Sarah, 102
conversivity, 79, 84–85, 131–38, 150, 152, 165n9
Cook, Coralie Franklin, 123
Cooper, James Fenimore, 11, 69, 94, 155
copyright legislation, 126

Cott, Nancy F., 46
Cove, Carmony, 141–42, 145
Cowan, Bud, 157
cowboys: B. M. Bower's portrayal of, 55, 59–63, 75, 128; Clayton Bower with, 57; Emma Curtis's portrayal of, 20–22, 25–27; female versions of, 101, 102; Mourning Dove's portrayal of, 86–87; as political figures, 14, 15, 19–20; and range wars, 31–37, 40, 46; as readers, 150; reputation of, 15–20, 31–32; as subjects, 3–5, 7, 11–12, 31, 43, 75, 107, 116, 128; work ethic of, 18, 31. *See also* men
Cowboy Stories, 138
Cow Country (Bower), 66
cowgirls, 102, 138, 150, 165n2. *See also* women
"Cow Woman" (Gilbert), 129
Coyote, 97
Coyote Stories (Mourning Dove), 77, 97
Crane, Stephen, 31
"Crescent Moon" (Brown), 128
criminals, 12, 15–19, 27–28, 43, 46, 52, 147–49
The Crux (Gilman), 121–22
culture: and authenticity, 54–56, 59–60, 93; of Colorado politics, 14, 19–20; of Johnson County War, 42; of patriarchy, 105, 114, 120–21; of popular western, 67, 75, 155, 156, 158, 160; preservation of Native American, 76–78, 81–83, 86–99; production in West, 63–65; of women writers, 7, 54, 60–62, 68, 101–2
culture, American: cowboys in, 31, 59–60; reading in, 85, 133; representation of, 56–57, 62–63; women in postfrontier, 101, 104–5
culture, popular: heroines in, 102–3; and oral tradition, 165n7
"Cupid and the Camp Wagon" (Noy), 145
Curtis, Emma Ghent: background of, 12, 21; career of, 1, 12, 13, 101, 154, 157; death of, 13; and frontier club, 6; politics of, 12–15, 21–22, 160; portrayal of cowboys, 15–16; portrayal of West, 5, 56, 75
Curtis, James, 12
Curtis, Mary, 12

INDEX 185

dance halls, 22, 25, 26, 147. *See also* square dance
Daniel Everton, Volunteer Regular (Putnam), 156–57
Davey, Frank, 55–56
Davis, Robert Murray, 153
Davitt, Michael, 156–57
Dawes General Allotment Act (1887), 86–87, 91, 96, 165n12. *See also* property ownership
Dean, Janet, 4
democracy, 47–52, 117, 162n7
Democratic state convention (WY), 41
Densmore, Frances, 87–88
Denver CO, 13, 18
"Desert Rose" (Bechdolt), 144, 146
Destry Rides Again (film), 159
detective stories, 128
Dillingham, 61, 62
dime novels, 1, 3, 5, 16, 31, 126, 127, 129, 155
Dinan, John, 153
Doke, Dele Newman, 58, 158, 163n3, 163n5
Doke, Reed, 163n5
domesticity, 2–4, 24–25, 44–46, 49–52, 60, 61, 114–16, 146–49. *See also* motherhood
Douglas WY, 41
Douglass, Frederick, 23
Dubois, Ellen Carol, 106–7
Dymond, Justine, 77

Eagleton, Mary, 2
East (U.S.): *The Branding Iron* in, 117–19; cattlemen from, 11, 35; media in, 5, 156; in range war novels, 45; readers from, 55, 133; westerners from, 12, 20, 24–25, 32, 34, 43, 56, 59, 62–63, 68, 71–72, 86–87, 102, 107, 142–45; woman suffrage in, 105, 166n5
"The Element of Chance" (Hofflund), 129
elite class, 11, 15, 19–20, 55, 56, 63, 75. *See also* cattlemen; frontier club; social class
Ellis, Edward S., 155
England, 12, 36, 42
English language literacy, 91–93, 165n7
Estleman, Loren D., 169n93
ethnography: and colonization of Native culture, 76–77, 81–83, 87–91; of Mourning Dove, 6, 78, 80–82, 92, 99; on oral tradition, 79, 97–98; written tradition of, 84–88
Etulain, Richard W., 156
eugenics, 103–5, 117, 120–22
Europe, 11, 18–19, 35, 117, 166n9

farmers, 19, 87, 147
Farmers' Alliance, 14
Farmer's Wife, 25
Farnsworth, Mona. *See* Newhall, Muriel
The Fate of a Fool (Curtis), 12, 21
feminism: and patriarchy, 114, 120–21; and race, 103–10, 120–23; in range war novels, 45, 48–52, 107; and western genre, 2, 63, 101–3, 122–23, 151, 154. *See also* women
Fetterley, Judith, 55–56
Fifteenth Amendment, 104. *See also* woman suffrage
film industry, 65, 101–3, 146–47, 166n8
Finnegan, Ruth, 83–84
fire, 110, 113–14
Fisher, Dexter, 85
Flagg, Jack, 32, 37, 41, 44
"Flapjack Meehan Rounds 'Em Up" (Pierce), 128
Flathead Reservation, 86–87, 95
folklore, 81, 87–88
Foote, Mary Hallock, 155–56, 158–59
Fort Garland CO, 17
"For the Girl He Left behind Him" (Bennauer), 129
Fremont County CO, 12
French, Warren, 16
frontier, American: closure of, 3, 4–5, 31, 33, 51–52, 162n7; *Cogewea* set on, 87; culture of, 56, 60–61; heroes of, 11, 34; myth of, 1, 4–5, 104–5, 117, 121, 166n9. *See also* West, American
frontier club: and authenticity, 77; Christine Bold on, 5, 11, 42, 75, 77; Owen Wister in, 42; racism of, 75; and women writers, 5–8, 101–2. *See also* elite class; masculinity; men
"Fugitive's Daughter" (Spencer), 145–46
Funk & Wagnalls, 156–57

gender: and abolition movement, 104–5, 109; in *The Administratrix*, 15; and pseudonyms, 129–30; and race, 119–23; in range war novels, 42, 45–48, 51, 52; of readers, 8, 125–28, 132–38, 151–53; of Sheriff Minnie, 147–49; and western genre, 125–26, 151–54; and writers' authenticity, 53–57, 60–64, 68, 70–74. *See also* masculinity; men; sexuality; women; women writers
Gender and Genre (Yates), 2–3
Georgi-Findlay, Brigitte, 75
Geyserville CA, 135
Ghent, Ira, 12
Ghent, Mary Palmer, 12
Gilbert, George, 129
Gilman, Charlotte Perkins, 8, 101, 106, 120, 121
"A Girl in the Rockies" (Lockhart), 68–69, 72, 73
Godfrey, Laura, 80
gold. *See* prospecting
Goldman, Emma, 8, 101, 102
Goldwyn, 166n8
Good Indian (Bower), 64
Goodwin Catholic Mission, 92
Gordon, Ann D., 104
Green, Andy, 159–60
Green, Edna T. *See* Newhall, Muriel
Grey, Dolly, 157–58
Grey, Zane, 2, 66, 156–59
guns, 26–29, 34, 70, 132

habitus, 63
Hall, Robert Henry, 146
Halloway, Zinza "Slim," 132
Handley, William, 7, 54
Happ, Bertha May. *See* Bower, B. M. (Bertha Muzzy)
The Happy Family (Bower), 128, 159–60
Harrison, Benjamin, 19, 41, 162n5
HAT brand, 37–38
Haymarket massacre, 36, 37
"Heart Brand" (Cameron), 146
Hersey, Harold Brainerd, 131–32, 138, 140, 150–51
Hispanics, 14–17, 20, 56–57. *See also* Mexicans; race

History of Woman Suffrage (Stanton, Anthony, and Gage), 106
Hobomok (Child), 94, 155
Hofflund, Raymond Ward, 129
"The Hollow Tree," 131–38
Hope Leslie (Sedgwick), 155
"The Horse and the Man" (Lathrop), 128
horses: Caroline Lockhart on, 70; in *Cogewea*, 89; and cowboys, 16–19, 60; and patriarchy, 120, 122; stories about, 128, 129, 132, 137, 145–46
Houghton Mifflin, 111, 166n8
Hubbard, Alice, 13

Idaho, 132, 166n4
Illinois, 57, 68
immigrants, 14–15, 19, 56–57, 92. *See also* Chinese
Indiana, 12, 21
Ingram, Prentiss, 31
"Into the Unknown" (Anderson), 128–29
Irish Americans, 92. *See also* immigrants
Ives, Muriel. *See* Newhall, Muriel

Jackson County IN, 12
Jackson Hole WY, 111
Jefferson, Thomas, 118, 166n10
Jenkins, Will F., 130
Jews, 117–19
Johnson County Rustler Wars of 1892: cause of, 33, 37–41, 162n4; and Chicago labor disputes, 36; history of, 31, 162n2; as subject, 1, 5, 31, 32, 42–44, 75, 107, 160. *See also* rustlers; Wyoming
juvenile fiction, 76, 125, 126, 127, 131

Kaestle, Carl F., 133
Kansas, 17, 25, 57, 68
Kaplan, Amy, 75
Kelly, Florence Finch, 31
Kent, Alicia, 77
Kettle Falls WA, 92
Kimbrough, Alex, 165n9
Kitson, Lela Cole. *See* Loya, Lupe
knowledge, philosophies of, 98–99
Kolodny, Annette, 165n3

labor unrest, 31, 32, 36, 37

Lacan, Jacques, 122
The Lady Doc (Lockhart), 7, 71–74, 159
L'Amour, Louis, 2
The Land before Her (Kolodny), 165n3
Lane, Frances, 71–74
Lara Croft: Tomb Raider, 102
lassos, 19
The Last of the Mohicans (Cooper), 69, 94
"The Last Ride" (Cove), 141–42, 145
The Last Stand, 63
Las Vegas NV, 65
Lathrop, Harley, 128
Lawdon, Tom, 165n9
Leatherstocking tales, 11, 69, 94, 155
Lee, Louisa Carter. *See* Jenkins, Will F.
"The Lemon and the Lioness" (Morrison), 142–43
Leonard, Orville, 128, 129
Lévi-Strauss, Claude, 122
Lewis, Nathaniel, 7, 54, 55
Lewis and Clark expedition, 97
Library of Congress, 159
Life, 139
Lippincott's, 68
Little, Brown, 3, 61, 62, 64–67, 107, 158, 163n3, 166n7
Lockhart, Caroline: authenticity of, 7, 54, 57, 69–74; B. M. Bower compared with, 7, 67–68; career of, 54, 67–74, 101, 129; civic engagement of, 68, 70, 72; contributions of, 159; and Frances Lane, 71–74
Lomawaima, K. Tsianina, 91–92
Lonesome Land (Bower): as autobiography, 163n3, 163n5; plot of, 60; success of, 64, 107, 111, 128, 166n7; women characters in, 103, 107–17
"Look Who's Here" (Ives), 147
Los Angeles CA, 65, 129
"The Lost Squaw Man" (Leonard), 129
love stories: in *The Administratrix*, 12, 20; in *The Branding Iron*, 117–19; in *Chip, of the Flying U*, 62; in *Cogewea*, 87, 89, 93–95; in *The Crux*, 121–22; in *The Lady Doc*, 72; magazines for, 125–31, 138–54; by men, 130; in range war novels, 32, 34, 42–44, 50–51; westerns as, 8, 138; women's representation in, 102, 140–48. *See also* marriage; sexuality

Love Story Magazine, 131
Loya, Lupe, 130, 151–53
MacLean, Charles, 61–62, 64
Madison, Nathan, 127
magazines: B. M. Bower's writing for, 58–59, 67, 139–40; conversivity of, 85, 131–32, 150–51, 165n9; Emma Curtis's poetry in, 13; illustrations in, 133, 137–38, 140–41, *141–44*; pseudonyms in, 129; westerns in, 53, 126–51; writers' profiles in, 65, 132; yellowback, 165n8. *See also* pulp fiction magazines
Malaeska (Stephens), 155
Malone, Carmen, 130
"The Man from Cloud Peak" (Burrell), 145
Marilley, Suzanne M., 105
marriage: cattle roundups compared to, 102, 104, 108–15, 118; of Charlotte Perkins Gilman, 120; in *Cogewea*, 87, 90–91, 94–98, 165n14; in love stories, 139, 145–49; protection through, 103–4, 107–8, 111–17; in range war novels, 34, 42–51; slavery compared to, 105, 116–17; of western women, 20–22, 24–26, 60, 121–22. *See also* love stories; men; women
Marsden, Michael T., 156
masculinity: of American West, 2–8, 53–54, 60; of professional women, 72, 73; symbolism of, 113; of western genre, 48–51, 125–27, 130, 145–49, 152–54, 159–60; and woman suffrage, 15. *See also* frontier club; gender; men
mavericks: character named after, 44, 107, 111–12; law governing, 35, 36, 39–42; in range wars, 32–33, 38, 45–46, 48. *See also* cattle; motherhood
McClure's, 58
McElrath, Frances: career of, 101, 154; and frontier club, 6, 8; on patriarchal power, 113; politics of, 160; portrayal of cowboys, 31; and *The Rustler*, 1, 5, 31–35, 42–52, 75, 102, 103, 156–57; on women's commodification, 107, 111
McIntyre, Alfred R., 65, 66
McVeigh, Stephen, 156
McWhorter, Lucullus, 6, 77, 80–81, 88, 92–94, 99, 102, 164n4

Meadow Lark, 97
media. *See* newspapers
memoir, 2
"Memory Trail" (Farnsworth), 147
men: African American, 104; authentication of women, 72, 73; in love stories, 140–45, *142*, *144*; moral reform of, 21–24; on range wars, 34–35; as readers, 127, 131–34, 137–38, 149–52; in West, 120; and woman suffrage, 14–15, 106; women characters as, 26–29, 44, 103, 146; on women writers, 65–66; women writers as, 53, 61, 64, 67, 129; as writers, 55, 56, 130, 132, 151–57. *See also* cowboys; frontier club; gender; marriage; masculinity; patriarchal power
Mercer, A. S., 35–36
Me—Smith (Lockhart), 57, 67, 70, 73, 159
Mexicans, 3, 128. *See also* Hispanics
mining, 17, 65, 71, 145. *See also* prospecting
Minnesota, 57, 61
El Mirasol Ranch, 135
Mitchell, S. Weir, 120
mixed-bloods, 76, 77, 82–83, 86–87, 93–96. *See also* race
Momaday, N. Scott (Kiowa), 77
money, 38–39
Montana, 55–59, 64, 68, 70, 86–87, 108, 165n9
Moore, Jacqueline, 16
morality: in *The Administratrix*, 15, 23–29; of cowboys, 31–32, 60; in *Me—Smith*, 67; of popular western, 85; in range wars, 33, 34, 40, 45–47, 50–51; in *The Rustler*, 44–45; of western women, 21–26, 44–46, 50–51; and woman suffrage, 106
Morrison, Paul Randall, 142–43
motherhood, 62, 63, 114–16, 122, 133, 146. *See also* domesticity; mavericks
Mourning Dove (Okanagan): as activist storyteller, 81, 82, 87, 97, 99; autobiography of, 76, 85; background of, 76, 79–80; career of, 101–2, 157; on class tensions, 6, 160; editor of, 76–77, 80, 93–94, 99, 164n4; education of, 91, 92; goal of, 86; social status of, 75–76
Munsey, Frank, 3, 127

Muzzy, Washington, 57
Native Americans: appearance of, 20; Caroline Lockhart with, 69; colonization of, 76–78, 81–83, 86–99, 165n14; education of, 79, 91–92; lesson stories of, 85, 96–97, 98; as magazine readers, 136; property ownership of, 86–87, 91, 96, 165n12; race conflicts of, 6; representations of, 62–63; on reservations, 76, 81–83, 86–87, 95; rights of, 76, 80, 81, 82, 160; stereotypes of, 166n10; violence against, 18; as writers, 54–55, 77–79, 84, 86, 92, 99, 164n4. *See also* Abenaki Indians; Okanagan Indians; race
native informants, 60, 81, 89–93
New Ground (Bredahl), 169n93
Newhall, Muriel: contributions of, 154, 159; pseudonyms of, 129, 130, 139, 143, 147, 168n75; and Sheriff Minnie, 8, 147–49; "To a Girl's Heart," 143–44, 149–50
Newman, Louise Michele, 103
newspapers: in Colorado, 12, 16–19; Emma Curtis in, 13, 21, 25; Frances Lane in, 71; and Frances McElrath, 156; Mourning Dove in, 86; portrayal of West, 5; range wars in, 31, 37
New York, 20, 36, 57, 61, 117–19, 136, 156
Nordoff, Charles, 162n7
novels. *See* dime novels; "quality" novels; sentimental novels; yellowback novels
Noy, Edith M., 145

Oakley, Annie, 102, 165n1
O'Hearn, Marion. *See* Allen, Anita
Okanagan Indians, 76, 81, 85, 92, 97. *See also* Native Americans
Oklahoma, 129
Omaha NE, 18
Ong, Walter J., 83–86
oral tradition: in *Cogewea*, 77–80, 96–99; continuity of, 84, 165n7; in Native culture, 78–82, 85–88, 91, 96–99; of popular western, 76, 78, 83–85, 93–94, 165n9
"Overland Mail." *See* "Pony Express"
Owens, Louis (Choctaw-Cherokee), 77, 79, 82, 92
Owl Woman (Native American legend), 85, 97

Pacific Northwest, 76, 80, 160
pacifism, 23
Paris, 19
Parker, Dorothy, 65
patriarchal power: in *The Administratrix*, 27; in *Cogewea*, 90, 96; feminists on, 114, 120–23, 151; in range war novels, 48; and slavery, 105–7; symbolism of, 8, 102, 109–17; in westerns, 103–4, 145, 146, 149, 151. *See also* men
"Pecos Pete." *See* Malone, Carmen
periodicals. *See* magazines; pulp fiction magazines
Philadelphia, 36, 68
poetry, 13, 130, 132
"Pony Express," 150
Popular magazine: audience of, 127; B. M. Bower in, 7, 59, 61, 64, 128, 140; conversivity of, 85, 165n9; westerns in, 53
populism, 12–15, 19, 22, 25
Powder River WY, 31. *See also* Johnson County Rustler Wars of 1892
Powers, Paul S., 129–30
property ownership: of Caroline Lockhart's family, 68; in *Cogewea*, 86–91, 95, 96, 165n12; in love stories, 141–45; in range war novels, 33–36, 45–51; in Sheriff Minnie story, 147; through branding, 38–40, 101, 107–14, 118, 119, 122; of women's bodies, 48–50, 101–19, 122. *See also* Dawes General Allotment Act (1887)
prospecting, 128, 144, 149–50. *See also* mining
prostitution, 21–22, 25, 48, 60, 105
Pryse, Marjorie, 55–56
pseudonyms, 6–7, 53, 57, 68, 125, 129–30, 139, 147, 168n75
publishers: of B. M. Bower, 54, 57, 59, 61, 64–67; of Caroline Lockhart, 74; marketing of westerns, 53, 56, 60–61, 67, 75, 85, 125–30, 156, 165n9; Mourning Dove's contact with, 80–81, 164n1
Publishers' Weekly, 156–57
Pueblo narratives, 78
Pullman strike, 36
pulp fiction magazines: advertising in, 131, 149–50; audience of, 3, 125–28, 131–32, 138–51; authors' identity in, 129–30; B. M. Bower in, 64, 67; collapse of market, 130, 139–40, 158; ghettoization of feminine, 151–53; love stories in, 138–39; Mourning Dove's reading of, 102; westerns in, 8, 125–26, 138–53, 159. *See also* magazines; western, popular; yellowback novels
"Puncher vs Poet" (Loya), 130
Putnam, Israel, 156–57

"quality" novels, 1, 5, 8, 31, 53, 125, 139, 153–54
"quality" publishers, 3, 58, 126–28, 155–56
Quick and the Dead, 101

race: and feminism, 103–10, 120–23; of magazine readers, 135–36; in popular westerns, 94–98, 117–19, 165n14, 166n9, 166n10; and writers' authenticity, 53–57. *See also* African Americans; Hispanics; mixed-bloods; Native Americans; whites
racism, 20, 75
Radway, Janice, 126, 133, 149
Raimi, Sam, 101
ranchers: Caroline Lockhart with, 70; in love stories, 142–45; marriage to, 21, 25, 42, 107; and range wars, 31, 32, 40, 45. *See also* cattlemen; cattle ranching, open
Ranch Romances, 138, 151–53
"Range Secret" (Green), 146–47
range wars. *See* cattle ranching, open; Johnson County Rustler Wars of 1892
"Ransom Oil" (Green), 145
Ray, Nick, 32, 33, 41, 44, 162n5
reading: conversivity of, 84–85, 131–38, 150–52; of *Romantic Range*, 149–50, 152; of westerns, 125–27, 131, 152–53
region, 7, 53–57, 61, 64, 68, 73–74
Remington, Frederic, 63
rescue plots, 98–99, 106, 112–13, 141–49
revenge, 27–28, 41, 44
Reynolds, Quentin, 126–27
Rice, Louise, 133, 134
Riley, Glenda, 21, 24–25
rodeo cowgirls, 102
rodeos. *See* tournaments
Roe, Vingie E., 130–31

190 INDEX

romances. *See* love stories
Romantic Range: content of, 138–52; cover illustrations of, *141–44*; pseudonyms in, 129
Roosevelt, Theodore, 53, 56, 117, 166n9
Rosaldo, Renato, 83, 89–90
Rosowski, Susan, 165n3
Ross, Ivan, 163n5
"The Round-Up," 131–32
Royal Gorge Review, 12
Rubin, Gayle, 102, 122
"A Running Account" (Leonard), 128
Russell, Charles, 63
The Rustler (McElrath): comparison to *The Branding Iron*, 111–12, 116–17; comparison to *Lonesome Land*, 113–17; comparison to *The Virginian*, 31–35, 42–52; marketing of, 156–57; plot of, 42–44; subject of, 1, 5; women characters in, 103, 107–16
rustlers: in *The Administratrix*, 27; cowboys as, 35–38, 46; in *Lonesome Land*, 114; in love stories, 143; and Maverick Law, 39, 40; in *The Rustler*, 34, 43–45, 48, 50, 75, 102, 108, 109, 112–15; as subjects, 5; vigilante justice against, 41, 44; in *The Virginian*, 32, 33–34. *See also* Johnson County Rustler Wars of 1892
Ryan, Jimmy, 92

Salish language, 76
salvage ethnography, 76–77, 81, 82, 90. *See also* ethnography
Sánchez-Eppler, Karen, 104, 108–10
San Francisco, 61
San Juan River, 18
The Saturday Evening Post, 139
Scotland, 36
scouts, frontier, 11, 126
Sedgwick, Catharine Maria, 155
Seitler, Dana, 120, 121
sentimental novels, 77
sentimental power, 23, 27–29
Seth Jones (Ellis), 155
sexuality: in abolitionist literature, 108–10; in cowboy culture, 60, 107; emphasis of female, 121, 122; of Frances Lane, 71–74; of magazine readers, 150–51; and racial differences, 94–96, 119; of Sheriff Minnie, 147–49; symbolism of, 113. *See also* gender; love stories
Shaw, C. K. (Chloe Kathleen), 130
Sheriff Minnie, 8, 147–49, *148*
Sho-Pow-Tan. *See* McWhorter, Lucullus
short stories, 13, 61
Shuler, Nettie Rogers, 106
Silko, Leslie (Laguna Pueblo), 77, 78
silver. *See* prospecting
Sinclair, Bertrand, 55, 59, 60, 163n5
slavery, 101–10, 116–17, 120–23. *See also* African Americans
Smart Set, 128
Smith, Christine Hill, 156
Smith, Helena Huntington, 40, 162n2
social class: in American West, 11–12, 51; of cowboys, 16–17, 60, 75; and racial differences, 95; in range wars, 32–42, 45–50; of readers, 126–27, 131, 149–50; of western women, 22–28, 47–48, 62–64; and women writers, 6, 7, 32, 57, 58; and writers' authenticity, 53–57, 67–68, 72–74. *See also* elite class; working class
social Darwinism, 47, 95, 103, 117, 118, 121–23, 166n10
South Dakota, 132
Spencer, Stella, 145–46
square dance, 102. *See also* dance halls
Steamboat (rodeo bucking horse), 132
Stegner, Wallace, 158–59
Stephens, Ann S., 155
Stewart, Elinore Pruitt, 102
Stewart, Jimmy, 159
Stone, Sharon, 101
"The Story of Green-Blanket Feet," 97
Storyteller (Silko), 78
storytelling. *See* oral tradition
Stowe, Harriet Beecher, 23–24, 113
Street & Smith: love stories of, 8, 138–52, *141*; publication of B. M. Bower, 59, 64, 139–40; readers of, 126–27; series of, 3, 126
"The Strike of the Dishpan Brigade" (Bower [Happ]), 61
Stuart, Granville, 36
sublime objects, 38–39

subliterate fiction, 76, 126
Suffragist, 105
survivance, 85
Suzette. *See* Lockhart, Caroline
Swift Current Pass MT, 70

Taylor, Mary Imlay, 151, 152
teachers, 21, 25, 43, 44, 50, 57, 68, 85. *See also* boarding schools
Teall, Edward N., 131
Teit, James, 88
television, 165n7
tenderfoot narratives, 69–70, 89
Terminator films, 102
Terrell, Mary Church, 123
Teuton, Christopher B., 79, 98
Teutons, 117, 166n9
Texas, 16, 19, 20, 25, 128
"A Thousand a Plate" (Chisholm), 128
Timmons, William, *148*
TL Ranch, 55, 59
"To a Girl's Heart" (Bailey), 143–44, 149–50
tobacco cards, 5, 16, 19
Tompkins, Jane, 2, 4, 23
Touching Liberty (Sánchez-Eppler), 108–9
tournaments, 16, 18, 102, 165n2. *See also* rodeos
"The Traffic in Women" (Rubin), 122
True Grit (film), 160
"A True Story" (Catt), 105
Turner, Frederick Jackson, 56, 117, 166n9
Tuttle, Jennifer, 120

Uncle Tom's Cabin (Stowe), 23–24, 113
Unforgiven (film), 160
U.S. Census, 12, 31
U.S. military, 41, 162n4
Utah, 18, 166n4
Ute Tribe, 18. *See also* Native Americans

"Valley of Sinister Blossoms" (Wilson), 151
Vanity Fair, 65
A Victorian Gentlewoman in the Far West (Foote), 158–59
Viehmann, Martha L., 77
violence: in *The Administratrix*, 15, 25–28; in *The Branding Iron*, 118–19, 166n10; in *Cogewea*, 87, 96, 98; of cowboys, 17–18; in *Lonesome Land*, 116; and range wars, 36, 38, 41, 50; in *The Virginian*, 32, 34; in westerns, 12, 16, 94, 165n3
Virginia City CO, 17–18
The Virginian (Wister): comparison to *The Rustler*, 31–35, 42–52; cowboy hero in, 11–12, 55; influence of, 1, 5, 53, 59, 126; marketing of, 156; social Darwinism in, 95
Vivian, Charles. *See* Cannell, Charles
Vizenor, Gerald (Anishinaabe), 77–79, 85, 86
VR Ranch, 42

Walla Walla WA, 80
Walsh, Mary Ellen Williams, 158–59
War on Powder River (Smith), 162n2
Washington (state), 76, 80, 87, 92, 166n4
Washington DC, 19
Watson, Ella, 38
Welter, Barbara, 24
West, American: Charlotte Perkins Gilman in, 120–21; colonialism in, 82; cowboys in, 11; domestic authority in, 33, 44–45; economy of, 11, 12, 21–28, 31, 33, 35–40, 44–46, 68, 72, 88–91, 96, 107; insiders and outsiders in, 69–77, 136–37; landscape of, 55, 56, 62–63, 140; living conditions in, 24–27, 42, 68, 83, 111, 132, 145–46; magazine content about, 129, 132–39, 145–46, 150; race in, 118; woman suffrage in, 15, 105, 166n4; women's representation of, 1–2, 5–7, 34, 53–57, 60–63, 67–70, 103, 122–23, 160, 165n3. *See also* frontier, American
West, Calvin M., 165n9
western, popular: authenticity of, 6–7, 20, 53–55, 59–60, 63, 68–74, 132; culture of, 155, 156; formats of, 8, 76, 80, 83–84, 93–94, 97–99, 125–51; history of, 1–9, 155; illustrations of, 127, 140–41, *141–44*; marketing of, 58–61, 65–67, 85, 126–28, 139–40, 155–57, 166n8; "original" versions of, 8, 125–26, 153, 154, 169n93; politics of, 47–52, 76, 77, 82, 83, 87, 119, 154, 160; popularity of, 53, 68; scholarship on, 53, 55, 67, 77–80, 103, 119–20, 126, 131, 156,

165n3; social class in, 11, 16–17, 42, 47; themes of, 2–5, 12, 75, 84, 93–94, 116–20, 128, 139–51, 155, 159. *See also* pulp fiction magazines; yellowback novels
Western Story, 128–38, 150–53
West of Everything (Tompkins), 2
White, Richard, 165n12
whites: and abolition movement, 103–9; B. M. Bower's portrayal of, 7; in *Cogewea*, 86–87; experience of West, 54–57, 67–68, 117–20, 166n9; marriage of, 104, 110; and Native culture, 77, 78, 81–82, 86, 87, 90–96, 165n14; race conflicts of, 6, 75, 76, 82–83, 95–97, 111, 119–23; and range wars, 31, 32, 35, 40; as readers, 135–36; social class of, 24, 28; as western heroines, 146. *See also* race
Wichita KS, 17
"Wild Freedom" (Baxter), 128
wild west shows, 16–19, 31, 102
"Will and Testament" (Ives), 149
Williams, Sylvanie, 123
Wilson, Cherry, 130, 151, 152
Wilson, Michael, 77
Winning of the West (Roosevelt), 166n9
Wister, Fanny Kemble, 157–58
Wister, Owen: B. M. Bower compared with, 55; career of, 53, 157–58; Caroline Lockhart compared with, 70; cowboy heroes of, 11, 15, 31–32, 34, 75; influence of, 1, 2, 5, 53; and Mary Hallock Foote, 155–56; and range wars, 42, 46; social Darwinism of, 47; as westerner, 56, 59, 117, 120. *See also The Virginian* (Wister)
The Wister Trace (Estleman), 169n93
Wolcott, Frank, 42, 59
womanhood, cult of true, 24, 108–10, 145–48
Woman's Christian Temperance Union, 14, 23. *See also* alcohol
Woman's Journal, 13
"A Woman's Place" (Ives), 148–49
woman suffrage: and *The Administratrix*, 23, 28; in Colorado, 12–15, 19–21, 160, 166n4; and morality, 24; and slavery, 104–5, 122–23; as subject, 151; in West, 105, 166n4. *See also* women's rights

Woman Writers of the American West (Baym), 156
women: bodies of, 8, 101; in cowboy culture, 60; domestic authority of, 33, 46, 50–52, 114–16; as moral reformers, 21–26, 44–46, 50–52, 60, 106; portrayal in westerns, 4, 20, 101–4, 107–10, 118, 120–23, 128–29, 140–51, 165n1, 166n10, 166n12; professions of, 21–25, 43, 51, 57, 58, 72–73, 102, 133, 165n2; as property, 48–50, 101–21; as readers, 125–28, 132–39, 149–53; and social Darwinism, 95, 121–22; western experience of, 68–70, 120–21. *See also* feminism; gender; marriage
Women and Economics (Gilman), 120, 121
women's rights, 15, 23, 26–29, 103–6, 119, 151. *See also* woman suffrage
women writers: careers of, 7, 8–9, 53, 58–59, 74, 139–40, 152–53, 157–58; in fiction, 115; and frontier club, 5–8; genres of, 2–3; in history of western genre, 1–9, 34–35, 103, 108–9, 122–30, 139, 151–55, 158–59; importance of Native American, 77; interaction of, 101; invisibility of, 2, 4, 126, 155–59; political activism of, 32, 120, 160; pseudonyms of, 6–7, 53, 57, 68, 125, 129–30, 139, 147, 168n75; publicity of, 64–68; publishers of, 127–31; representation of West, 1–2, 5–7, 34–35, 53–59, 65, 67, 68, 102, 122; scholarship on, 55, 74, 103, 156, 165n3; on sexual taboo, 109. *See also* gender
working class, 11, 14–15, 19, 36, 92, 107, 126, 131. *See also* social class
World War I, 139, 164n1
World War II, 3, 140, 149
Writings (Jefferson), 118
written tradition: of ethnography, 85–88; vs. oral tradition, 78–85, 88, 91, 98–99, 165n7; preservation of Native culture in, 92, 93, 98–99; racial differences in, 94; social networks in, 101–2, 133
Wrobel, David, 5
Wyoming: Burt ranch in, 111; Caroline Lockhart in, 70–73; cowboys in, 17, 37; Democratic convention in, 41; Maverick Law in, 35, 40; Owen Wister in, 42, 59; *The Rustler* set in, 43, 107; women in,

Wyoming (*continued*)
   105, 121–22, 166n4. *See also* Johnson County Rustler Wars of 1892
Wyoming Stock Growers Association, 35, 37, 38, 40

Yates, Norris, 2–4

yellowback novels, 76, 79, 82, 85, 92, 126, 165n8. *See also* pulp fiction magazines; western, popular
"You Never Can Tell" (Ives), 147
Young Wild West series, 76

Žižek, Slavoj, 38–39

In the Postwestern Horizons series

The Places of Modernity in Early Mexican American Literature, 1848–1948
José F. Aranda Jr.

Dirty Wars: Landscape, Power, and Waste in Western American Literature
John Beck

Post-Westerns: Cinema, Region, West
Neil Campbell

The Rhizomatic West: Representing the American West in a Transnational, Global, Media Age
Neil Campbell

The Comic Book Western: New Perspectives on a Global Genre
Edited by Christopher Conway and Antoinette Sol

Weird Westerns: Race, Gender, Genre
Edited by Kerry Fine, Michael K. Johnson, Rebecca M. Lush, and Sara L. Spurgeon

Positive Pollutions and Cultural Toxins: Waste and Contamination in Contemporary U.S. Ethnic Literatures
John Blair Gamber

A Planetary Lens: The Photo-Poetics of Western Women's Writing
Audrey Goodman

Dirty Words in Deadwood: *Literatures and the Postwestern*
Edited by Melody Graulich and Nicolas Witschi

True West: Authenticity and the American West
Edited by William R. Handley and Nathaniel Lewis

Teaching Western American Literature
Edited by Brady Harrison and Randi Lynn Tanglen

Manifest Destiny 2.0: Genre Trouble in Game Worlds
Sara Humphreys

Speculative Wests: Popular Representations of a Region and Genre
Michael K. Johnson

We Who Work the West: Class, Labor, and Space in Western American Literature
Kiara Kharpertian
Edited by Carlo Rotella and Christopher P. Wilson

Captivating Westerns: The Middle East in the American West
Susan Kollin

Postwestern Cultures: Literature, Theory, Space
Edited by Susan Kollin

Westerns: A Women's History
Victoria Lamont

Manifest and Other Destinies: Territorial Fictions of the Nineteenth-Century United States
Stephanie LeMenager

Unsettling the Literary West: Authenticity and Authorship
Nathaniel Lewis

Morta Las Vegas: CSI and the Problem of the West
Nathaniel Lewis and Stephen Tatum

Late Westerns: The Persistence of a Genre
Lee Clark Mitchell

María Amparo Ruiz de Burton: Critical and Pedagogical Perspectives
Edited by Amelia María de la Luz Montes and
Anne Elizabeth Goldman

In the Mean Time: Temporal Colonization and the Mexican American Literary Tradition
Erin Murrah-Mandril

Unhomely Wests: Essays from A to Z
Stephen Tatum

To order or obtain more information on these or other University of Nebraska Press titles, visit nebraskapress.unl.edu.

OTHER WORKS BY VICTORIA LAMONT

Judith Merril: A Critical Study (McFarland, 2012)

www.ingramcontent.com/pod-product-compliance
Lightning Source LLC
Chambersburg PA
CBHW030109170426
43198CB00009B/553